MW01283253

Amelia McNutt is a hardworking researcher and writer. Traveling to the sites of America's military history she finds the lesser-known places, people, and stories that are hidden in America's military history. Amelia engages the reader to follow her into these overlooked, little-known, under-reported, and quite fascinating events. Think you know the story – read on and find out what really happened. She introduces the reader to compelling, unpredictable events that will intrigue the learned and novice students of military history.

This book is dedicated to all the American soldiers who chased Rommel across Normandy and into history. On the land, sea, and in the air, they came from all over the United States of America. They changed the world and inflicted a fatal wound on Hitler and his tyrannical Nazis. Some stayed in Normandy and rest in peace above Omaha Beach. They are all heroes to me. As are these soldiers that I knew personally:

My father, Donald "DJ" McNutt (U.S. Army, Korean Era), and my uncle, Frederick "Fred" McNutt (U.S. Air Force, Korean Era), and the World War II guys—my uncles, John "Jack" McNutt (Royal Air Force, Canadian and the American Army Air Force), William "Bill" McNutt (U.S. Army), Edward "Eddy" Wall (U.S. Army Air Corp), James "Jim" Wall (U.S. Army), and William "Willie" Wall (U.S. Marine Corps). And two very dear friends, Anthony "Tony" Fassi Sr. (U.S. Army), Normand Hamel Sr. (U.S. Navy—Pacific).

My mission statement was inspired by those I knew, and those I will never know. It is dedicated to all the American veterans and as I work to keep their memories alive, I say to you.

"Learn the Stories. Don't let their Glory Fade."

Amelia McNutt

CHASING ROMMEL

AUSTIN MACAULEY PUBLISHERS™

LONDON • CAMBRIDGE • NEW YORK • SHARJAH

Ordering Information
Quantity sales: Special discounts are available on quantity purchases by corporations, associations, and others. For details, contact the publisher at the address below.

Publisher's Cataloging-in-Publication data
McNutt, Amelia
Chasing Rommel

ISBN 9781685624286 (Paperback)
ISBN 9781685624309 (Hardback)
ISBN 9781685624316 (ePub e-book)
ISBN 9781685624293 (Audiobook)

Library of Congress Control Number: 2022923620

www.austinmacauley.com/us

First Published 2023
Austin Macauley Publishers LLC
40 Wall Street, 33rd Floor, Suite 3302
New York, NY 10005
USA

mail-usa@austinmacauley.com
+1 (646) 5125767

I want to express my sincerest thanks to: Rosanne Crowley as well as my family and friends who have listened to me endlessly speak of the stories contained in this book. I want to remember my mother, father, brother Don as well as an old and wise teacher named Mr. Boyd. They taught me that humility and hard work will empower one to succeed, this done by countless examples.

I wish to thank Major (Honorary) Ellwood von Seibold who opened my eyes to Normandy and the bigger story that is needed to be told, and retold. Thank you, Major.

Thank you to Karen Ruggiero and the memories she shared with me of her father, US Army Ranger Antonio Ruggiero, our hometown hero in Plymouth, Massachusetts. I would also like to thank Doug McCabe, Curator of manuscripts, Mahn Center for archives and special collection, Alden Library, Ohio University, Athens, OH.

Table of Contents

Note to the Reader

Thank you for taking the time to read this book. Please do not confuse any of my accounting of these events as supporting in any way Hitler and his Nazis.

This is the story of the American soldiers in Normandy. But it is a story with a very British beginning that starts with the struggle at Dunkirk, because without Dunkirk, there would never have been an invasion of Normandy. These are the stories of the Americans sent to France to liberate a people conquered and subjugated by the tyrannical Nazis.

It was in Normandy, driven by the breathtaking American and British sacrifices on the battlefields, and all the unselfish support of the American and British people at the home front, that began the decisive final act of Hitler and his Nazis.

Amelia C. McNutt
25 March 2021

Prologue—Meet Rommel

No other German General came close to preoccupying the military leaders of Great Britain and the United States in World War II as did Erwin Rommel. To this very day, his exploits in the North African deserts attract and fascinate many who study or read military history.

From February of 1941 until March of 1943, German General and later, Field Marshal Erwin Rommel, dominated the wartime strategy of Great Britain and the United States in the European and Mediterranean theaters of operations. Churchill, Britain's wartime leader, was once heard to exclaim:

Rommel, Rommel, Rommel, Rommel, what else matters but beating him?

Rommel made what was initially regarded as an Italian sideshow in North Africa into, perhaps, the most fascinating armored warfare campaign in history. Churchill, the British Prime Minister spoke before the House of Commons in January 1942 declaring, *"We have a very daring and skillful opponent, and may I say across the havoc of war, a great general."*

That was when Erwin Rommel began his transformation from feared enemy soldier to respected *Desert Fox*, ultimately falling into the pages of military history not as a man, but as a mythical military legend.

Introduction—Normandy

It was the hope of General George C. Marshall, (1880–1959) US Army Chief of Staff (1939–1945) that the US Army would invade the occupied continent of Europe as soon as 1942 (Operation Sledgehammer). General Marshall understood, from his experiences in World War I, working on General of the Army, John J. "Black Jack" Pershing's staff, that the German Army had to be destroyed. A glaring oversight as World War I ended with an armistice in 1918.

Despite Marshall's power as one of President Roosevelt's prime military advisors, and his personal experiences in the First World War, General Marshall did not get his way. His principal sources of resistance were the British generals who believed they knew better than Marshall.

They insisted that the timing as well as the location had to be perfect for such an enormous and breathtakingly dangerous military feat. They were correct, and those same British military minds found the perfect man to begin the process of the invasion of the continent of Europe.

He was the most important D-Day soldier you have never heard of, as he was the man who made the plans, picked the places, and started the entire massive effort while others were still just dreaming and talking. In March 1943, British General Frederick Morgan (1894–1967) was appointed Chief Of Staff Supreme Allied Commander (COSSAC), despite the fact that there was no Supreme Allied Commander at that time.

Morgan assembled a team and went to work creating the framework for the Allied invasion of the continent of Europe. It was British General Morgan who choose Normandy and began to prepare for an invasion in 1944. General Morgan can rightfully be called the architect of D-Day.

After months of planning and training, he was replaced by the Supreme Allied Commander and his staff known as Supreme Headquarters Allied Expeditionary Forces, (SHAEF) in January 1944. Now, General Morgan's plans would be expanded as Eisenhower was appointed Supreme Commander, and British General Bernard Montgomery came aboard as the Supreme Ground Forces Commander. With those appointments, General Morgan was all but forgotten. But to know the Normandy story one must begin with the men that initiated the story, US General George C. Marshall and British General Frederick Morgan.

As we have learned, before Normandy no single soldier held the attention of the British and American war machines as the man the British soldiers called, *The Desert Fox*. Rommel's successes in North Africa led to TIME magazine putting him on their cover, 13 July 1942, as the conqueror of the British port of Tobruk.

Eventually, North Africa was lost to the Germans and the Italians, and with that, Rommel was ordered home to Germany. After a very brief posting in Italy, Rommel was given a special assignment by Hitler himself. In November of 1943, Hitler ordered Rommel to inspect the German defenses along the coastal areas from Norway to the Spanish border.

By the end of December 1943, Rommel's inspection was complete. Rommel had become an authority on Hitler's Atlantic Wall, and shortly thereafter, Hitler ordered Rommel to defend the Atlantic Wall.

From December 1943 until D-Day on 6 June 1944, Field Marshal Rommel did his best to shore up the incomplete German defenses along the coast of France. Rommel focused on stopping the Allies at the water's edge, where he believed he held the only advantage of defending Hitler's Fortress, Europe.

On 6 June 1944 the Allied forces found Erwin Rommel again, this time as the commander of German Army Group B in the northwestern area of France, an area that encompasses Normandy. During the summer of 1944, the American Army, Navy and U.S. Army Air Forces were all in France—*Chasing Rommel.*

From 6 June 1944 until he was wounded on 17 July 1944, Rommel held the Allied armies near the coast. His defense, combined with the difficult terrain the French call the *bocage* and we know as the hedgerows, kept Eisenhower's massive force from breaking out of the Normandy area. This continually frustrated the British commander General Bernard Montgomery and the American Commander General Omar Bradley.

Rommel seemed to have an answer for each of their attempts at the breakout. When the breakout did occur, it was at the end of July 1944 and was spearheaded by the brilliant American armored warfare commander, General George S. Patton, Jr.

From Tuesday 6 June until Monday 17 July 1944, just forty-one days, Rommel denied the Allies the breakout they needed to ultimately win the war. Rommel was very seriously wounded by two British Royal Air force fighter planes on 17 July 1944. His staff car was strafed, and he was thrown from the open top vehicle nearly dying in the process. He was sent home to Herrlingen, Germany. Rommel would die there on 14 October 1944, after being implicated in the attempt to kill Hitler on 20 July 1944.

For forty-one days, the success of the Normandy invasion was questionable. For all those days, the world watched as the Allies threw everything they had at one man and his strategy, tactical responses, and defensive operations. These are just a small sampling of the men, the places, and the stories of the remarkable American warriors who began *Chasing Rommel* on D-Day.

Our journey through time begins with the astonishing British evacuation at *Dunkirk—Their Beach.* There nearly four years before D-Day we find Montgomery and Rommel. Rommel is at the spearhead of an invasion, while the Montgomery is methodically trying to escape with an army back to Britain. Together, we will learn of *Rommel's Defense of Normandy*, as he shapes his strategic, tactical, and operational plans to defend Hitler's crumbling empire.

We will understand the lessons Rommel experienced in North Africa and beyond, and how, in his desperate defense of Normandy, he applied those lessons. We will meet *D-Day's Old Man*, the oldest son of one of America's favorite Presidents.

We will get to know a small-town hero who was one of the exceptional US Army Rangers who assaulted *Point-du Hoc* and lived a long and colorful life in America's hometown. Together, we will walk *D-Day's Forgotten Place*, and explore its circumstance in a history nearly erased by intention and time. A place rediscovered and today, it is emerging from the D-Days shadows, its role once neatly buried, it now unearths questions that need to be asked and answered.

We will travel to a place that is on the peripheral of the Normandy story, *Oradour-sur-Glane*. It is the story of a group of German monsters, masquerading as men, who on their way to Normandy, committed an unspeakable act. It is a painful place, and a sorrowful story that supports why America sent her brave sons to France in 1944.

We will end this journey together at *Bloody Omaha Beach* and learn why so many men were killed on the cold wet sands of France. The questions and the answers are painful. Together, we will learn why D-Day at Omaha Beach was the day and place more Americans died – than any other day and place in World War II.

Chasing Rommel is our first trip together. There are more places and stories we will share in the future as we continue *Chasing Rommel—Again.*

Looking toward the beach at Dunkirk from the Mole.

Chapter 1
Dunkirk: Their Beach

Introduction

"You can practically see it from here. Home."

Commander Bolton, portrayed by actor Sir Kenneth Branagh
Dunkirk, Motion Picture 2017
Director: Christopher Nolan

Arriving late into the evening, I met Dunkerque on the darkest of nights. The moon and the stars were hidden by a damp lingering blanket of clouds. My drive from Paris was much slower than it should have been, the rain, wind, and the cold were my companions on what seemed like an endless journey.

Lamentations as the visions of Dunkerque I wanted to see were exchanged for time surrendered to airport delays, lost luggage, and unrelenting traffic. The images of Dunkerque I wanted to see, faded into the blackness of night. I walked in blinding darkness towards the sea as the city rested peacefully behind me. The sounds and smells of the ocean were my sensory compass guiding me to the water's edge.

Scanning the darkness, I looked left and saw red and green navigational lights. I was looking at the historic Mole. That is when it hit me, I realized *they* stood here in the daylight and the darkness. They were driven here by an enemy determined to annihilate them.

Here they stayed, prayed, and hoped for a miracle. In that complete darkness at land's end, on a moonless, starless, cloudy, wind driven night my disappointment abated, my imagination was ignited. The black and white images, and books full of words came to life—I am on *Their Beach*.

It is *Dunkerque* to the French, a harbor on the northern coast of France beside Belgium and across from the English Channel from the British port of Dover. It is remembered by history as Dunkirk, where on June 4, 1940, the last of over 338,000 British and French soldiers were evacuated from the beaches, and the harbor, escaping the grasp of Hitler's rampaging *Blitzkrieg*.

I am *Chasing Rommel* to the north coast of France, far from Normandy in distance but not in importance and relevance. I am in Dunkerque, trying to understand an event of nearly unparalleled importance when an entire World was marching toward the calamities of war for the second time in twenty years.

Part I: Fading History

"We shall defend our island, whatever the cost may be, we shall fight on the beaches, we shall fight on the landing grounds, we shall fight in the fields and in the streets, we shall fight in the hills; we shall never surrender."

Winston Churchill (1874–1965)
Prime Minister, United Kingdom (May 1940–July 1945) and (October 1951–April 1955)
Speech at the House of Commons—4 June 1940

The histories of Great Britain and France are full of remarkable military victories. France was the land of Napoleon and Jeanne d'Arc (Joan of Arc). They were the brave, brilliant and tragic military leaders who vanquished the enemies of France.

The military history of Great Britain is equally full of heroes. Field Marshal Arthur Wellesley, the Irish born Duke of Wellington, was the man who led the Allied armies that eventually defeated the French military genius Napoleon at Waterloo.

Wellington was proclaimed, *The conqueror of the world's conqueror.* The British had another hero, Vice Admiral Horatio Nelson, the victor of the Battle of Trafalgar. The naval battle that saw him lead the out gunned British fleet to victory over the combined navies of France and Spain. Nelson's victory would solidify Britain's Royal Navy as the World's greatest sea power for over 100 years.

But neither France nor Great Britain and their celebrated warriors were famous for retreats, and yet, by 1940, each nation had had a famous retreat.

Some retreats are a signaling of the end, like Napoleon's retreat from Moscow in 1812. Facing a desolate winter and a Russian policy of scorched earth that left nothing of value for the invading French forces, Napoleon's arrival in Moscow was a bitter pyrrhic victory as best.

He and his grand army retreated, chased by the Czar's weary forces and the relentless bitter cold of the Russian winter, memorialized perfectly in Peter Tchaikovsky's 1812 Overture.

Other retreats like the British Army that evacuated Gallipoli in 1916, ensured that they would continue to fight on, during World War I. One of the architects of the Gallipoli invasion, but not the Gallipoli withdrawal of the British Forces, was *First Lord of The Admiralty*, Winston Churchill.

On 10 May 1940 Winston Churchill, who had recently been reappointed the *First Lord of the Admiralty,* became the leader of a coalition government in Great Britain. Churchill had been out of political power and influence for over a decade, however, with his country facing war with Germany for the second time in twenty years, he was selected and replaced the aging, sickly Prime Minister Neville Chamberlain.

Churchill, the man some believed to be a glory seeking, callous warlord was in, and Chamberlain who had negotiated a *faux* peace with Hitler six months earlier proclaiming, *Peace in our time* was out. Chamberlain, now a beaten and weary man would never see his country at peace again. In six months, he would succumb to bowel cancer.

On the day Churchill became the Prime Minster of the United Kingdom, Germany invaded France.

The Germans were unstoppable and in a matter of weeks, Churchill watched as the Belgium Army surrendered, and large parts of the British and French Armies were surrounded. Now, it would be Churchill who would preside over one of the most important and successful retreats in History.

A withdrawal of unprecedented size and scope, through but a brief open window of time. When the British and French Armies were chased by Hitler's forces to land's end, the British had just days to do the impossible. The Second World War on the Western Front was just weeks old, and Hitler's forces were poised to hand Great Britain and France an overwhelming, unprecedented defeat. A defeat that could change the world.

Part II: The Trap

"As a correspondent I have seen all the great armies...but those armies...were made up of men. This was a machine, endless, tireless, with the delicate organization of a watch and the brute power of a steamroller. It is, perhaps, the most efficient organization of modern times; and its purpose only is death. Those who cast it loose upon Europe are military-mad."

With The Allies
Richard Harding Davis (1864–1916)
C. Scribner's Sons, 1914.
Pages 24–26

Richard Harding Davis's description of the German Army is his eyewitness account of the German invasion of neutral Belgium in 1914, opening World War I. The invasion was highly organized, swift, and remarkably brutal.

So effective was Germany's invasion of Belgium in 1914, it was repeated by Adolph Hitler's forces in May 1940 as World War II broke out in Western Europe. Except that Hitler's forces used tanks and trucks that moved at record speed.

To the French and British forces, defending Western Europe from Hitler's modern blitzkrieg armies—history was repeating itself only moving much, much faster, robbing the Allied Forces of the time they required for recovery.

In 1914, as World War I began, the Germans invaded France on its Western Front. They arrived quickly using an old war plan drawn up a decade before the war. Although it was greatly modified, the *Schlieffen Plan* directed the German armies to sweep quickly into France from neighboring and neutral Belgium.

They would begin their advance traveling north and west and then turn to the south in an attempt to capture Paris, the French capital. With many cavalry divisions in the lead, it was believed that the French would be crushed in as little as six weeks. It did not work, and the German Army became locked into a deadly war of attrition against the Allied British and French Forces, creating the horrific trench warfare that defined the Western Front for the duration of the First World War.

In 1940, the Germans attacked France. Like the 1914 plan, it seemed they were coming through Belgium and it was believed they would attack north to south repeating the movements of 1914. But 1940 was in so many ways different from 1914. *Schlieffen's Plan* had been a failure, and it was the Germans who learned the most from its mistakes.

The Germans loosely followed a plan whose architect was a relatively unknown, but brilliant strategist, General Erich von Manstein. Manstein would go on to great fame for his plan to invade France in 1940. He would achieve the rank of Field Marshal while battling the Soviets on the eastern Front.

In March of 1944, he was retired by Hitler for being a defeatist, and uncooperative to Hitler's growing madness. After the war, Manstein was found guilty of war crimes and was imprisoned in Germany. But Eric von Manstein was so respected by Allied political and military leaders, such as Winston Churchill that his sentence was commuted in 1953 in exchange for helping the Allies rebuild the German Army and create the plan that would repulse an expected Soviet invasion through Germany into France.

In 1940, Manstein's plan, *Sichelschnitt* (cut of the sickle) was very different from the failed World War I *Schlieffen Plan*. It began with a movement the British and French believed the Germans would make. But in 1940, the opening move through Belgium was a diversionary action only. The French Generals, who were in command, saw history repeating itself and ordered the British forces and some French forces to meet the German movement into Belgium.

And very early on 10 May 1940, *German Army Group B* with twenty-six infantry divisions attacked Holland and Belgium in the opening hours of World War II in Western Europe. And as the eyes of the world turned toward history repeating itself in Belgium, the French and British armies furiously moved towards the German advance. This set the stage and blinded the French military leaders to the primary attack of the fast-moving Panzer divisions further south.

As the predicable was happening, so too was the impossible, as German armored units began their burst through the Ardennes Forrest just north of where France's famous and useless *Maginot Line* ended. The Ardennes Forrest is so dense and hilly, the French ended their famed *Maginot Line*, a line of concrete forts and gun emplacements where the dense forest and rolling hills nearly obscure the French border with Luxembourg.

I have visited the Ardennes in Luxembourg. There I was instantly struck at how crammed and overgrown the vegetation is. The trees grow tall and completely full of branches so covered in dense foliage, they sometimes hang to the ground.

Driving the Ardennes in May offered scenery so breathtaking, that you slowed down to see such a beautiful natural setting. I easily thought—You could get lost or hide here forever. Even today, nearly 80 years removed from the events, it is easy to speculate how the French believed a modern army could not pass through this area quickly. The Ardennes offered a perfect place to hide Germany's Army Group A.

Hitler and his Generals created German Army Group A, which was comprised of forty-five divisions, including *three Panzer Corps totaling seven Panzer Divisions.* The Panzer Divisions were full of armored vehicles including tanks. These modern mobile armored armies were the future of warfare and they crossed the uncrossable Ardennes Forrest with record speed.

The French believed the Ardennes to be nearly impassable with modern trucks and tanks and in one study, the French military high command believed it would take the attacking Germans many, many days to pass through the forests. It took the Panzers of Army Group A, just 2 days to exit the Ardennes and dash into the open.

The Germans broke through at the Ardennes encountering little serious resistance from the overwhelmed French forces. The Panzers rushed across the Meuse River, smashed through the French city of Sedan and the race to the coast was on. Thousands of armored and motorized vehicles rolled into the open and attacked from the south moving west and north.

The German attacks in May of 1940, introduced the world to names that became synonymous with German World War II military successes including: General Eric von Manstein, General Heinz Guderian, and the little known Major General Erwin Rommel.

Part III: Rommel's Ghost Division

"The enemy is exposed to annihilation…"

Major General Erwin Rommel,
Commander 7th Panzer Division
Outside Lille, France
June 1940

By 1940, Heinz Guderian was an experienced leader of motorized troops. He believed that fast moving armored units, coordinated with attack aircraft held the future of warfare. His theories proved correct in the 1940 invasion of France.

He had written the book *Achtung Panzer* (Attention Tank!) a guide to motorized warfare and was considered one of the preeminent experts on mobile warfare in the German Army. He commanded a Panzer Division when the Germany invaded Poland in 1939. For the invasion of France, he commanded a *Panzer Korps*—three Panzer Divisions.

One of the Panzer Divisions that attacked France in 1940 was the 7th Panzer Division. It was led by a highly decorated World War I infantry officer. He had never commanded a division, let alone one of the new Panzer formations. But he was one of Hitler's favorite soldiers, and like Guderian, he was a published author, writing about his infantry experiences in the First World War.

Major General Erwin Rommel published, *Infanterie Greift.* (Infantry in Attack – 1937) and that is how Rommel came to attention of Adolf Hitler who was also a published author. Hitler's book, *Mein Kampf* (My Struggle) was published in 1925.

(Note: In the 1970 movie *Patton,* a book we are led to believe was written by Erwin Rommel is on Patton's nightstand as he is awoken on the morning of the *Battle of El Guettar* in Tunisia. The title of the book is, *The Tank in Attack.* A book Rommel planned to write—but did not. When Patton says, *"Rommel, you magnificent bastard, I read your book!"* was he referring to the book Rommel wrote *Infanterie Greift (Infantry in Attack-1937)* or the book Guardian wrote *Achtung Panzer (Attention Tank-1937)?*

Rommel planned on writing a book about his tank warfare experiences in World War II but did not live to see the war's end. Perhaps, the screenwriter of the movie *Patton*, Frances Ford Coppola who also was the screenwriter and director of the *Godfather* films would know.)

Major General Erwin Rommel was given command of the 7th Panzer Division for Germany's invasion of France. The command of a Panzer division was a gift from Hitler himself, after Rommel had served as the leader of Hitler's personal protection battalion during the German invasion of Poland on 1 September 1939. This brought Rommel into very close proximity to Hitler, and they bonded over military events of the past and strategy in the Polish Campaign.

Rommel was fascinated with the speed and success he saw in the new Panzer formations. He asked Hitler if he could command a Panzer division, and Hitler gave his favorite general, command of the 7th Panzer Division. This *favor* from Hitler to Rommel was deeply insulting to the men who were passed over by such favoritism.

Rommel wasted no time and began training the 7th Panzer Division as soon as he arrived to take command in February of 1940. He had learned from his days as an infantry commander that speed, maneuver, firepower, and combined arms actions got results. He drilled and trained his soldiers until May of 1940 when it was time to go do battle in France. His division was now ready.

At dawn on 10 May 1940, Major General Erwin Rommel and the 7th Panzer Division began their legendary assault across the French countryside. Their objective was the crossing of the Meuse River. By 12 May Rommel was at the Meuse River. He was moving furiously between armored and infantry units, organizing and coordinating local attacks.

With the bridges destroyed by the retreating French, the Germans were trying to cross the Meuse in small boats. Without a smoke screen, the soldiers were literally sitting ducks for the well dug in French across the river. Rommel ordered that some houses on the French side of the riverbank be shot into flames, creating dense smoke that provided the cover to cross the river.

Quick thinking and pragmatic results would become Rommel's trademarks as his legend grew from his exploits in France to his days in North Africa, wheeling his vaunted *Afrika Korps* across the top of the African continent in 1941 and again in 1942.

With his Division crossing the Meuse, Rommel was on the move into open country. He pushed himself and his men, engaging and destroying the retreating French wherever he found them. Fighting for four straight days by 17 May, Rommel was crossing the Sambre River.

Rommel was moving faster than the French could blow up their bridges, and by 18 May 7th Panzer had reached the historic city Cambria. By 20 May, Rommel and his Panzers reached the *La Bessee Canal* on the outskirts of the city of Arras.

(Note: Arras is where several World War I's battles occurred. And just outside of Arras is Vimy Ridge. There, you will see a massive and striking memorial to the Canadian troops who fought and died at the Battle of Arras and Vimy Ridge.

On that memorial, carved amongst the thousands of names is *M. R. McNutt*. PFC Morton Ross McNutt was assigned to the *1st Canadian Infantry Division,* a tough hard fighting group nick-named by their enemies the *Little Black Devils*. He was killed in action in April 1917. PFC McNutt was my great grandfather.)

At Arras, Rommel encountered British troops who counterattacked the Germans to try to slow the remarkable advance of the German Panzer forces racing towards the English Channel. The British attacked the Germans at Arras on 21 May. The Battle for Arras was fierce, and it was at Arras that Rommel faced British soldiers and their Matilda tanks for the first time.

The Matilda tanks grounded Rommel's less protected or armored Panzers. These were the very tanks Rommel would face in Africa where the British Army nicknamed him, *The Desert Fox*. Rommel quickly understood his tanks were being outmatched and outgunned.

Rommel's career was defined by his ability to think quickly and differently. Outside of Arras, in May of 1940 was another example as Rommel found a battery of German 88s, the notoriously accurate and effective anti-aircraft guns. The German 88 (*8.8 cm Flak 36*) became legendary for its accuracy in shooting down enemy aircraft.

The German 88 was one of World War II's most feared artillery pieces and yet, they were originally built to be only anti-aircraft guns. The *Krupp 8.8 cm FlaK* gun fired an 8.8 mm projectile (3.6") at a speed of 2,700 feet per second or well over twice the speed of sound. The incredible speed of the projectile is what did the extraordinary damage to the British tanks.

The 88 as an anti-tank gun was amazingly accurate and had a range much greater than comparative tank mounted guns in 1940. Rommel quickly approached the commander of the anti-aircraft battery. He demanded to know if the gun barrel of his 88s which was highly elevated to shoot into the sky, could be lowered and still fired.

He explained his need to fire the guns at tanks not airplanes, the gunners said it was possible to fire the gun at lower trajectory. He moved them up and lowered the nearly vertical barrels to horizontal positions and thereby turned them into anti-tank guns. Rommel used the guns to destroy over two dozen British tanks.

The fighting around Arras against trained and determined British soldiers was the costliest for Rommel and his 7th Panzer Division during the Battle of France. He would carry memories of his encounters with the determined British armored units the rest of his remarkable career.

In North Africa, it was the British armored units that consistently stopped him, offering resistance that nearly always matched his battlefield cleverness.

With the Battle of Arras over, and the 7th Panzer ready to roll on, incredulously on 24 May, Rommel and all the other rapidly advancing German forces were ordered to stop. Hitler ordered all German forces to halt. Deemed to need rest and refit, the three days off would be a welcome relief to the Germans who believed the British were on their heels, backed up to the English Channel at a place called Dunkirk.

The Germans surprised, pushed, and nearly surrounded their enemy so quickly, their only reaction was a steady fighting withdrawal. The only direction they could retreat was towards the sea, to French ports on the English Channel like Calais, Boulogne, and Dunkerque.

As the British Expeditionary Force moved closer to the Channel coast, the Germans tightened the noose. They had elements of the British, French and some of Belgium Armies encircled and were pushing them towards the English Channel.

The trap was closing. Set in historical precedent and executed with fast moving Panzer Divisions on the ground, supported by a blanket of attacking aircraft from above. It was Lighting War—*Blitzkrieg*, and Germans were quickly becoming the masters of the battlefields of 1940 Europe.

German Bunker at Dunkirk Harbor

Part IV: The Retreat

"For us Germans, the word "Dunkirchen" (Dunkirk) *will stand for all time for victory in the greatest battle of annihilation in history...for the British and French* (it will stand as) *a defeat that was heavier than any army had ever suffered before."*

Editorial, German Magazine *Der Adler*,
5 June 1940

There was very little space left to trade for time. By 26 May, just 16 days after the German invasion began, Britain's new Prime Minister, Winston Churchill ordered *Operation Dynamo* to begin. In just 16 days, the Germans seemed to have accomplished two unthinkable events.

First, they had routed the combined forces of France and Great Britain in just two weeks. Secondly, they were about to run the British Army off the European continent for the first time in history. Churchill, his generals, and admirals knew they must save the BEF from annihilation and get them off the coast of France. The loss of the British ground forces in 1940 would have surely forced the collapse of Churchill's government and created lopsided peace talks between Germany and Great Britain.

But before they can be saved, they would have to get to the coast. And in order to get to the coast some units would have to be left in the rear—*The Rear Guard*, to hold back the Germans, something that thus far in this short war had been impossible.

The French hoped the retreating British and French armies would join together and maintain a small piece of France. Just enough for a base of operations against the Germans. That would be tried in the Normandy region of France, as some of the British and French forces just barely held out.

But it was too late, the trap was closing, and the British knew what the French did not; it was all over, the battle lost. As May 1940 was ending, the only hope for the future would be determined by the successful evacuation of as many soldiers as possible.

To be evacuated successfully, the British and French forces would need to get to a safe harbor on the French coast, where they could be protected by the Royal Air Force working from bases on the English coast. They would have to trade selected soldiers, strategies, and space for time. They would exchange the lives of some for the lives of many.

Many of Britain's most experienced generals were in France in May of 1940. Along with Allan Brooke and Harold Alexander was a highly respected infantry division commander, Major General Bernard Law Montgomery. Montgomery led the 3rd Infantry Division in a fighting, tactical withdrawal to Dunkirk.

Like Rommel, Montgomery was a veteran of the First World War. Monty, as he was affectionately known by his troops had been in France since September of 1939 and had spent all his time training his division for a multitude of scenarios, including the eventually of a fighting retreat.

Montgomery, like Rommel, would survive the hard fighting in France in 1940. Each had the trajectory of their remarkable careers altered just miles from one another in May and June of 1940. They would meet again on the sandy plains of the North African desert, where each would move from man to legend.

On 14 May, just 4 days after the Germans attacked France, it was Montgomery and his 3rd Division that halted a German advance near the town of Louvain. This was the first of many times Monty knocked the Germans back on their heels. II Corp Commander, General Allan Brooke used Montgomery to patch or hold the lines many times as the perimeter was collapsing through attacks and withdrawals.

Nearing the end of May, things seemed hopeless for the British Expeditionary Force retreating to the Channel Coast. When II Corps Commander General Brooke was told that Belgium surrendered, it created a massive gap in his lines. Knowing how well Montgomery had trained his division, Brooke asked Montgomery to make a 25-mile night march, and move completely across the defensive perimeter to close the gap.

Brooke could not have asked any other divisional commander to do what Montgomery was about to accomplish. Montgomery was a man greatly respected by his troops for his preparedness and willing to keep his men out of needless danger. Already known for his pride, Montgomery never needlessly endangered any soldier for his personal vanity.

With his entire division moving in total darkness, on unfamiliar roads, and at times barely skirting around the German lines, Montgomery brilliantly moved 3rd Infantry Division into place to hold the line. At times, perilously close to their enemy, Montgomery's soldiers marched in a blackout march and into place to close the gap in Brooke's tenuous defensive lines.

It is hard to overstate the importance of what General Montgomery and his troops accomplished. They may have made the evacuation of Dunkirk the incredible success it became by extending the time available for the troops to embark onto the waiting flotilla.

Brooke was recalled by Churchill, and on 30 May 1940, Montgomery was promoted to Commander II Corps. Montgomery and his 3rd Infantry Division were eventually evacuated from Dunkirk, but not before their remarkable achievement helped ensure that the evacuation would occur. Montgomery's career rapidly escalated after the British Army's 1940 campaign in France.

Eventually, Rommel would find and face Montgomery in El Alamein, a dusty, old, unknown rail town in North Africa. The results of that contest would be very different from the experiences they each shared in France.

Lighthouse at Dunkirk Harbor.

Part V: The Rescue

"If you can force your heart and nerve and sinew
To serve your turn long after they are gone,
And so hold on when there is nothing in you
Except the Will which says to them: "Hold on!"

IF by Rudyard Kipling (1865–1936)

Rising before the sun, I step out to the small balcony of my old seaside hotel. I can see the blinking green and red lights at the end of the long Mole. On a cloudy morning, they are shrouded against a background mist, as darkness lifts slowly from the English Channel. The lights are a reminder that Dunkirk was, and remains, a vibrant seaport on the coast of Northern France.

My morning walk leads me from land's end where the wind-blown dunes surrender to the concrete walkway on the top of the mole. The relentless, barreling wind has reduced my stroll to a stop and go contest of my will. The sand from the nearby beach and dunes is driven into my hair, and eyes so strongly that I have to cover my face with my arm.

I determinedly defy nature, walking on a low angle into the howling wind. I feel I am in a blizzard of sand. Head down, hood over my head, I am looking down to the sand covered sidewalk. I am determined to walk in their footsteps. It is why I am here.

From the Mole, you can study the seemingly endless expanse of beach, as the coastline seems to go for miles. Engaging my imagination, I can see a city that is in ruins with columns of smoke easily defining a target for the German Luftwaffe closing in for the kill. Closing my eyes, I conjure an image of thousands of British soldiers on the very beach I am gazing onto. My mind's eye suddenly shares the Mole with those brave men in those desperate hours.

Again, I think—this was *Their Beach*. And for admirers, historians, authors and tourists it is still *Their Beach*. What gallantry such an undertaking requires, I choke up with emotion, and just stare at the crashing waves, and endless expanse of sandy shores.

Then, looking out to the sea, I am thinking how could rescue be achieved here at land's end, before annihilation came from land and sky? It was achieved by other extraordinary men, the sailors of the Royal Navy, the pilots of the Royal Air Force, and ordinary yet exceptional British citizens.

Operation Dynamo was the name chosen for the most amazing military rescue operation in history. Without the Dunkirk evacuation, there would not have been an Allied Invasion at Normandy nearly four years to the day in June of 1944.

Without Great Britain remaining to oppose Hitler, there would be no base for the military operations on land, sea and air. It was having those bases in England that brought the total destruction of Hitler's Nazis.

On 26 May 1940, as the British nation joined with King George VI in a day of national prayer, Prime Minister Winston Churchill and the man he personally selected, Admiral Bertram Ramsey to bring the British Army home, began their impossible task. As the battle on land around Dunkirk was drawing to its enviable conclusion, the challenges that would be faced and mastered by the Royal Navy were just beginning.

By 26 May, the battle on land had not concluded but the Germans had stopped advancing. For four days beginning 26 May, the German Army just stopped. This has created a million conversations, and thousands of contrary opinions.

The truth probably contains many parts of the stories that have grown around the Dunkirk evacuation. But simply put, the truth is that Hitler stopped his Panzers short of the coast. Many say his administrative generals, not his field commanders believed the Panzers needed rest and refit.

This would give the army infantry units following behind a chance to consolidate and reinforce the Panzer's lighting fast gains. Some German generals feared a concerted Allied counter attack and wanted the army prepared for that event.

Others have argued that Hitler wanted to give peace negotiations a chance. In an interview after the war, Hitler's confidant, and Minister of Munitions Albert Speer said plainly, "...*anyone who believed that Hitler wanted to let the English escape didn't understand the Führer very well.*" [1]

Hitler decided his vaunted Luftwaffe should finish off the British Army. This pleased his early and important supporter, *Reichsmarschall* Hermann Göring the commander of the Luftwaffe. Further, this action saved his Panzers for the conquest of what remained of France.

So, Hitler unleashed his fighters and bombers to do the job. First the German Air Force destroyed the French Forces holding Lille, and the remaining British forces in areas like Calais. Next, the Luftwaffe headed to Dunkirk to annihilate the stranded British and French forces fighting for their survival amongst the vanishing hopes of rescue.

Meanwhile, Admiral Ramsey sent Captain William Tennant to organize the beach and harbor. It all began with the expectation of removing 45,000 soldiers from Dunkirk. His assessment was that the shallow water at the beaches was not good for larger ships, but the Mole was perfect.

He also assessed that smaller craft, when found, would shuttle soldiers from the beach to the higher capacity ships offshore. By the operation's end,

---

[1] Lord, Walter. The Miracle of Dunkirk. The Viking Press; New York. 1983 Print. Page 203.

over 98,000 men, or nearly 30% of all evacuees would be removed from the beaches. [2]

Another very pressing problem facing Ramsey and Tennant was that the shortest route from Dunkirk to England was a 39-mile sea route then known as, *Route Z*. It was a very dangerous route as the Germans had artillery on the coastal areas surrounding Dunkirk and beyond.

The ship's next option was *Route X*, a route that spared the dangers of German shore artillery but was 55 miles long, 41% longer, and subject to German sea mines. It was most dangerous at night when the mines were very difficult to observe.

The last option was *Route Y*, it was 87 miles long, 125% longer than Route Z, and placed vessels at a danger from attack by German ships and planes. *Route Y* doubled the time from Dunkirk to England, and the British were already nearly out of time. Pragmatically, the British chose to use all three routes.[3]

Although Ramsey ultimately acquired nearly 850 vessels of all types and descriptions, the operation began with just a handful of Royal Navy ships. Some ships were staffed with British sailors, or professional sailors—merchant marines. Others were small private vessels of all accounts, skippered by their owners. Fighting the unforgiving clock and ruthless Germans, Ramsey needed anything that could float.[4]

They came from all over England. They came from seaports, and fishing villages, they came from rivers like the Thames in London, they came by motor, by sail, and by tow: tug boats, fishing boats, passenger steamers, private yachts, and ferries. They came with navy sailors and weekend captains, professionals, and amateurs and they all came to get their boys off that beach.

The flotilla was described by one author as, "*Between May 27 and June 4, a ragtag fleet of 850 barges, ferries, fishing boats, lifeboats and pleasure craft, all summoned by the small-craft section of the British Ministry of Shipping, set sail from Ramsgate and made its way 40 kilometers across the English Channel...Manned by naval officers, ratings and experienced volunteers—*

---

[2] Thompson, Julian Major General. (Ret). Dunkirk: Retreat to Victory. Arcade: New York. 2011. Print. Page 306. Appendix C.

[3] Thompson. Dunkirk: Retreat to Victory. Page 223

[4] Ibid. Page 224

mostly fishermen, a few yachtsmen and one legendary seaman—they navigated the shallow waters into Dunkirk[5]

Those ships and their crews were exactly what Ramsey's navy needed. The flotilla was supported by the Royal Air Force. Over the years, the Royal Air Force has been falsely maligned at Dunkirk. The disappointment of British soldiers in France was voiced immediately after they were evacuated.

Conversely, their role was more accurately portrayed by British Royal Marine Major General, historian, and author, General Julian Thompson when he wrote, *The Royal Air Force Flew 3,500 Missions.* This number represents the total number of missions flown in support by British Royal Air Force.

These missions were to cover the withdrawal and containment on the beaches of the beleaguered British and French armies. Unfortunately, the contribution of the RAF has been minimized or in some cases overlooked, being labeled as inadequate.

Nothing could be further from the truth, as Thompson lists the Royal Air Force activity as, "*Coastal Command flew 171 sorties, Bomber Command 651, and Fighter Command 2,739, all directly in support of Operation Dynamo.* (Total of 3,561 sorties)."

Thompson continues as he reminds us of the price paid by the men of the Royal Air Force. The air commanders knew every pilot, every plane they lost on France, was one less for the coming battle of Britain. *The RAF lost 145 aircraft...*[6]

Often, the RAF was fighting battles inland from Dunkirk, where the Luftwaffe bases were located, and out of sight of the soldiers on the beaches, or on board the ships trying to extract the British army from its paramount danger. The RAF was also outnumbered. The Luftwaffe had a large advantage in attacking Dunkirk. They had bombers, dive bombers (Stuka JU-87) and fighters like the BF109.

The RAF was also greatly concerned with what they knew was coming— the battle for Britain. It would require the British to be masters of the sky to keep the Nazis off British soil. On 1 June 1940, with Naval and air losses mounting the evacuations concentrated on night movements. From June 1–4,

---

[5] Thorne Stephen, J. The "Miracle of Dunkirk" Came at High Cost. June 9, 2020 https://legionmagazine.com/en/2020/06/the-miracle-of-dunkirk-came-at-high-cost/ Retrieved March 2021

[6] Thompson. Dunkirk: Retreat to Victory. Page 228.

143,606 soldiers, over 42%, would be evacuated from Dunkirk in the black of night.

When it ended, over 338,000 British and French soldiers had been evacuated over the course of nine miraculous days: 27 May–4 June 1940. [7]

But that is not the last of the British in France in June of 1940. It is a little-known fact that General Alan Brooke went back to France on 13 June to help the French Army which was in total disarray. Brooke arrived in Cherbourg at the tip of the Cotentin Peninsula in the Normandy region of coastal France.

It did not take General Brooke long to assess that the situation in France was fatal, and no force could turn around the defeat they had already suffered. When Churchill intervened and tried to talk Brooke into making a stand in France with British troops, Brooke refused.

Churchill implored Brooke telling him, *"he (Brooke)...had been sent to France to make the French feel that the British were supporting them."* Brooke's reply was very direct. Brooke told Churchill the unvarnished truth *"...it is impossible to make a corpse feel, and that the French army was, for intents and purposes, dead..."*

By 17 June, just four days after General Brooke returned to France, the French government, with the aged Marshal Pétain at its head, agreed to surrender to Germany.[8]

General Brooke departed France for England on 18 June. He would be evacuated again, this time on an English trawler, because the destroyer sent to pick him up was already full. It is not widely known that there were more evacuations from the coast of France, which went on until 25 June 1940.

These evacuations were not from Dunkirk, but from other areas of France. In a rich irony, some were evacuated from the Normandy region, where General Rommel and his 7th Panzer Division was bearing down on the Cotentin Peninsula towards Cherbourg. When this second wave of evacuations was completed, *"144,171 British, 18,246 French, 24, 352 Polish, 1,939 Czech, and 163 Belgians were transported to Britain."*

---

[7] Lord. The Miracle of Dunkirk. Page 275.
[8] Thompson. Dunkirk. Pp. 292-293.

This additional action of saving these troops was the direct result of General Brooke's refusal to needlessly engage the British and French in an already lost cause.[9]

As his words have so often been the best description the English language can offer. We turn to Churchill, who in Britain's darkest, most perilous hours stayed the course of recovering his army from the war-torn shores of France. But Churchill cautioned his fellow countrymen and the world when he said, *"We must be very careful not to assign to this deliverance the attributes of a victory. Wars are not won by evacuations. But there was a victory inside this deliverance, which should be noted..."*[10]

But from the cinders and broken lives of the defeat in France in 1940, something extraordinary happened. The British people saved their soldiers, sailors and airmen, and those brave men went on to save the British people.

When it was over one report in Germany claimed, *"As for escape of 'a few men' back to England...this was no cause for alarm. 'Every single one of these completely demoralized soldiers is a bacillus* (a disease-causing bacteria) *of disintegration'...they would never be back..."*

What an astonishing conceit and misjudgment, as the Germans soon discovered the war was not over, it had, in fact, just begun.[11]

In May and June as they fought, and then retreated the British Army lost an incredible, irreplaceable amount of war material. In the fields of France, and on the shores of Dunkirk the British lost:

Ammunition (tons):	*76,697 of 109,000*	*70%*
Artillery Pieces:	*2,472 of 2,794*	*85%*
Motor Vehicles:	*63,879 of 68,618*	*93%*
Supplies (tons):	*415,940 of 449,000*	*93%*
Petrol (tons):	*164,929 of 166,000*	*99%* [12]

---

[9] Thompson. Dunkirk. Page 294.

[10] Churchill, Winston S. Prime Minister of the United Kingdom. Speech at House of Commons, June 4, 1940 https://winstonchurchill.org/resources/speeches/1940-the-finest-hour/we-shall-fight-on-the-beaches/ Retrieved March 2021.

[11] Lord. The Miracle of Dunkirk. Page 275.

[12] Thompson. Dunkirk. Page 300.

The human cost was tragic. In just a matter of weeks, the British military had lost 66,000 killed, wounded, missing, and taken prisoner. It was a stark reminder of the casualties of the Great War, World War I. Despite it all, the British people saw it as the miracle of Dunkirk. [13]

Rescued from France and the Nazi grip were names forged into British military history. General Alan Brook, General Harold Alexander, and General Bernard Montgomery worked to save their Army. These warriors of the Battle of France in 1940 had to align themselves with the weary fates of war. Names were written into and out of the glorious histories of France and Britain, but the whole story remained untold.

The final act of this sea-borne drama would unfold four years later. And before that final act, the English and Germans would face each other on land, sea, and in the air. They battled on the high seas in the Battle of the Atlantic, Battles of Crete, Malta, Sicily, Italy, and in the skies over first Britain then Germany, and of course, in the deserts of North Africa. The final act between them would begin on 6 June 1944 as the sun began to rise over the beaches of Normandy.

Across the beaches, just like those you find in Dunkirk, tens of thousands of American and British soldiers cracked Hitler's vaunted Atlantic Wall and began *Chasing Rommel* and his German Army into the ashes of history.

---

[13] Sebag-Montefiore, Hugh. Dunkirk's Darkest Day: when the evacuation came close to disaster. Guardian Sunday, 16 July 2017.
https://www.theguardian.com/world/2017/jul/16/dunkirk-darkest-day-29-may-1940-evacuation-came-close-to-disaster Retrieved March 2021.

Part VI: Conclusion

"...until, in God's good time, the New World,
with all its power and might,
steps forth to the rescue and the liberation of the Old."

Winston Churchill, 4 June 1940

At 06:15, on the morning of 4 June 1940, a blanket of dense fog lifted off the English Channel, revealing the last of the last ships leaving from Dunkirk. It was the last day of the historic evacuations, and the ships were carrying members of the beleaguered French Army.

Now, it was their turn to leave France as the hated Germans finished what they had begun just weeks earlier and closed the port of Dunkirk, sealing off the once vital place of rescue. Relief was felt by those leaving, so was sadness, and more than a little shame in having been defeated so fast and so thoroughly by the dreaded Germans.

Suddenly, a massive explosion tore through the small French ship. In less than 60 seconds, seventy five percent, over 400 of those onboard the *Emile Deschamps* were lost, disappearing forever into the unforgiving seas they thought held their rescue. Amazingly, the *Emile Deschamps* was the last of the 243 vessels lost in the evacuation of Dunkirk.[14] [15]

On 16 July 2017, a column in the British newspaper *The Guardian* featured a piece describing the price paid for the Battle of France and holding back Hitler's forces as they closed on Dunkirk. Below are listed the killed, wounded, missing, and captured by country:

French casualties: approximately 300,000
British casualties: approximately 66,000
Belgian casualties: approximately 23,000
Dutch casualties: approximately 10,000

---

[14] Wragg, David. Sink the French: The French Navy After the Fall of France 1940. Page 95.
[15] Lord, the Miracle at Dunkirk. Pp. 268-269.

For their part, *The Guardian* lists German casualties as about *155,000 killed,* wounded, missing, or captured in their short and violent conquest of France in 1940.[16]

Britain's losses on the continent were extreme, to say the least.

Germany's victory was seen as Hitler's finest hour, his Nazi Government's most successful triumph. He was greeted in Germany as a conquering hero, the man who led Germany to crushing the enemies of the Fatherland, forever removing the stigma of failure in the First World War and casting off the punitive Treaty of Versailles.

From 10 May to 22 June 1940 a mere forty-four days, seven calendar weeks is all it took Hitler and his Blitzkrieg forces to undo decades of failures. But what Germany ultimately experienced was not the happy ending they believed they had found. Disaster awaited Hitler's forces, because he failed to defeat the British people and their fearless leader, Winston Churchill.

As Churchill had predicted, *The New World* came to the rescue and liberation of *The Old World.* The United States entered the war against Germany after Hitler and his German sycophants declared war on the United States. This they did on 8 December 1941, the day after the surprise attack by the Japanese at Pearl Harbor.

Nearly four years to the day the Dunkirk evacuations ended, the Allies arrived on the coast of France. On 6 June 1944, empowered by the remarkable efforts of the American and British people on the home fronts to build all that was necessary to invade Europe, the American and British forces fell from the skies and charged from the sea to liberate a continent from Nazi tyranny.

Admiral Bertram Ramsey, the man who got them out at Dunkirk brought them back at Normandy. Admiral Ramsey was appointed Commander of all Naval forces for the Invasion of Normandy. His remarkable plan, *Operation Dynamo* that brought them home was equaled by his planning and executing of the largest seaborne invasion in the history of the world, *Operation Neptune.*

By September of 1944, the invading Allies finally reached Dunkirk by land. But there were not enough Allied forces to attack and liberate the strongly defended port city of Dunkerque. The city was never liberated. From September of 1944 until the surrender of all German forces in May of 1945

---

[16] Sebag-Montefiore. Dunkirk's Darkest Day. Guardian Sunday 16 July 2017. Web. Retrieved March 2021.

Dunkerque was put under siege, the Germans held their prize until the very end of the War.

Today, there is much to see in Dunkerque. There, you find an excellent museum, full of relics and images that reminds one of what happened here. You can stroll the old city streets hunting for the right souvenir from the many shops. Unlike the images in the movies, Dunkerque was badly destroyed by the fighting in 1940 but it was rebuilt and today Dunkerque is a very modern metropolis, and still a busy seaport as well as a tourist attraction.

You can walk the beach, walk the mole, stroll along the old streets imaging what it was like in June of 1940. But it is the beach that draws me—*Their Beach*.

On the beach you will find the same sand, and sea that held their fates, and cast onto our history a remarkable reversal of fortune for Hitler and his Nazis invaders. Here, men defied a tyrant and his destructive war machine. From these sands alone, the British Nation delivered a most remarkable victory that was the foundation of the defeat of Germany in the Second World War.

Part VII: Epilogue

A soothing glass of French red wine accompanied me into my reflective reverie, as a long day slowly melted into passing images. Visits to France and the history she holds always lead me to reflective moments set in historical places. A peaceful, cerebral time to capture lasting sights, sounds, and thoughts before I move on to another adventure of *Chasing Rommel.*

Sitting back in an old, uncomfortable, wrought iron chair and gazing into history from my hotel balcony I observe a most remarkable sight. Under a lone, dimly lighted streetlight where the worn cobblestone street ends and the sandy beach begins, slightly shrouded with the incoming ocean fog, I saw them. At first, I thought they were in an embrace, then they moved, together and I watched as they danced.

Twisted tightly into each other's arms, their pace was slow and deliberate, as her head rested upon his chest. His eyes seemed closed from my distance, and he seemed to savor the touch and smell of her hair, as he tenderly turned her toward the sea.

It was not their first dance, I thought as they moved in unison, mindless of everything except themselves. They rhythmically moved to a soundless song, music that was only theirs, they shared a tempo, perhaps, that has been shared over a near lifetime together.

I could hear only the sounds of the crashing waves, and see only what was illuminated by the antique streetlight. *How French,* I think, and how perfect to close my visit to this historic place, a last and lasting image is of two lovers enjoying the liberties provided by men now ghosts.

My wine glass emptied, their dance over I realize I have been a witness to the place that changed the course of our history. My last thoughts are of them, on *Their Beach*, standing steadfastly, fearless, and hopeful that a nation would, and could bring them home.

They stood just a few miles from home with only the perilous English Channel, that dangerous and unforgiving body of water that has protected England, separating them from their beloved homes. They were freedom's last hope as they stood on *Their Beach*—resolute and unyielding, the British soldiers who defied German tyranny, on a thin strip of sand on the French coast.

For this author the hallmark of British fortitude and determination, centuries in the making, can still be found in its perfection on the beaches of Dunkirk. And if you stand on *Their Beach* and pause for a moment, the winds carry the words that has defined a country, her people, and inspired millions more:

"We shall defend our island, whatever the cost may be, we shall fight on the beaches, we shall fight on the landing grounds, we shall fight in the fields and in the streets, we shall fight in the hills; we shall never surrender."

Winston Churchill
4 June 1940

Bibliography

Adams, Perter Caddick. *Monty and Rommel Parallel Lives*. Overlook Press: New York. 2012. Print

Evans, Martin. *The Fall of France: Act with Daring*. Osprey Publishing: Oxford. 2000. Print.

Lord, Walter. *The Miracle At Dunkirk*. The Viking Press: New York. 1982. Print.

Luck, Hans von. *Panzer Commander*. Memoirs of a Panzer Commander. Praeger: New York. 1989. Print

Stasi, Jean-Charles. *Dunkirk 1940 Operation Dynamo: The Evacuation 340,000. British and French Soldiers to England.* Heimdal: Bayeux, 2018. Print.

Thompson, Julian. Major General. (Ret) *Dunkirk: Retreat to Victory*. Arcade: New York. 2011. Print.

Thorne Stephen, J. *The "Miracle of Dunkirk" Came at High Cost. 9* June 2020 https://legionmagazine.com/en/2020/06/the-miracle-of-dunkirk-came-at-high-cost/ Retrieved March 2021.

Wragg, David. *Sink the French: The French Navy After the Fall of France 1940.* Pen & Sword Books, Ltd.: South Yorkshire, UK. 2007. Print.

Warner, Philip. *The Battle of France: Six Weeks That Changed the World.* Hugh Sebag-Montefiore. *Dunkirk*. Sun 16 Jul 2017. www.theguardian.com

German Tiger Tank I Museum in France.

Chapter 2
Rommel's Defense of Normandy

Introduction

In the 2001 documentary film about the first Gulf War in 1991, *Inside the Kill Box,* an American armored unit commander reminisced about a remarkable experience,

"*...in the first Gulf War, a Bradley (*American armored personal carrier*) had a picture of German Field Marshal Erwin Rommel inside. A captured*

*Iraqi officer asked...why (a picture of) America's enemy. The driver replied
that if he had studied Rommel's campaigns, perhaps, he wouldn't be an
American prisoner.* "[17]

I am over seventy years behind the D-Day Invasion, and I am *Chasing
Rommel* across Normandy, trying to understand his defense of Hitler's
crumbling empire, a defense the Allies did not break until Rommel was
wounded and removed from his Normandy command.

---

[17] Sayenga, Kurt. Inside the Kill Box: Fighting the Gulf War. Arc Welder Films, LTD.
for Discovery Communications, LLC. 2001.

Part I: Rommel's Road to Normandy Allied Air Superiority

*"In the future...the battle on the ground will be preceded
by the battle in the air. This will determine which of the
contestants have to suffer...operational and tactical disadvantages...and
thus, be forced...into adopting compromise solutions."*
General Erwin Rommel (1891–1944)
1940—Quote on airpower
Rommel May Guide U.S. In Desert Warfare
19 February 1991 By Charles Leroux. The Chicago Tribune

From February 1941 until May 1943, General and later Field Marshal Erwin Rommel and his vaunted *Deutsches Afrikakorps* rampaged across North Africa not once but twice. Initially, Hitler sent Rommel with a meager two division force to North Africa to help the faltering Italians.

In September of 1940, the Italians invaded the British colony of Egypt. Mussolini's dreams of a second Roman Empire were promptly crushed by the British Army in the North African deserts. Desperate for Italian glory, Mussolini asked Hitler to help his armies in North Africa as the British had nearly wiped them out.

In February of 1941, upon arrival in North Africa, Rommel and his forces were subordinated to Italian command. Rommel was instructed by the German High Command in Berlin to help the Italians with defensive action only. Rommel's idea of defensive action was to immediately attack the British Army. At the outset, he was remarkably successful.

He surprised his British enemy constantly, engaging in fast-moving armored battles and fought his way over one thousand miles east to the outskirts of Tobruk. The British held onto their coveted deep-water port, defeating numerous German attacks. Rommel and the seemingly invincible *Afrikakorps* were forced to retreat, eventually surrendering nearly all of the ground they had gained.

In January of 1942, Rommel attacked again. This time, along with his army's one-thousand-mile advance, he captured Tobruk. Hitler awarded him the rank of Field Marshal, in German—*Generalfeldmarschal*, the highest rank in the German Army. At fifty-one years old, Erwin Rommel was one of the youngest men ever to achieve such a rank. From Tobruk the new Field Marshal continued easterly trying to capture further British territory.

Rommel's plans included taking Alexandria, Cairo, the Suez Canal, and then the rich Middle East oil fields. But Rommel's plans would be subjected to the same threat that so convincingly destroyed his supply lines a year earlier, and constantly hammered his advances—The British Royal Air Force.

Known as the Western Desert Air Force (WDAF), it was formed in late 1941 and would ultimately turn the tables against Rommel in the North African campaign. In a word, the air support from the WDAF was—overwhelming. It was in the barren, open plains of North Africa's desert that Rommel learned first-hand of the destructive power of Allied air supremacy. As he was defeated at El Alamein and began his retreat, he quickly realized that he had no answer for an enemy who ruled the skies above a battlefield.

In his book, *Rommel's Desert War: The Life and Death of The Afrika Korps*, author, professor, and retired US Army officer, Samuel W. Mitcham, Jr. bluntly describes the fate of Rommel's forces facing Allied air superiority, *"The RAF had so badly mauled Rommel's transport and supply columns that all his captured* (from the fall of Tobruk) *stockpiles did him little good, because he could not get them to front-line soldiers. In fact, the British Air Force operated so successfully that it must be given the major credit for saving Egypt from* (Rommel's) *Panzer Army."*[18]

North Africa was Rommel's first lesson in Allied air power, it would not be his last. Rommel became more experienced than most German generals in the Second World War with the destructive capabilities of an unchallenged enemy air force. The lesson quickly blasted into Rommel's personal life.

Rommel's wife and son were everything to him. And as the fortunes of war turned against him in North Africa, the war came home to his wife and son living in the family home near Stuttgart. In 1943, as the Afrika Korps were struggling for their very survival, Stuttgart was bombed by the Strategic Allied Air Forces.

On the night of March 11–12, 314 RAF strategic bombers pounded the city of Stuttgart. Although most of the bombs fell outside the city, nearly one hundred and twenty houses were destroyed, and five hundred people were

---

[18] Mitcham, Samuel W. Jr. Rommel's Desert War: The Life and Death of The Afrika Korps. Mechanicsburg, PA: Stackpole Books, 2007. Print. Page 102.

killed, wounded, or missing. It was this kind of massive attack that the Allies used to demoralize the German people.[19]

April brought more terror from the skies to Rommel's homeland and April brought bigger raids to Germany. On the night of April 4–5, 577 bombers struck at Kiel. A week later, 502 bombers attacked Frankfort on the night of April 10–11. It was back to Stuttgart which was hit by 462 bombers on the night of April 14–15. These unprecedented air attacks continued. [20]

This was happening all over Germany in 1943. Rommel knew it would get worse and it did. The numbers of planes the Allied air forces could send over German skies was frightening even to an old soldier like Erwin Rommel. July of 1943 brought hell to Hitler's cities, on the night of July 3–4, 653 bombers hit Cologne, 300 hundred planes hit one of Italy's jewels—Turin, on July 12–13.

The next day, nearly 400 bombers pounded the German city of Aachen. In the RAF diary the entry states, "*Aachen appeared to burst into flames.*" The diary lists another attack this one at Hamburg, on the night of July 24 and 25, "*728 aircraft dropped (their) bombs in 50 minutes. Approximately 1,500 people were killed.*"

On July 27–28, the Allies bombed Hamburg again with about 800 Allied bombers. The results were breathtaking as revealed in the achieved RAF diaries, "*Approximately 16,000 (sic) multistoried apartment buildings were destroyed. There were few survivors from the firestorm area and approximately 40,000 people died, most of them by carbon monoxide poisoning when all the air was drawn out of their basement shelters. In the period immediately following this raid, approximately 1,200,000 people—two thirds of Hamburg's population—fled the city in fear of further raids.*"

[19] National Archives of the Government of Great Britain. Royal Air Force Bomber Command 60th Anniversary. Campaign Diary March 1943.
http://webarchive.nationalarchives.gov.uk/20070706011932/http://www.raf.mod.uk/bombercommand/nov43.html retrieved April 2021.

[20] National Archives of the Government of Great Britain. Royal Air Force Bomber Command 60th Anniversary. Campaign Diary April 1943.
http://webarchive.nationalarchives.gov.uk/20070706011932/http://www.raf.mod.uk/bombercommand/nov43.html retrieved April 2021.

The devastation of a German city was nearly complete.[21]

Charles F. Marshall author of, *Discovering the Rommel Murder: Life and Death of the Desert Fox,* captures the Desert Fox's second lesson in the overwhelming power of the Allied Air Forces. Marshall writes, "*...Allied bombing squadrons were reaching deep into German air space and rendering vast destruction. Rommel's home...was near a Messerschmitt aircraft plant...He feared for the safety of his family and arranged...to move their residence...to southern Germany...*"

The war had come home for Rommel. The man who had become a legend in 1940, leading the German 7th Panzer Division—The Ghost Division (*Gespensterdivision* in German), and sweeping aside superior British forces in the deserts of North Africa, was now nearly powerless to protect his family. His enemy became all but unreachable in the skies above him and Germany.

In Marshall's book, we find a deeply concerned Rommel writing to his wife on 10 October 1943, "*Dearest Lu...thank god your trip (out of Stuttgart) was successful...That you had to experience the air raid in Stuttgart was not so wonderful. Only when you have moved, will I be able to rest...*"[22]

Rommel's last lesson in Allied air power would occur in Normandy. Before, during, and after the D-Day invasion of France, air power would greatly influence the outcome of the Allies most important military campaign. For Germany, her Armed Forces, and Rommel himself, Allied air power in Normandy would have fatal consequences.

---

[21] National Archives of the Government of Great Britain. Royal Air Force Bomber Command 60th Anniversary. Campaign Diary July 1943.
http://webarchive.nationalarchives.gov.uk/20070706011932/http://www.raf.mod.uk/bombercommand/nov43.html retrieved April 2021.

[22] Marshall, Charles. Discovering the Rommel Murder: The Life and Death of the Desert Fox. Mechanicsburg, PA: Stackpole Books, 2002. Page 116.

Massive German Tiger II Tank in French Museum.

Part II: Defending the Undefendable Fortress

*"When asked, "Why We Lost the War?" he reduced it to a
single formula: What was decisive in itself was the loss
of air supremacy...Everything depends on air supremacy,
everything else must take second place."*

German General Karl Koller (1898–1951)
Luftwaffe Chief of Staff (1945)
Why the Allies Won, Overy—Page 322

Adolph Hitler's dreams of Nazi conquest and world domination were unraveling very quickly in early 1943. Just months before, in the summer of 1942, it was all so different. His armies were still on the attack all over Russia, albeit attacks that could not and would not be supported. And in North Africa, in June of 1942 Hitler's favorite general Erwin Rommel, had captured the prized city and harbor of Tobruk in Libya, from its British defenders.

But by early 1943, everything had changed, and Hitler's armies were on the defensive after stinging defeats at Stalingrad, in the Soviet Union and at El Alamein, in the desert of North Africa. Meanwhile, in 1943, the Americans and British were bombing German cities, nearly at will.

It was within that context that drew Hitler, Germany's Supreme Military Commander to write his Führer Directive No. 51 on 3 November 1943—

"...The threat from the East remains, but an even greater danger looms in the West: the Anglo-American landing! In the East, the vastness of the space will, as a last resort, permit a loss of territory even on a major scale, without suffering a mortal blow to Germany's chance for survival...If the enemy here succeeds in penetrating our defenses on a wide front, consequences of staggering proportions will follow within a short time..."[23]

Found within those words, is the reality of Germany's war in November of 1943. Hitler's words were issued as a warning of the land war that was looming in the West. But the prelude to invasion was the battle being fought in the skies over occupied Europe and Germany, a battle Hitler was badly losing.

Before the Allies would invade Hitler's *Fortress Europa*, they had to have command of the skies over France and beyond. The more the Allies bombed cities, infrastructure, industrial plants, and military targets, large groups of German Air Force fighters moved closer to Germany to protect these vital assets. As Hitler was writing his Fuhrer Directive, Germany's air defenses had already been breached on a massive scale.

On the night of 22–23 November 1943, just three weeks after issuing his Führer Directive, the British RAF flew 764 aircraft over Germany's Capital Berlin. The resulting destruction caused insidious firestorms that left 175,000 people homeless.

The RAF diary entry reads, *"A vast area of destruction stretched from the central districts westwards across the mainly residential areas of Tiergarten and Charlottenburg to the separate suburb city of Spandau. Because of the dry weather conditions, several 'firestorm' areas were reported and a German plane next day measured the height of the smoke cloud as 6,000 (sic) meters (nearly 19,000 ft)."*

---

[23] Ambrose, Stephen E. D-Day June 6, 1944: The Climactic Battle of World War II. New York: Simon & Schuster, 1994. P. 28

Three days later, 383 aircraft bombed Berlin, the diary entry reports "...*crews aimed their bombs through the cloud at the glow of 11 major fires still burning from the previous night. Much further destruction was caused in Berlin.*" Two days later 262 aircraft attacked, and then two more days later, 450 airplanes attacked Berlin. The results were the same as the devastation in Germany reached the nearly defenseless capital city.[24]

It is within the context of massive arial attacks that Hitler and his Generals know the Allied invasion of Europe is pending. In November of 1943, Hitler ordered Germany's most famous soldier, Field Marshal Rommel to inspect the coastal defenses the Allies would have to attack.

The Atlantic Wall was Hitler's believed impregnable series of structures running nearly 2,000 miles from arctic Norway to the Spanish–French border. Rommel only covered the areas he believed the Allies could possibly invade. One of his prerequisites was the ability of the Allies to use their overwhelming air superiority.

Distance to known airfields in England held the key to the Allies choosing an invasion site. Rommel and his staff toured from Denmark to the Brittany coast of France, ruling out all areas beyond the reach of Allied air power.

Rommel was now an expert on Hitler's impregnable Atlantic Wall. Who would be a better choice to defend the wall? Author Stephen Ambrose, on Page 58 of his excellent work, *D-Day, June 6, 1944 The Climatic Battle of World War II,* describes Rommel's thoughts as he finished his inspections of Hitler's Atlantic Wall. *Rommel denounced the Atlantic Wall as a farce.*

Ambrose then quotes Rommel as he confided to close associates, "... (The Atlantic Wall) *is a figment of Hitler's Wolkenkuckucksheim* (cloud—cuckoo land imagination)...*an enormous bluff...more for the German people than the enemy...and the enemy through his agents knows more about it than we do.*"

On 15 January 1944, Adolph Hitler appointed Field Marshal Erwin Rommel to command Army Group B, the defenders of the French northwestern coast. And on that very same day RAF Bomber Command sent 498 large two and four engine bombers over Germany. The air war over Germany was a disaster for Hitler's military.

---

[24] National Archives of the Government of Great Britain. Royal Air Force Bomber Command 60th Anniversary. Campaign Diary November 1943 http://webarchive.nationalarchives.gov.uk/20070706011932/http://www.raf.mod.uk/bombercommand/nov43.html retrieved April 2021.

It was just a matter of time before such an enormous advantage ended the war. Nearly all of Germany's generals understood the devastation of bombing German civilian targets. But even in January of 1944, most of them had not faced the weight of the Allied air forces in combat. Erwin Rommel was one of the few Germans who had. [25]

Hitler's Third Reich was fatally broken. Since 1942, German cities, factories, infrastructure, as well as known or suspected military targets had been under devastating Allied Air Force bombing missions. Hitler's promised 1000-year Reich was unraveling by an enemy who ruled the skies.

Beginning in March of 1944, the Allied Air Forces began the systematic destruction of the rails and roads leading to Normandy. General Eisenhower was creating a *Strategic Island*, isolating Normandy from its supplies and the German Army's ability to resupply the area after the invasion. Rommel had other worries as well, such as the time and specific locations of the invaders.

In contrast to the massively growing Allied Armada in England, Rommel and his army in France were low on most everything. The German occupiers could gather very little beyond what was already in France, a devastating result of the Strategic Allied bombing campaign.

Realizing he was low on oil, gasoline, ships, planes, trucks, tanks, and other motorized equipment, Field Marshal Erwin Rommel had a simple plan to defend the western edge of Hitler's quickly crumbling Third Reich.

Rommel, the master of armored warfare, a genius of offensive, fast moving fluid battles fought with a combination of tanks, artillery, aircraft, and infantry would do what he always did; attack his enemy. He would attack the attackers.

He would attack the invading forces at the shoreline, where he was confident, they were most vulnerable. Here his limited use of movement was not a hindrance because the Allies suffered from the same limited area of movement.

A good examination of the Germany Army situation in Normandy is explained by the way they primarily moved soldiers, materials, and supplies in the Spring of 1944. Detailed in his book, *Mechanized Juggernaut or Military Anachronism? Horses and the German Army of World War II*, author R.L.

---

[25] National Archives of the Government of Great Britain. Royal Air Force Bomber Command 60th Anniversary. Campaign Diary January 1944
http://webarchive.nationalarchives.gov.uk/20070706011932/http://www.raf.mod.uk/bombercommand/nov43.html retrieved 10/21/16

DiNardo describes the reality of the German Army in the west, charged with defending the expected Allied Invasion:

"...*It* (the use of thousands of horses) *was a measure of the seriousness of the German situation that what was once the most modern army in the world was reduced to the use of horsepower.*"[26]

Another way to think of the German Army on D-Day is to remember the scene in the movie the *Longest Day*. In the film we see an older, fat, German soldier on a horse. He is trying to deliver breakfast to the Germans guarding the Normandy coast. He is mocked by a local French resident who sees the rich irony of his German occupiers needing a horse to deliver supplies, as the Allies begin the invasion with modern warships sitting unopposed off the French coast.

Another revealing example is found in the first moments of combat in France for the famed, *Band of Brothers*, Easy Company, 506 PIR, 101st Airborne Division. Lieutenant Winters and a small group of paratroopers attack German soldiers on a horse drawn wagon in the second chapter of the HBO TV series, *Band of Brothers, "Day of Days."*

And at the end of that same episode, the viewer sees a group of dead horses being pulled from blocking the roadway. A roadway filled with American soldiers, tanks, and trucks—a modern mobile motorized army that arrived on the European Continent in a matter of hours, after crossing an ocean. The contrast is amazing.

How does one of history's most famous armored warfare specialists win a 20th Century battle with horses? A battle that will foretell the outcome of humanity's most deadly event, World War II. With greatly limited mobility, Rommel began to plan his defense.

If the Allies could travel thousands of miles and cross the vast Atlantic Ocean, a weak wall would not stop them. Rommel's only chance was to improve that wall, to improvise obstacles, and use or create geographic barriers that would generate blockages.

In doing so, he planned to slow down or stop the attackers on the beach or as they tried to move inland. He would create kill zones on the beaches and

---

[26] Dinardo, R.L., Mechanized Juggernaut or Military Anachronism?: Horses and the German Army in World War II. Mechanicsville, PA: Stackpole Books. 2008. Page 112.

beyond, to trap the American and British forces charged with destroying the Atlantic Wall. After all, the Allies had the mobility and Rommel did not.

By slowing, stopping, or funneling the invaders into preselected areas, Rommel hoped he was balancing the scales to some equal measure for his static defenders.

How would Rommel disrupt the seaborne invaders? How would he slow, stop, and kill as many as possible on the shoreline? Returning to Ambrose's book *D-Day The Climatic Battle of World War II*, on Pages 63–64 the author quotes a conversation Rommel had with his chief engineer officer in Normandy, General Lieutenant Wilhelm Meise:

"Drawing on his experiences in North Africa, Rommel told his Chief Engineer Officer, Wilhelm Meise, Allied control of the air would prevent movement of reinforcements to the battle area. Our only possible chance is at the beaches—that is where the enemy is always weakest."

Rommel knew his enemy would dominate the skies above his coastline defenders. Ambrose continues and captures Rommel's words demanding action from his Chief Engineer, *"I want anti-personnel mines, anti-tank mines, anti-paratrooper mines. I want mines to sink ships and mines to sink landing craft. I want some minefields designed so our infantry can cross them but no(t) enemy tanks. I want mines that detonate when a wire is tripped; mines that explode when a wire is cut; mines that can be remote controlled; and mines that will blow up when a beam of light is interrupted."*

Rommel reluctantly surrendered the skies above the invasion, but would offer to his enemy something that very few amphibious invasion forces in history had ever encountered. They would be attacked while invading. The invaders would be slowed or stopped on the beach and then attacked while still wet, disoriented, and having finite supplies of ammunition.

Ambrose brings us into Rommel's mind as he addresses his staff officers, *"Rommel predicted the Allies would launch their invasion with aerial bombings, naval bombardments, and airborne assaults, followed by seaborne landings."*

It was clear to the Desert Fox that the Allies would press their overwhelming advantage and attack under a deadly blanket of thousands of aircraft.

Rommel knew the bulk of the invading forces would be from the seaborne side. His only answer for that was to place his static and mobile troops, as well as armored divisions, close to the beaches to deliver a fast and decisive counterattack at the shoreline. With his ideas of repelling the invasion in place, Rommel understood in the late spring of 1944—he was nearly out of time.

By the spring of 1944, years had been wasted as the German Forces in France failed to build an impregnable barrier between the sea and the land. And what of the defenders of that barrier, what soldiers were left to defend Hitler's most vulnerable flank, the Western Front on the French Coast?

The best troops and equipment had been removed and sent to the Eastern Front in Russia and replaced by an amazing array of German and non-German fighting forces, under a scattered not centralized command.

First, there were some elite units in France. The best ground forces the German Army had in France on D-Day were the German Paratroops (*Fallschirmjäger* in German). Also, there were Panzer Divisions, mostly under the direct control of Hitler, or Geyr von Schweppenburg, Commander of *Panzer Group West.* There were also SS (*Schutzstaffel*) units in France, and they, like most of the Panzer Divisions, were under separate SS command until assigned to an army group or corps.

The German Navy, the *Kriegsmarine* and German Air Force, the *Luftwaffe* were also not under Rommel's direct command. The Luftwaffe Field Divisions were commanded by Luftwaffe officers, and they were poorly trained as infantry soldiers. The bulk of Rommel's defenders were infantry units, and many of those were immobile or static, and one in six of them was a Non-German.

A large part of the men defending Germany in France were not Germans, could not speak German, and were very poorly trained. They were also for the most part unarmed and remained that way until the invasion. They were called volunteers and labeled *Osttruppen*—troops from the east.

In his D-Day book on pages 33–34, Ambrose describes the foreign soldiers fighting for Germany in France, "*the Wehrmacht had 'volunteers' from France, Italy, Croatia, Hungary, Romania, Poland, Finland, Estonia, Latvia, Lithuania, Asians, North Africa, Russia, Ukraine, Muslim Republics...and Koreans.* Ambrose continues describing some of the Germans in Normandy...*increasingly   unreliable...relaxed   physical standards...convalescing soldiers, stomach and lung ailments, and older men and boys* (one division the average age was 36)."

Hitler had more divisions fighting the Soviet Union than all his other remaining forces combined. And the once feared German Air Force, the vaunted *Luftwaffe*, had been recalled to defend the skies over the Fatherland. As we have seen, the destruction of Germany from the endless Allied aerial bombing campaigns was conducted night and day with deficient resistance.

But as the winter of 1943 turned to spring of 1944 along the northwestern French coast, Rommel's most oppressing problem was his lack of time. Rommel understood the magnitude of his challenge, and the coming campaign in France. Interestingly, one day along the English channel, Rommel gazed out in the direction of Britain.

Detailed in his epic D-Day account, *The Longest Day*, author Cornelius Ryan quotes Rommel standing on a Normandy Beach, on 22 April 1944, just weeks before the D-Day Landings, "*The first twenty-four hours of the invasion will be decisive...the fate of Germany depends on the outcome...for the Allies as well as the Germans, it will be the Longest Day.*"

It was a prophetic realization and the inspiration for the title of Ryan's Book—*The Longest Day*. This quote underscores the Desert Fox's belief that the significance of time had no parallel in the successful defense of the coast of France. Simply stated, Rommel wanted the struggle decided on the beaches on the very first day—The Longest Day.

That April day in 1944, standing along the cold and windy beach, Rommel looked out at the rushing seas and pointed where the sands and sea meet, "*The war will be won or lost on the beaches.*" Not the battle will be won or lost— but "the war will be won or lost," Rommel knew, as did every German or Allied soldier who could read a map, that the coast of France was close to Germany, and that a successful invasion would represent victory or loss in the war.[27]

Even Hitler had drawn that conclusion in his, Führer Directive No. 51 on 3 November 1943. Hitler wrote, "*...If the enemy here* (Invading France) *succeeds in penetrating our defenses on a wide front, consequences of staggering proportions will follow within a short time...*"[28]

Rommel was determined to kill, stop, or slow the invading Allies between the tide lines at best or just inland at the least. His weapons were composed of old and new artillery pieces, mortars, machine gun installations, and Panzer

---

[27] Ryan, Cornelius. The Longest Day. Simon and Schuster: New York. Introduction.
[28] Ambrose, Stephen E. D-Day June 6, 1944. Pp. 28-29.

divisions he hoped to move just behind the static beach positions. With this thin shoreline defense in place, he hoped his troops would defeat the most powerful seaborne force ever assembled.

What Rommel found in Normandy, and all along the French coast appalled him. He understood that by 1944 the Allies had already launched a number of successful invasions in the both the European and Pacific Theaters of the war.

His own forces in North Africa had been defeated when the Allies launched *"Operation Torch"* in late 1942. *Torch* was the nearly unopposed amphibious invasion of North Africa that surrounded the German Army and forced its surrender in less than six months. Next, it was the more difficult seaborne landings at Sicily in July of 1943, code named *"Operation Husky."*

Then *"Operation Avalanche"* in September of 1943, just nine months before D-Day, it was the seaborne invasion of mainland Italy. All the while, the US Navy, Marines and Army had launched many successful invasions of Pacific Islands. The Allies were coming and sooner not later. Rommel knew he was nearly out of time.

World War I artillery used by Rommel's forces in Normandy.

Part III: Crumbling Fortress

"The Battle for Normandy was the most complex and daring military operation in the history of modern warfare. Two years of intense, detailed planning reached its successful conclusion when the Allied forces took the beaches on D-Day. But the seventy-six-day campaign that followed...was one of the bloodiest of the war and its true story has been concealed in myth."

Decision In Normandy
Carlo D'Este—1983

Artillery was a major problem all along Hitler's Atlantic Wall and Rommel ordered guns from every conquered territory. What he ultimately had was an unsupportable mixture of calibers and kinds: German, British, French, Czech, Hungarian, and Russian. It was mockingly referred to as, *Rommel's Traveling Artillery Circus*, by some of his German peers. In 1942 and 1943, much of the movable, wheeled modern artillery had left the Atlantic Wall for the failing

Eastern Front. Rommel and his operatives gathered as much artillery as they could find, including some World War I relics.

They assembled artillery from all over the Reich, many were obsolete and with a very finite supply of ammunition. Rommel had successfully used captured Russian guns in North Africa as his German equipment was destroyed. The German Army shipped captured Russian 76 mm guns to Rommel for his 1942 campaign in North Africa. He put them to use in the desert. Hitler's war against the Soviet Union consumed vast quantities of Germany's military assets from its beginning in June of 1941 until the war ended in May of 1945.

Also, it is often overlooked and is an important piece of the Normandy story, that the Allied air attacks over Germany forced thousands of anti-aircraft guns to remain in Germany to protect German cities. Thousands of artillery pieces, tens of thousands of tons of ammunition, and thousands of experienced artillery soldiers to man these guns were unavailable to protect the coast and skies of Normandy.

The material vacuum created by the day and night bombings in Germany by the Allied Air Forces was critical to creating the opening that the D-Day invading forces exploited in the skies above Hitler's Atlantic Wall.

One of the best examples of the artillery shortage in Normandy is that even the guns at Pointe-du-Hoc, the cannons that Eisenhower made job number one to destroy on D-Day, were French built, World War I, 155 millimeter, wagoned wheeled howitzers. These famous guns were destroyed by US Army Rangers on D-Day. They never fired a single shell on the invading US forces at Omaha and Utah beach.

Lacking soldiers, guns, and air power, Rommel mined vast swaths of the beaches and areas inland. He knew from experience mines, or even the suspicion of mines could slow an advance. Any mines made by any supplier would be fine. Antitank, antipersonnel, metal, wooden, and delay fuse mines were all used. He also used artillery shells in creative manners, such as hanging them from trip wires at Pointe-du-Hoc and placing them on beach and airborne obstacles.

Metal, wooden, and sometimes concrete barriers were placed in belts along the beaches. Some were topped with mines and some old artillery shells. He also positioned the beach obstacles so they would be covered by a high tide.

When this was learned by the Allies, it was one of the determining factors to invade at low tide, a course of action that only slowed the invading troops.

Now, instead of a narrow strip of beach they would have to cross 400 plus yards of open beach to the sea walls. Slowed by wet clothes, wet and sandy weapons, being sick and disorientated, this played into Rommel's plans.

On the beaches, all of his defense obstacles were narrow. Those with multi support legs had narrow legs, never wider than the average soldier's body. They lulled a soldier into thinking that cover could be found there. It was rather a place where the invaders were slowed or stopped and that made them a stationary and easier target.

If an invader or his landing craft made it to shore, he would have to contend with the mines. Mine fields were just beyond the open beach, and usually marked. From the base of the seawall to the rising bluffs, Rommel placed his deadly static killers.

By D-Day Rommel and his defenders were nearly out of mines, but had nonetheless buried millions of hidden killers in the Normandy sands. They had also developed fake mine fields which could slow down an invader as quickly as a live mine field. They were all marked, *Achtung Minen*—caution mines.

Behind those mines were infantry, machine guns, mortars, and artillery spotters connected by tunnels, trenches and telephones. The effect, especially on Omaha Beach, was devastating.

To combat the threat of an airborne landing Rommel gathered concrete and wooden poles. He also ordered trees cut down and turned into deadly poles whittled into points to impale gliders or falling paratroopers. They were called *Rommel's Asparagus* and some also had artillery shells or mines so if struck by a glider they would explode injuring or killing many aboard.

Next, he ordered streams and rivers dammed up. Unable to drain into the sea, they filled low lying areas, thereby creating large and often deep swamps and lakes. The roads not flooded over by Rommel, created a shortage of roads that led inland from the beaches.

These lonely roads could be mined, or have artillery zeroed in on them. The raised dry roads were the only way to move men and supplies inland and were often death traps. Conversely, these isolated roads limited Rommel's counter movements costing him time he did not have as he tried to reach his enemies invading from the sea.

And finally, close to the beaches Rommel would place his Panzer divisions. He felt it was a critical piece of his defense of the coast. And it was a constant source of contention between Rommel and his direct superior in Normandy, Field Marshal Gerd von Rundstedt, and his superiors in Berlin. Rommel knew he had no answer for Allied air power, and only one hope—to have Panzers close enough to strike the beaches immediately.

This too was dangerous, because it put massive Panzer formations within reach of the Allies destructive naval guns. But Rommel had to gamble he would win on the beaches, but his superiors would have none of it, the Panzers were never moved close enough to the beaches to make any difference on D-Day.

On the morning of 6 June 1944, Erwin Rommel was at his home in Herrlingen, outside of Ulm in southern Germany. Rommel was not in Normandy on D-Day. Believing the weather was impossible for an Allied attack, he was granted permission to leave Normandy by his superior, Field Marshal von Rundstedt.

He also had been told repeatedly by the weather experts in Berlin that an invasion was not possible for the next few days as the seas were too rough for small ships, and the clouds were too thick for aircraft. But unknown to Rommel was that the Germans had lost their weather stations out in the Atlantic.

Before 1944, they had U-Boats and small surface ships to gather weather data. But by 1944, that was no longer an option, and the weather charts were created and read in Berlin, and were of little value in an area like Normandy.

With rainy, cloudy, stormy weather expected for the foreseeable future, Rommel went home to Germany to be with his wife and son and celebrate her fiftieth birthday—6 June 1944. He stopped at home, because he was on his way to see Hitler in East Prussia, at his military headquarters at Rastenburg, The Wolf's Lair—*Wolfsschanze* in German.

There, he was to argue for more Panzer divisions and to move them into coastal areas like Normandy, close to the beaches, for the expressed purpose of attacking the invaders at the water's edge. Rommel wanted as much armor as he could get from his commander in chief, Adolph Hitler. Rommel's plan included moving the fanatical 12th SS Panzer Division to the area of Carentan, close to Omaha and Utah Beaches.

On the morning of 6 June 1944, the day of Mrs. Rommel's 50th birthday celebration, the phone rang at the Rommel house. It was Rommel's Normandy

Chief of Staff, General Hans Speidel who informed Rommel the invasion had seemingly begun.

Rommel never made it to Rastenburg, to meet with Hitler. The Panzers were never installed behind the beaches in Normandy. Rommel returned to his headquarters in Normandy late at night on 6 June 1944. By then, the *Longest Day* was nearly over, and the battle for the beaches had been decided. Rommel's weak and scattered forces were overrun on all the landing beaches except Omaha, which into the evening of June 6, was just barely in Allied hands.

From 6 June through 17 July 1944, Rommel tried to slow the Allied advance from a beachhead to a breakout. With every passing day, the Allies grew stronger, and the German army, navy, U-boats, and air forces grew weaker.

In a matter of weeks, the Allies' opposition to the German resistance was becoming overwhelming. The Normandy front was crumbling. Yet, Rommel managed to prevent a breakout. Regardless, every day that passed, Rommel knew Germany was that much closer to total defeat in the west and the loss of the war.

Knowing the end seemed a mere formality, Rommel played his last desperate card. A daring, and deadly assault on the power of the man who had helped to create the Rommel legend, his military commander and chief—Adolf Hitler. He would offer the Allies peace on the Western front.

On 15 July 1944 Field Marshal Erwin Rommel did what no other German Field Marshal dared to do, he directly challenged Hitler's absolute power. Rommel wrote a document now remembered as, *The Ultimatum of July 15.* Author and retired US Army officer Samuel Mitcham writes on page 184 of, *The Desert Fox in Normandy* that Rommel addressed his Chief of Staff, General Speidel, that he would take independent action against the Nazi dictator.

Mitcham tells us, *"Rommel summarized the deteriorating military situation in Normandy."* (Rommel wrote), *"Army Group B had sustained 97,000 casualties…and lost 225 tanks…*(of which only 7% were replaced).*"*

Rommel concluded his ultimatum, *"The troops are everywhere fighting heroically, but the unequal struggle is approaching its end. It is urgently necessary that the proper political conclusions to be drawn from this situation.*

As C & C of the army group, I feel myself duty bound to speak plainly on this point."

The next day, 16 July, Rommel visited one of his trusted subordinate commanders. The officer asked Rommel what he would do if the Fuhrer refused to agree with his assessment. Rommel snapped back that he would open the Western Front and seek peace with the Allies himself, in isolation from Hitler. But before he could do that, he had one last rendezvous with the Allied Air Forces that had so bitterly defeated him in North Africa, in Germany, and in Normandy.

On 17 July 1944, early in the evening, Rommel was speeding back to his headquarters. He had been visiting the front in the area of Caen. His open top staff car drew the attention of two Allied fighter aircraft hunting for any signs of German movement.

The Allied air power that had defeated Rommel in North Africa, bombed his German homeland into tatters, and reduced his Normandy Armies to barely effective defensive action was now bearing down on him. With a series of machine gun blasts, the two staff cars were destroyed, killing or wounding all the occupants.

Although he survived the attack, he would not survive Hitler's vengeance for his implication in the 20 July 1944 attempt to kill Hitler with a bomb. Hitler and many on his staff believed Rommel was involved in the failed ill-fated assassination attempt.

Part IV: Conclusion

"Unlike other senior army leaders, Rommel had had experience with the air power the Anglo-American powers would bring to the battlefield, as well as with their immense logistical capabilities. For other German leaders, especially Hitler, American and British military capabilities simply did not appear nearly as threatening as they did to Rommel...From early 1944, Rommel argued that the Germans must defend against the coming invasion on the beaches. If the Wehrmacht failed to defeat the Allies at the water's edge, the superiority of Anglo-American air power and logistics...would be an inevitable defeat that would end whatever chance the Reich had to achieve a compromise peace."

Williamson Murray
June 2006 issue of World War II magazine

The Allied air power that nearly killed Rommel would only continue to dominate the struggle on the ground. Just a week after Rommel's wounding, the Allies preceded their breakout with a breakthrough. Air power was chosen to create the vital opening that would free the Allied armies stuck in the bocage country. In a plan called *"Operation Cobra."*

The Panzer Lehr Division were the unfortunate German ground forces opposite Bradley's American forces set to pass through a gap that would be created in the German's fragile defense lines. For all of Rommel's preparation, planning, building, and creative defenses, there was no defense for what happened on 25 July 1944.

Samuel Mitcham describes the ultimate blow that the Allied Air Power would deliver in Normandy. It was the fatal blow of destruction in the Normandy ground war and it arrived from the skies which grew dark as the incredibly enormous modern air Armada blotted out the Normandy sun.

It was the decisive blow that the Germans could not imagine and Germans could not possibly defend. It was *Blitzkrieg* on steroids as the American army and army air forces pulverized a narrow strip of the German lines. It was what Rommel feared most in his final showdown with the Allied Air Power in Normandy.

We find on page 187 in Professor Mitcham's The Desert Fox in Normandy, "*On July 25 1944, the heaviest tactical employment of strategic air power during World War II was concentrated against the Panzer Lehr Division…1,600 B-17 Flying Fortresses dropped thousands of tons of high explosive on Bayerlein's* (German General Fritz Bayerlein) *units. They were followed by hundreds of medium bombers and Jabos* (German slang for Allied fighter planes). *In all, the air forces dropped 12 bombs for every German soldier in the target area. Tanks were hurled in the air…Entire companies were buried alive and completely wiped out…The massive carpet bombing continued on an unprecedented scale…the entire area resembled the surface of the moon.*"

The air power that drove Rommel from North Africa, drove his family deep into southern Germany, and drove him off the Normandy battlefield would be one of the deciding factors of the Second World War. Rommel's defense of Normandy, considering that he had very little time and materials, was a remarkable military accomplishment. He held lines, using natural geographic barriers like hedgerows and barriers of his own devices like flooded areas. With all his inventiveness, it was the Allied Air Forces that he could not stop.

The Allies breeched the Atlantic wall on a fifty-mile front by sea in a matter of hours. They also landed in Hitler's *Fortress Europa* from the skies, as three airborne divisions arrived and remained to protect the flanks of the invasion force.

In the end, Rommel's defense of Normandy was a failure. He was unable to stop the Allies on the ground, by the sea, and most importantly—from the air.

Bibliography

Ambrose, Stephen E. D-Day June 6, 1944: The Climactic Battle of World War II. Simon & Schuster: New York, 1994. Print

D'Este, Carlo. *Decision In Normandy*. E. P. Dutton: New York. 1983. Print

Dinardo, R.L., *Mechanized Juggernaut or Military Anachronism?: Horses and the German Army in World War II*. Stackpole Books: Mechanicsville, PA. 2008. Print.

Hargreaves, Richard. *The Germans in Normandy: Death Reaped a Terrible Harvest*. Pen & Sword Military: South Yorkshire, UK. 2009. Print.

Marshall, Charles. *Discovering The Rommel Murder: The Life and Death of the Desert Fox*. Stackpole Books: Mechanicsberg, PA2002. Print.

Mitcham, Samuel W. Jr. *Rommel's Desert War: The Life and Death of The Afrika Korps*. Stackpole Books: Mechanicsburg, PA, 2007. Print.

Overy, Richard. *The Bombing War: Europe 1939–1945*. Penguin Books Ltd: London. 2013. Print.

Overy, Richard. Why The Allies Won. W.W. Norton: New York. Print

Ryan, Cornelius. *The Longest Day*. Simon and Schuster: New York. 1995. Print.

Williamson, Murray. *Field Marshall Erwin Rommel's Defense of Normandy During World War II* WWW.HISTORYNET.COM/FIELD-MARSHALL-ERWIN-ROMMELS-DEFENSE-OF-NORMANDY-DURING-WORLD-WAR-II.HTM

The Longest Day. Producer Daryl Zanuck. Director Ken Annakin. 20th Century Fox. 1962. Film.

Day of Days. Band Of Brothers. HBO. September 2001. TV Miniseries.

Big German gun at Maisy Battery.

Chapter 3
D-Day's Forgotten Place, Battery Maisy

Introduction

"Man is not what he thinks he is, he is what he hides."

André Malraux (1901–76)
French novelist and politician

This is a story you were not meant to know. It is the story of a place still being unearthed and with every shovel full of dirt removed, we find more truth. That truth makes some historians uncomfortable and even combative. It is a narrative that some say does not fit the D-Day story. Yet, it has a growing place in the history of D-Day and a few days beyond that historic day.

Questions linger at the mention of its name. It is the square peg that many try to fit into a round hole, and then dismiss it disdainfully. Some claim it is a fantasy developed by the man who discovered this long lost massive German gun battery. It is not.

Maisy is a place still being excavated, still being uncovered, rediscovered, and still being debated.

Just before they departed Normandy, US Army engineers were ordered to take bulldozers and bury this place. Many places in Normandy were left exactly as they were after the battles were over. Pointe-du-Hoc, for example, is still covered in bomb craters from the endless Allied air and naval bombings.

As the Allies advanced towards Germany, they slowly departed the Normandy coast and moved beyond the wreckage of coastal France. But Maisy was not left as it had been conquered. The bunkers, gun platforms and trenches were not destroyed, just covered over by many feet of soil. It was buried, and that is out of place in Normandy, it leads us to question—did someone want it erased, deleted from the D-Day stories that would grow from the remarkable loss of American lives defeating Hitler's forces on the coast of France?

The man who rediscovered Maisy calls it a "cover-up". He refers to not just the act of physically burying Maisy, but intentionally removing the history of Maisy on D-Day. That is a strong statement, especially for Americans, we don't like the words cover-up; they have an ominous illegal sound and remind many of a troubling period in American history. It smacks of corruption and sinister double dealing, lying politicians.

Regardless of the label you assign this place, it follows that the first questions to be asked about Maisy are not what it did or did not do on D-Day. The first questions are why was it buried? What was or is still there, that in 1944 needed to be covered? Most importantly, who ordered the Maisy Battery buried?

The D-Day story has become a monolith of legendary, nearly unparalleled sacrifice. On 6 June 1984, at the Fortieth Anniversary of D-Day, at the American Cemetery overlooking Omaha Beach President Ronald Reagan spoke as authentic emotion pushed out the words.

He said, "*We stand today at a place of battle…that saw and felt the worst of war. Men bled and died here for a few feet of—or inches of sand, as bullets and shellfire cut through their ranks…*" Mr. Reagan also spoke at Pointe-du-Hoc on that day. He was standing before the survivors of the attack on the cliffs and guns of the Pointe.

Reagan said, "*These are the boys of Pointe du Hoc. These are the men who took the cliffs. These are the champions who helped free a continent. These are the heroes who helped end a war.*" The legends of Pointe-du-Hoc, and Omaha Beach were intact and growing.

Thirty-five years after that another President would speak at the D-Day Anniversary. On 6 June 2014, President Obama said, "*…on these shores…the tide was turned…We say it now as if it couldn't be any other way. But in the annals of history, the world had never seen anything like it…Omaha—Normandy—this was democracy's beachhead…our victory in that war decided not just a century, but shaped the security and well-being of all posterity…future generations, whether 70 or 700 years hence, will gather at places like this to honor them and to say that these were generations of men and women who proved once again that the United States of America is and will remain the greatest force for freedom the world has ever known.*"

With their soaring and eloquent words, these two Presidents framed the sacrifices in Normandy, searing the collective memories of generations of proud Americans. The legends and myths of D-Day that had grown over the decades were not just unimpaired, or even unflawed, they were unbroken. Then a place called Maisy called into question the role of certain ghosts of men during and after the heroics of D-Day.

I am in an active historical excavation site in Normandy. Maisy is raw, it is open and basic, no frills as you follow the semi-excavated German trenches. It is incomplete, with weeds and tall grass all around. It wants to tell you its story as you walk through mud to navigate the primitive trenches. It has gun platforms and all the support bunkers you can imagine.

It is a very big place that seems out of place in Normandy. Most gun batteries in Normandy are much smaller than the sprawling Battery Maisy. I am *Chasing Rommel* to *D-Day's Forgotten Place,* the massive German gun battery at Maisy looking for answers to a 75-year-old question that many still will not ask.

Part I: A Little Disguised

"Seldom, very seldom, does complete truth belong to any human disclosure; seldom can it happen that something is not a little disguised or a little mistaken."

Jane Austen (1775–1817)
Emma
1815.

I met Maisy in a book. It was a short sentence, on an old, photocopied page identified as, *Headquarters 1ˢᵗ Infantry Division.* The copied document covered two pages—214–5, in one of the photo sections of the book. It was a timeline from D-Day morning, it read like a diary, a tragic diary. *"Batrys* (sic) *at Maisy still in commission. Being kept under fire."*

Each line lists all that went wrong on the sands of Bloody Omaha Beach. The Maisy entry is near the bottom of the first page and it has an entry time of 08:24, or two hours after H-Hour. Two lines down from the Maisy entry was the last entry on the page, *"08:33 Failed to unload* (LCT 538-Landing Craft Tank) *due to indirect fire of 88s* (German artillery pieces).*"* Reading an entry about a third of the way down on the second page I see Maisy again. *"09:45 Batrys* (sic) *at Maisy completely destroyed."*

The next line seemed to contradict that Maisy was out of action. *"09:46 Firing on beach Easy Red is keeping LCIs* (landing Craft Infantry) *from landing."* A few lines down, and only ten minutes from claiming Maisy Battery was destroyed the entry reads, *"09:55...Many LCTs* (Landing Craft Tank) *standing by but cannot unload because of heavy shell fire on beach."*

I questioned—Was Maisy destroyed or not? Most all the entries listed the bad news of the landings on Omaha, and these were more failures on a tragic morning of failures. I continued reading my book, a first edition, first printing of *The Longest Day* by Cornelius Ryan. I loved every page of his work, and the Maisy Battery slipped from my memory as Ryan masterfully told the story of *The Longest Day.*

The next time I met Maisy was on a movie screen. Well, I think it was maybe Maisy, because the name Maisy was never spoken. I, like so many others, had waited for Steven Spielberg's seminal, D-Day film, *Saving Private*

Ryan, and although the movie was a fictional story, his portrayal of Omaha Beach was startling. Even for someone who had read hundreds of stories, the violence he depicted on screen seemed other worldly.

We meet the US Army Rangers of C Company, 2nd Battalion on Omaha Beach as they land with the 29th Infantry Division. We follow them through that hell and then watch them assault the German gun positions. When they make it to the top of the bluff, the Rangers administer the unbridled retaliatory savagery that the Germans have earned.

After the landings on Omaha Beach and before he is sent to find Private Ryan, fictitious Captain John Miller (Tom Hanks) Commander of C Company, 2nd Ranger Battalion reports to his superior officer at the HQ, 2nd Rangers Battalion. This is at the 36:19-time mark of the movie and we see on screen, "*OMAHA BEACH D-DAY PLUS THREE*." (D-Day plus three is 9 June 1944).

Captain Miller reports to his superior officer, Lt. Colonel Walter Anderson (Dennis Farina) about the difficult fight he and his soldiers had just finished. First, he explains the dense mine fields, and the vast array of mines employed by the Germans to protect the guns he was sent to destroy. He never looks at the Lt. Colonel, rather he addresses a map on the table in front of him, as he points out where the three the guns were located.

He is asked about casualties and lamenting his dead and wounded comrades, he stares blankly at a map. Miller answers the question of casualties as he pulls a large group of Dog-Tags from his pocket. Miller never looks at his commanding officer he says softly, "*They just didn't want to give up, those 88s.*"

At the time, I did not understand the reference, Captain Miller does not identify the German battery by name. He is staring at a map we cannot read well and it does not look like a map I have seen of Omaha Beach. My mind cannot make the association of his references to an actual place.

Inherent in the conversation between the Ranger officers is that these guns were firing on Omaha Beach until they were captured. My lasting impression is that 2nd Rangers were sent to attack a gun battery with three separate gun emplacements that had fired on Omaha Beach. It included 88s and the fight ended on 9 June 1944. [29]

---

[29] Saving Private Ryan. Dir. Steven Spielberg. Produced Steven Spielberg. Written by Robert Rodat. Perf. Tom Hanks, Edward Burns, and Tom Sizemore. DreamWorks Pictures, 1998. DVD.

Maisy was not on my mind as time passed. Its transient, yet contradicting, note in Ryan's, *The Longest Day* slipped from my memories as irrelevant. The vague and passing scene in Spielberg's *Saving Private Ryan* also faded from my thoughts, unless that is, I was in Normandy.

There, it was a mystery that encouraged me to travel from gun battery to gun battery hoping to find some similarities. It presented a fun search criterion as I was *Chasing Rommel* in Normandy. These are some of the places I looked for *Saving Private Ryan's* Captain Miller and his Rangers.

Firstly, I thought of the big guns between the British Gold Beach and the US Omaha Beach. *Longues-sur-Mer* Battery is located between the American Omaha Beach and the British Gold Beach. The battery is still very impressive to see in person. It is composed of four large naval guns enclosed in massive concrete casements.

I have visited this site many times, having once toured this important gun position with a World War II German Army veteran. The four guns and their casements are very impressive and draw many tourists and enthusiasts alike. The battery is unique in that the four guns are still in their massive concrete structures. It is a fascinating to look at what the Germans put on the coast of France to defend themselves from the invasion they knew would come from the sea.

Historians know the battery as, *Widerstandsnest* 48, or WN-48. The guns are immediately recognizable as naval guns in enclosed steel turrets. When I walked the site with the old German veteran, he thought the idea of fixed gun emplacements was just a better target opportunity for the Allies to bomb.

He was correct. You can easily see where Allied Naval guns impacted the casements and rendered at least one gun inoperable. But while they were firing, these guns could have shelled the approaches to Omaha Beach.

On D-Day morning, the Allied air forces dropped over a thousand tons of high explosives at the battery site. Throughout D-Day the Royal Navy, two French cruisers, and the US Navy Battleship USS Arkansas fired on the four guns of the battery.

The German guns were neutralized, and the battery was captured by British soldiers on 7 June 1944, or D-Day plus one. The guns at Longues-sur-Mer certainly did not fit into the narrative cast by Captain Miller. I remember leaving the site, and I have never forgotten the word that my German Army tour guide used to label these weapons, "*useless*."[30]

Another battery I visited is at the village of Marcouf. It is remembered as, Battery Crisbecq. This is a sprawling well restored site, and you get the idea of the serious threat artillery posed to the invasion. The guns at Crisbecq could hit ships at sea or the troops landing on Utah Beach.

It has numerous open gun pits that would hold a field piece like very large 155 mm wheeled or towed gun. The 155 mm guns were accurate and fired a great distance.

At Pointe-du-hoc, the Germans had six 155 mm guns. Three other guns in place at Crisbecq were the Czech built, 210 mm monster of a cannon. The big 210 mm guns were imposing and threatened all of Utah Beach and the shipping lanes well offshore.

The 210 mm guns were housed in a huge concrete casement that covered three sides and the top. It is opened only towards the English Channel. Crisbecq also had 75 mm field pieces, and many anti-aircraft guns. It was well-staffed and fired on the invasion fleet and Utah beach.

On June 7th, elements of the 4th Infantry Division that landed on Utah Beach were tasked with attacking the still firing battery. They attacked in the morning and were repulsed, they attacked again on June 8th, with support of US Naval gun fire. This time, they got closer but could not break the German defense.

The results of battling the Americans left the Germans short on ammunition and they abandoned the battery to the Americans on the night of 10–11 June, D-Day plus four or five days. The stories of the Battery, and the restored sites are fascinating and worth a visit. But they did not fit the criteria spoken by Captain Miller in *Saving Private Ryan.*[31]

I have also visited and explored the German battery at Azeville. It is well-preserved and you can visit the casemates and a bunker. On D-Day, it held four 105 mm guns that fired on Utah Beach. Like its close neighbor, Battery Crisbecq, Azeville was attacked by elements of the 4th Infantry Division as they moved inland.

---

[30] Battle of Normandy, Guns at Longues sur-Mer.
http://www.normandy1944.org.uk/longues_sur_mer.htm,
[31] Battle of Normandy, Crisbecq Battery - Marcouf. http://www.batterie-marcouf.com/fr/test-histoire-de-la-batterie/ Retrieved March 2021.

The Americans attacked the Germans on June 7th, but the defensive positions were too much for the Americans and the attack was driven back. Again, the Americans attacked the Germans on June 8th, and the results were the same.

On June 9th, with the help of naval guns off the coast of Utah Beach, and some local artillery the Americans attacked again. This time the German resistance broke, and the guns of Azeville Battery were silenced on 9 June D-Day plus three days. The story has an ending that slightly matches Captain Miller's explanation for June 9th. But key pieces were missing, especially the 2nd Rangers. [32]

The Crisbecq, or the Marcouf Battery, and the Azeville Battery were closer to and sighted on Utah Beach. These batteries are just too far from Omaha Beach to have had any impact. These guns never fired at Omaha Beach, because they were too far away and busy defending themselves from the Utah Beach attackers.

The artillery at Pointe-du-Hoc, Longues-sur-Mer, Azeville, and Crisbecq did not fire on Omaha Beach. So, where were the guns that rained so much death and destruction onto Bloody Omaha? I could not find such a place in Normandy or in any books I read—except two. These were older accounts, written while many of the D-Day soldiers on both sides were still alive.

In 1951, Gordon Harrison and other military historians wrote, *Cross-Channel Attack*. It is an excellent reference book because it was written from the testimonies gathered from the participants of the Normandy landings. Harrisons massive history of Normandy included a reference to the German Battery at Maisy on pages 353–6.

Harrison's account included the US Army Rangers, and elements of the 116th Infantry Regiment of the 29th Infantry Division. The fight for the battery he described as...*a nasty fight*. The battle ends with the Battery being silenced on June 9th—D-Day plus three days. Seems as if some of my criteria was reached as Harrison puts US Army Rangers there and tells us the fight ended on D-Day plus three.

Outstanding books on Normandy followed in the 1980s and 1990s. These books were meticulously researched and beautifully written without a mention of a battery at Maisy. Some examples include, Carlos D'Este's excellent read

---

[32] Route of Liberation: Battery Azeville. http://www.dday.center/d-day-review-batterie-d%27azeville.html Retrieved March 2021.

Decision in Normandy written in 1983, Max Hasting's *Overlord* in 1984, and Steven Ambrose's *D-Day 6 June 1944* written in 1994. Even as the century turned many more excellent books were written and many failed to mention a German gun position at Maisy.

It leaves me wondering why the earliest chroniclers of the Normandy Campaign knew of Maisy and those that followed decades later seemed to know nothing. Why was Maisy a modern historical blank? Logically, I determined the earlier books on D-Day had thousands of personal recollections and eyewitness accounts by the participants.

The later books often depended on the written accounts, and at that, official written accounts. This disparity exists in many cases to this very day, driven by the passing years, Maisy faded as years turned to decades. While some soldiers died, others grew old and frail with memories that dimmed fainter, forever absorbed into their growing shadows of old age.

The answers may have been found by accident, when an old map found new life, when it was removed from the pocket of an old pair of US Army pants by a military collector. Maisy would be discovered or rediscovered in 2004. Why it faded from memory is simple, time passed draining away those that remembered. Add to that, a meter deep entombment and Maisy had the perfect camouflage.

I have visited many historical places in Normandy and none of them was ever buried by three feet of French soil until I walked Maisy and saw history yielding to the shovel as bit by bit the ultimate historical disguise was revealed.

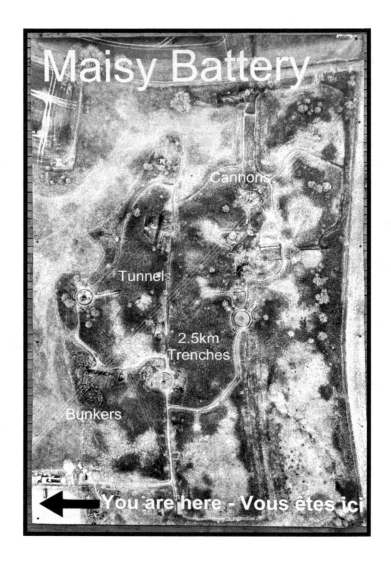

Map of modern-day Maisy Battery.

Part II: Lost and Found

"La plus belle des ruses du diable est de vous persuader qu'il n'existe pas."

(The devil's finest trick is to persuade you that he does not exist.)
Charles Baudelaire (1821–1867)
French Poet

Normandy is today, much as it has been for over a thousand years, an active farming and dairy region of northwest coastal France. Added to that are the museums, tourist sites, restaurants, tour buses, travelers, and pilgrims converging here to understand the momentous historical events that wrote Normandy into history beginning 6 June 1944.

Beaches, bunkers, cemeteries, villages, cities, all are visited for their historic contributions on the "*Day of Days*" all are visited for the completion of the stories we learned long ago.

For me, Normandy is a place of research, discovery, and endless curiosity. I return year after year as I pursue history and look for the little known or forgotten stories. Normandy is full of examples of bravery, heroism, and selfless sacrifice from the shoreline to the inland roads and bridges that carried the Allies to Germany.

Here intricate planning, and years and months of training became days then weeks of deadly warfare. Successes and failures intersected with lives lived and lost, some converted to legends and myths at the water's edge and inland as the battles raged.

Normandy has stories yet to be told, and in 2014 a new and controversial book was published, *The Cover-Up at Omaha Beach: D-Day, the US Army Rangers and the Untold story of Maisy Battery*. The book was written by British World War II militaria collector and historian, Gary Sterns. Mr. Sterns is the current owner of the large Maisy Battery site. Mr. Sterns revealed that the Maisy story was full of intrigue and surprise. He claims the Maisy story has changed the way we talk about D-Day and Omaha Beach.

At Omaha Beach, the American military planners believed they could supply a war winning offensive. They would build a Mulberry Harbor System, and miraculously land a railroad on the beach just 38 days after D-Day. Ships would anchor and unload the men and materials to win the war. But first, you had to win the battle for Omaha Beach.

This is the beginning of the story you were not meant to know. Maisy's rediscovery begins as mysteriously as it had disappeared, and we begin our search for Maisy on Bloody Omaha Beach at H-Hour.

Noted military historian General S.L.A. Marshall dispelled the myths that had grown up around Omaha Beach. In 1960 General Marshall wrote, "*The passing of the years and the retelling of the story have softened the horror of Omaha Beach on D Day.*"

Marshall went on to explain his conclusions, "...*their ordeal* (the soldiers at Omaha Beach) *has gone unmarked because its detail was largely ignored...overlooked...personal experiences were toned down...in a situation which was largely characterized by tragic failure.*"

Reading Marshall's description, we get our first serious look at why the Maisy story fits into the events on Omaha Beach. Marshal writes, "*Ignored, overlooked,* and *toned down*" and those words bite at us. Why were they *ignored, overlooked,* and *toned down?* Who chose to selectively record history and why?

General Marshall's gritty portrayal of the events on Omaha Beach were startling to some readers. His words uncovered a truth only known to the men who landed on Omaha Beach. Marshall continued to remove the sanitization that had turned truth into myth at Bloody Omaha Beach "...*Normandy was an American victory...which in the early hours bordered on total disaster...*"

In processing this statement, his intentions are on bold display. If he is correct and the early hours, "*bordered on total disaster*", we want to know why. We expect the truth.[33]

Those are serious words from a retired US Army Major General. His words have within them an invitation to look deeper at the events at Omaha Beach. Because they were in direct opposition to the official reports from 1945 and 1950.

First, we start with the 1945 report. It was developed by the US Army Historical Division, "*Omaha Beach Head*," and it was dated September 1945. Lt. Colonel Charles Taylor, a US Army officer who landed on Omaha Beach early on D-Day wrote, "...*the two assaulting regimental combat teams* (16th Regiment of the 1st Infantry Division landed at Omaha's east end, and 116th Regiment of the 29th Infantry Division landed at Omaha's west end) *lost about 1,000 men each.*"[34] Our conclusion is, about two thousand men were casualties on the entire Omaha Beach Head assault. It was a gross misrepresentation.

---

[33] Marshall, SLA. First Wave at Omaha Beach. Atlantic Monthly, Nov. 1960. https://www.theatlantic.com/magazine/archive/1960/11/first-wave-at-omaha-beach/303365/ Retrieved March 2021.

[34] Baloski, Joseph. Omaha Beach: D-Day, June 6, 1944. Mechanicsburg, PA: Stackpole, 2004. P. 342

Five years later, another official US Army historian refuted the 1945 conclusions of Lt. Colonel Charles Taylor. In October 1950, Gordon Harrison, US Army Office of the Chief of Military History, wrote, *Cross Channel Attack.*

In his book Harrison doubled the casualties that Lt. Colonel Taylor had reported in 1945. Harrison wrote, "*The V Corp* (16th Regiment) *losses for* (June 6) *were two thousand killed wounded or missing...*"[35] So Harrison claimed that one regiment alone suffered two thousand casualties. The casualty numbers at Omaha Beach have increased as the years have passed. Leading one to at least suspect they were covered over, like the battery at Maisy.

The point in introducing these conflicting reports is to understand why so many soldiers were killed or wounded on Omaha Beach. As one veteran, US Navy Quartermaster Peter Rossetti, 70 years removed from D-Day, recalled his experience on Omaha Beach: "*What makes Omaha important is the extent of the losses...Gen. Bradley, seriously thought of withdrawing his forces at one point.*"[36]

In his somber recollections, Rossetti plainly stated, "*Those poor guys never had a chance...we were all being shelled by the German artillery...*"[37]

Rossetti's recollections point directly to the German Artillery. The questions seem to jump out at you. What artillery? Where was the artillery?

Before D-day, Eisenhower decided the guns of Ponte-du-Hoc would be his number one target on D-Day. The Allied Commander feared that the massive guns atop the promontory that protruded out into the English Channel would potentially destroy the landings at both Utah and Omaha Beaches.

From early April 1944 until D-Day morning Pointe-du-Hoc was amongst the most heavily bombed places per square meter of earth during the entire Second World War.

"*This operation is not being planned with any alternatives...we're going to make it a success...*"[38] said Supreme Commander General Dwight D.

---

[35] Balkoski. Omaha Beach: P. 342

[36] Callahan, Marion. Recalling D-Day: The High Ground Was Won The Intelligencer (Doylestown, PA] 6 June 2014: Web. https://www.theintell.com/article/20140606/NEWS/306069762 Retrieved March 2021.

[37] Ibid

[38] National World War II Museum, D-Day June 6, 1944.

Eisenhower, the man who would be elected President of the United States in a landslide victory just eight short years after D-Day.

Beginning at 07:30 hours on D-Day, elements of the US Army Rangers landed on the beach at the base of the 100' cliffs at Pointe-du-Hoc. Three companies of the 2nd Battalion, US Army Rangers under the command of Lt. Colonel James Rudder attacked the six German gun casements on top of Pointe-du-Hoc.

Fighting up the cliffs, climbing ropes and ladders, the Rangers ultimately made it to the top. Once over the top, the Rangers attacked the massive gun positions covered in camouflaging netting.

To their everlasting astonishment, the "guns" under the netting were not guns, but telephone poles sticking out of the gun casements. By 09:00 hours (9:00 AM) US Army Rangers located the guns that were supposed to be at Pointe-du-Hoc.

Five very large, wheeled 155-millimeter guns were sitting unguarded in an apple orchard one mile from the promontory of Pointe-du-Hoc. The Rangers destroyed the guns. In the daring and successful assault of Pointe-du-Hoc, *"The US Army 2nd Ranger Battalion suffered over 50% casualties."*[39]

On D-Day morning, Eisenhower's number one target, *Canon de 155 Grande Puissance model 1917*[40] World War I, French made field guns were destroyed. The guns at Pointe-du-hoc never fired a single shell on D-Day.

Yet, Omaha Beach was very heavily shelled on D-Day as noted by historian and author, Steven Zaloga. Zaloga writing in his 2013 book, *The Devils Garden: Rommel's Defense of Omaha Beach on D-Day*, claims *"...that the most lethal weapons* (firing at Omaha Beach) *were motors and artillery."*[41]

---

http://enroll.nationalww2museum.org/learn/education/for-students/ww2-history/d-day-june-6-1944.html Retrieved March 2021.

[39] Ibid

[40] Chant, Chris. Artillery of World War II. Zenith: Minneapolis, MN 2001. P.

[41] Zaloga, Steven. The Devil's Garden: Rommel's Desperate Defense of Omaha Beach on D-Day. Stackpole: Mechanicsburg, PA 2013. P. 73-74.

Cornelius Ryan author of, *The Longest Day,* described Omaha Beach at H-Hour (06:30) on D-day, *"Artillery roared. Mortar shells rained down. All along the four miles of Omaha Beach German guns flayed the assault craft."*[42]

Author Sharon Cromwell in her book, GI Joe in World War II describes the chaos on Omaha Beach, *"Artillery…rained down."*[43]

All D-Day morning, Omaha Beach was raked by German artillery. Where was the firing coming from? In short, the answer is a lot of different places, and that was a defense implemented by Field Marshal Rommel. On 3 April 1944 at his Headquarters in La Roche-Guyon there is a conference on the use of artillery to repel invading forces.

The Germans had experienced in Italy where the Allies landed at Anzio and Salerno that, "(When) *'reasonably heavy artillery fire'* (was used) *Allied infantry on the beaches did not attack or even advance."* They determined that *"…they need to go to the outlying areas…"* Rommel understood, *"More batteries are needed…"*[44]

A week later, on 10 April 1944 Rommel was informed that the Allies have bombed one of his strongest gun batteries near the important harbor city of, Lé Hâvre at the Seine River estuary. Rommel was initially very disappointed, but from this attack, he determined that he needed to build not just more batteries, but he had to immediately build, *Scheinbatterien* (dummy batteries).

Before long, Rommel had drawn the Allies to his phony positions, sparing a few of his real batteries. This is pattern that begins and does not end until D-Day.[45].

On 25 April 1944 Rommel addresses soldiers preparing coastal defense works. He says, *"The enemy will have a confoundedly difficult time getting out of the water…then the moment comes when he tries to attack…Remember…artillery support…We must continue to fire! Fire! Fire!"*

---

[42] Ryan, Cornelius. The Longest Day: June 6, 1944. New York: Simon and Schuster, 1959. P. 207.

[43] Cromwell, Sharon. GI Joe in World War II. Minneapolis, MN: Compass Point. 2009. Page 5.

[44] Margaritis, Peter. Countdown to D-Day: The German High Command in Occupied France, 1944. Casemate Publishers: Havertown, PA USA. 2019. Page 289.

[45] Margaritis. Countdown to D-Day. Pp. 304-305.

Later in the day as Rommel continues his coastal inspections, he is told that some of the shore batteries have been bombed by the Allied Air Forces. But he is also told that his new dummy batteries in that area have been bombed. He departs knowing "...*the ruse seems to be working here and there.*"[46]

On Wednesday, 26 April 1944, Rommel is back at his headquarters in La Roche-Guyon. He is further informed of Allied Air Forces bombing his coastal gun batteries: "...*he orders the construction of more dummy batteries...*" But what he does next is part of the story of Maisy.

Rommel orders, "*There is to be a least one fake battery for every real one along the coastline. And to further throw off* (Allied Air Forces) *dummy foxholes...dug...around the real guns.*"[47]

By 9 May 1944, Rommel decides that the 352 Infantry Division which was located near Omaha Beach needed help. They had only "...*four coastal batteries...spread out...along eight major bunkers...Rommel wants them reinforced by June with a few dozen pill boxes, mortar pits...machine gun nests.*" That supplementing of the artillery batteries will exact a deadly price on Omaha Beach.[48]

Before his day ends, Rommel visits the Grandcamp-Maisy area near the River Vire. This is very close to the secretive Maisy Gun Battery. Rommel does not stop with his entourage at the Maisy site, but rather, he continues to Pointe-du-Hoc.

Rommel makes sure he is photographed at Pointe-du-Hoc, he wants the Allies to know it is there, waiting for them.

"*Rommel is told that fierce bombing...destroyed one of the* (Pointe-du-Hoc's) *battery's six 155 mm French guns. Because of this, the other five were covertly moved inland.*"

Where they remained until destroyed on D-Day morning.[49]

Rommel wants Eisenhower and his commanders to lock their gaze onto Pointe-du-Hoc. For Eisenhower, Pointe-du-Hoc becomes the sum of all his fears. He cannot look away.

The guns at Pointe-du-Hoc were moved inland. Those massive guns were replaced by massive wooden poles. Just like that, Rommel had created a ruse

---

[46] Ibid. Pp. 342-345.

[47] Ibid. Pp. 350-351.

[48] Ibid. Page 406.

[49] Ibid. Page 407.

to continue drawing the Allies attention to his latest dummy battery. As D-Day grew closer, Rommel was determined to build more artillery positions, and more believable dummy positions.

His 1 real to 1 dummy battery opens an interesting view from our historical perspective. The guns of Pointe-du-Hoc were moved inland to an apple orchard and protected by camouflaging nets. But the Allies did not know that the gun casements on Pointe-du-hoc were empty and would not until they captured those phony casements on D-Day. They did what Rommel wanted, attacked one place, and relatively ignored another.

Gun under net at Maisy Battery.

Part III: Finding the Ghosts of Maisy

"At that time, my virtue slumbered; my evil, kept awake by ambition, was alert and swift to seize the occasion..."

Robert Louis Stevenson (1850–1894)
"The Strange Case of Dr. Jekyll and Mr. Hyde"
Published 1886

With their *virtue slumbered,* and their *ambition awake and alert* the military officials *seized the occasion* to bury the Maisy Battery. In November of 1944, the Allies were done with Normandy, and the need to land supply ships at Omaha and Utah Beaches was replaced by captured ports along the coast of France and the Netherlands. Time to close the books on Normandy, and time to erase something that did not fit into the emerging narratives of the D-Day landings, a mistake, a very costly mistake.

Fast forward sixty years and on a cold rainy January day in 2004, two brothers from England were wandering around an old farm field in Normandy. They were collectors of World War II material, and they were searching for a place to build a museum. Their day had been long and fruitless. Tired, discouraged, and nearly ready to call it quits, Gary Sterne took one last look at the old map.

Stopping in a small clearing in the dense overgrowth of brush, he realized he was standing on a slab of concrete. He murmured to himself that Normandy was full of old German gun placements made of concrete. Nothing here, he figured as he turned to walk back to the car in the rain, cold and wind of Normandy.

But then he stumbled and looking down saw what he believed was the remnants of a chimney sticking out of the concrete slab. He realized he was not on a floor slab; he was on the roof of an old German concrete bunker! A German bunker that was not supposed to be there. He had literally stumbled onto a piece of World War II history, a German gun battery covered over and nearly forgotten. Sterne had found the buried and forgotten Maisy Battery.

The German battery at Grandcamp-Maisy was built under strict secrecy. Unlike most German gun positions in Normandy, it was not built with local conscripted French workers, but with Russian, Polish, Czech and other prisoners of war.

The German Army oversaw its construction and the area was restricted from the local French population. No one allowed in—and none of the men building the buildings was allowed out. Maisy was Surrounded by old tall hedgerows, and the local roads were blocked leading to or from the batteries. Maisy was blocked from the seaward side by a rising hill.

The concealed batteries at Maisy were mostly hidden from any casual French observer, or perspective French resistance prying eyes. Its open positions, with large field guns were covered by camouflage nets, and many of the cement grey structures had been painted black, to add to the camouflage. Maisy was purposely hard to see where Pointe-du-Hoc stuck out on purpose. Rommel was a master of making you look where he wanted you to look.

Maisy was unlike most shore batteries in other ways, not just its construction. Maisy was very large. It was three separate gun batteries including, Maisy-la-Martinière also known as WN84 and Maisy-la-Perruque also known as WN83, and Foucher Farm. Writing that sentence reminds us that the fictitious Captain John Miller of *Saving Private Ryan* pointed to three separate locations on a map before him and his commander on D-Day plus three.

According to author and historian Steven Zaloga in his book, *Devil's Garden,* WN84 had, four Czech built *100 mm IFH Field* artillery pieces. At WN83, Mr. Zaloga lists six French built *155 mm sFH414* heavy field artillery guns. In the same listing Mr. Zaloga has four *155 mm K20* French built heavy field guns at Pointe-du-Hoc.[50]

In that listing alone, the Maisy battery complex has 60% more fire power than the guns at Pointe-du-Hoc. Pointe-du-Hoc never fired a single shell on D-Day, but it was shelled by the Germans as the US Army Rangers assaulted the promontory cliffs. It is believed that Maisy, the mostly unknown battery shelled Pointe-du-Hoc as the Rangers attacked on D-Day, and on the next day as the Germans tried to drive the Rangers into the sea.

The three Maisy Batteries were connected with observation platforms including a local church bell tower and water tower. Maisy was large enough that it had its own telephone exchange building. Maisy was one of only two German shore batteries with its own telephone exchange, which was further connected to artillery observers closer to the shoreline at the area the Allies had designated, Omaha Beach.

The German observers on the bluffs at Omaha Beach called down the unprecedented death and destruction to a beach and landing area that was laid out with precise coordinates, many bearing a single word to simplify and speed-up the carnage.

In 1944, the battery at Maisy was massive covering over 144 acres including the large mine fields. It contained dozens of buildings, and over two miles of mostly covered trenches connecting it all together. It was staffed by elements of two German Army divisions, the 716th, and some elements of the veteran 352nd Infantry Division. It had its own small hospital and medical facility.

It contained large amounts of food, water and vast supplies of ammunition. It was one the best equipped and stocked shore batteries in all of Normandy. David Lesjak author of, *Does Pointe-du-Hoc Still Matter* notes, "*Maisy represents one of the largest batteries in the region* (Normandy)*, and by its very size is important.*"[51] Some of Maisy's guns were within easy reach of Pointe-du-hoc, Utah Beach and Omaha Beach.

---

[50] Zaloga, Devil's Garden. Page 251 - Appendix 3.

[51] Lesjak, David. Does Point-du-hoc Still Matter, History net.com

There were other guns at Maisy on D-Day. We already know about the 10 big 100- and 155-mm field guns. But on D-Day morning and until darkness fell late on D-Day evening there was another group of guns at Maisy. In his book, *The Cover-Up at Omaha Beach* author Gary Sterns has a section derived from the excellent notes of Cornelius Ryan.

Ryan interviewed German Colonel Werner von Kistowki, Commander of Flak Assault Regiment No. 1 in 1954 for his book, *The Longest Day*. Colonel Kistowki's command held an unusual distinction in Normandy in June of 1944, it was fully motorized.

All guns and men moved by trucks, at a time when the Germans were using tens of thousands of horses in Normandy. Stern quotes Ryan's notes, Colonel Kistowki said, *"The light group of batteries were placed at...La-Martinière* (which is part of Maisy)...*and the mixed groups at Maisy..."*

Maisy has three components, and the Colonels force's were mixed among the different batteries at Maisy. In the same interview, the Colonel explains what was included in his "mixed group" of artillery. *"Each of the two mixed groups had three batteries apiece. These had in them four 88s..."*

Although these 88s were assigned to an anti-aircraft regiment, they are the very same 88s that were used in infantry support and anti-tank roles. The fire power at Maisy on D-Day morning was enormous, with the addition of the twelve 88 mm guns.[52]

In total, Maisy had over 20 operational field guns, four times the fire power of Pointe-du-Hoc. All plugged into the German coastal artillery spotters around the invasion beaches at Utah and Omaha. On D-Day, all of Maisy's guns were functional, even though the Royal Air Force bombed Maisy that morning.

The Royal Air Force reported that the two *Widerstandsnest* (Resistance Nests) received another bombing on D-Day itself. But there is an additional report we should look at concerning Maisy on the days leading to D-Day.

It too, was generated by the Royal Air Force. This quote is taken from Bomber Command and presented to the British War Cabinet on 18 June 1944.

---

http://www.historynet.com/does-pointe-du-hoc-still-matter.htm   Retrieved   March 2021.

[52] Sterne, Gary. The Cover-Up at Omaha Beach: D-Day, the US Army Rangers, and the Untold Story of Maisy Battery. New York: Skyhorse Publishing, 2013. Pp. 207-208.

It was a summary of four weeks of bombing the coast of France. Within that summary was a report described as *"Incidental"* and it lists the following:

"259 aircraft...(sent) to bomb 4-gun positions; 3 of these were deception targets at the Pas de Calais, but the fourth battery, at Maisy was in Normandy between what would soon be known as Omaha and Utah Beaches, where American troops would land in less than 36 hours' time. Unfortunately, Maisy was covered by cloud...but was bombed by 52 Lancasters (British built 4 engine heavy bombers) *of No. 5 group..."*

In summing up operations for the War Cabinet on 18 June 1944, the report reveals the following, *"Bomber Command took a highly successful part in the attack of gun positions and coastal batteries in France during this period (4–5 June 1944) Very good results were obtained...On the eve of D-Day attacks were carried out by 1,136 aircraft on 10 coastal batteries to such good effect that, with the sole exception of the Battery at Maisy, not a single battery was able to offer any serious resistance to the invading forces."*[53]

We are closing in on the truth that was buried. Next up, was the US Army Air Force, who bombed Maisy at 06:25, five minutes before the H-Hour landings on Omaha and Utah Beaches. The 391st US bomber group attacked Maisy recording *"...more than 50 aircraft were dispatched in a threefold mission, striking simultaneously on Benerville, St. Pierre du Mont, and Maisy..."*[54]

These are examples of the Allied Command trying to destroy Maisy. And these bombing runs did bring results, especially to the dummy batteries Rommel had built around the Maisy complex. They damaged the massive mine fields that surrounded Maisy, and silenced some guns, but not all. That would have to be done by the US Army Rangers, on you guessed it—9 June 1944—D-Day plus three days.

---

[53] Sterne. The Cover-Up at Omaha Beach. Pp. 205-207.
[54] Ibid. Page 208.

US Army Ranger memorial—Maisy Battery.

Part IV: Maisy, Omaha, and D-Day

"Man is not what he thinks he is, he is what he hides."

André Malraux (1901–1976)
French Novelist and Politician

Jack Burke, A Company, 5th Rangers, who landed on Omaha Beach recalled: "*...we got closer to the beach...in range of German artillery...I can still hear...* (and smell) *odor of exploding shells...you begin to experience the worst day of your life...murderous machine guns...the 88s and 105s* (German artillery guns) *shelling the beach...I will never see anything like it again...*"[55]

There is no doubt that Omaha Beach was shelled causing enormous death and destruction. The shelling came from many different places, and many

---

[55] Ibid. Page 38.

different guns. The closest artillery pieces to Omaha Beach, beside the one 88 at each end of Omaha Beach, were the field guns of the 352nd Infantry Division.

The 352nd moved into the area at Omaha Beach just weeks before the Allied Landing. These were for the most part veteran soldiers from the fighting against the Soviet Union on the Eastern Front. In his assessment of the guns at Omaha Beach, Steven Zaloga writes in *The Devil's Garden*:

> *"They (352nd) brought with them divisional artillery...three batteries of the 1st Battalion were deployed immediately behind Omaha Beach...each of these batteries consisted of four 105 mm leFH 18/40 field howitzers..."*

That is a total of twelve 105 mm guns behind Omaha Beach.

He then writes that the standard ammunition supply is 225 per gun, with a total allotment of 2,700 shells for the battery. He continues describing another four artillery batteries of the 352nd. This group used 150 mm field guns which were placed in range of Omaha Beach with "*1,600 rounds.*" He also states that the Allies did not know that those guns were there.[56]

That was a powerful surprise for the men landing on Omaha Beach at H-Hour. When you add the additional guns at Maisy firing on Omaha Beach, you have a disaster. The seemingly endless morning of death slowly became the afternoon. The shelling and the killing at Omaha continued, with precious time slipping away, the intensity grew. On D-Day, time was the driver of mayhem on a five-mile-long French beach, time's passing hardening the resolve of both invaders and defenders.

The afternoon looked like the morning on Omaha Beach to Major Stanley Bach, HQ 1st Infantry Division, liaison officer with the 29th Division. In his Diary, 6 June 1944, between 12:15–16:00 hours (12:15 to 4:00 PM) wrote: "*...heavy mortar and 88s* (German cannons) *fire on the beach, from east end to west end...at burst of shell, two Navy men went flying through the air...direct hit on LCM,* (Landing Craft Mechanized) *flames everywhere men burning alive...direct hit on trucks gasoline load...for 100 square yard men's clothes on fire...others die in the flames...*"[57]

---

[56] Zaloga. The Devil's Garden. Pp. 87-92
[57] Baloski, Omaha Beach. P. 308.

In closing his diary entry for 6 June 1944 Major Bach writes, "...*nothing can approach the scenes on the beach...men being killed like flies from unseen gun positions...*"[58]

Explaining the results of shelling infantry men in combat, author Steven Zaloga, quotes a US Army Medical Department study that found, 80–92% of battlefield casualties can be a result of artillery and mortar rounds. Zaloga finishes stating that the men under fire at Omaha included "...*field artillery located some distance from the beach...*"[59] Among the guns firing, "*Some distance from the beach*" is the large German gun battery at Maisy.

In his article, *Does Pointe du Hoc still Matter,* author David Lasjak quotes radio reports from two US Navy Warships at Omaha Beach on D-Day, "...*USS Ancon* (landing zone command ship) *and the amphibious support ship Samuel Chase...both states regularly that* (the) *batteries at Maisy* (were) *still firing on Omaha Beach throughout D-Day morning.*"[60]

Captain John Raaen of the 5th Ranger Battalion remembered his ride into Omaha as "...*artillery shells were detonating all around us...adding to the inferno...the scene was one from hell...*"[61]

Captain Raaen and his fellow Rangers from 5th Ranger Battalion were headed towards Omaha Beach. The 5th Rangers were behind the 2nd Rangers headed towards Omaha under the command of Colonel Max Schneider. Schneider was a seasoned veteran by June of 1944. He had been a member of the 1st Rangers Battalion created in the early days of the war.

He landed in North Africa with the 1st Rangers, then as an officer in the 4th Ranger Battalion he fought in the Italian Campaign. As the Landing crafts were headed toward Omaha Beach, Colonel Schneider could see the 2nd Rangers being torn to pieces as they landed at the western end of the Beach. Schneider reacted coolly as he told the landing craft pilots to land about a thousand yards to the east of the 2nd Rangers. The navy man did as instructed and Schneider's fast thinking saved many, many lives.

In his recollections, Captain Raaen said: "*The sense on the beach was almost unbelievable. Shells of all kinds were hitting at the water's edge...dead and wounded lay in the water and across the sand...The noise was*

---

[58] Ibid. Page 308.

[59] Zaloga. The Devil's Garden, P. 74

[60] Lesjak, Does Point du Hoc still Matter.

[61] Sterne, The Cover-Up at Omaha Beach P. 34

deafening...an LCT was hit by artillery fire and burst into flames...Artillery was hitting all around us..."

Raaen continues his experiences landing with the Rangers on the Beach: *"The scene was from Hell... black ugly puffs from artillery bursting...As he approached the seawall, Captain Raaen looked back for the rest of his men, Artillery was falling...Bodies were strewn all over the beach."*

He saw a landing craft arriving at the water's edge, and the ramp flew down into the shallow surf. *"Wham! An artillery round caught the ramp...the ship burst into flames...* (Then again, he saw another landing craft get hit), *Wham! An artillery round* (hit another ship stuck on the beach) *the British crew paid with their lives."*[62]

The Artillery shells fell on Captain Raaen and his Rangers while they fought their way off Omaha Beach and up the bluffs. The intent of the Allied planners was to neutralize that artillery by D-Day. They did not. The Allied air power in Normandy was commanded by Commander and Chief Allied Expeditionary Air Forces, Air Chief Marshal Sir Trafford Leigh Mallory (1892–1944) Mallory was a very capable and experienced British officer who began his career as an infantry commander.

He was wounded in World War I and volunteered for the Royal Air Force. He and his staff of American and British air forces officers were dedicated to the destruction of as many German coastal gun batteries as possible. They attacked the known batteries nearly up to H-Hour on D-Day.

One of his reports notes: *"West of Omaha, the battery positions at Pointe du Hoc would receive a final attack by 18 medium bombers of the Ninth Air Force* (US Army Air Forces) *...In the same period, mediums would deliver a blow of equal weight at Maisy..."*[63]

The Allies knew Maisy was there and absolutely tried to destroy it by aerial attack before D-Day. They failed, and the result was that Maisy's guns fired at Pointe-du-Hoc, Omaha Beach, and Utah Beach on D-Day and to some extent during the three-day period after D-Day. But it was their contribution to the chaos, the sheer disaster at Omaha Beach which is most memorable.

---

[62] Raaen, John C. Major General, US Army (Ret). Intact: A First-Hand Account of The D-Day Invasion From A 5th Rangers Company Commander. Reedy Press: St. Louis, MO USA. 2012 Pp. 38-42.

[63] Sterne. Cover-Up at Omaha Beach. Page 226.

Beginning at H-Hour artillery shells of all calibers rained down on the men sent to break Hitler's Atlantic Wall on the Normandy Coast. The US Army Air Force and US Navy could not shell Maisy out of existence. The bunkers were made of solid steel reinforced concrete many feet thick.

They were expressly built to withstand aerial and Naval bombardments. Most of the bunkers were built into the ground, and they did not sit on top of the ground as exposed targets. Telephone exchanges, personnel barracks, command center, and even a hospital were still functional after D-Day.

It was determined that on D-Day plus three, the Batteries at Maisy that were surrounded by marshes, mine fields and Germans would be attacked by the 5th Rangers, with some 2nd Rangers as well.

Part V: Capturing Maisy

"There is nothing more deceptive than an obvious fact."

"The Adventures of Sherlock Holmes"
Sir Arthur Conan Doyle (1859–1930)

The battle of Omaha Beach ragged all morning and into the evening. The US Army's hold on Omaha Beach was the most tenuous of all the five landing beaches. The bloody victory on the sands of Omaha was yet incomplete as artillery continued to shell Omaha into the night of June 6th.

It was not the same furious shelling that marked the early hours on Omaha Beach, but it was still deadly artillery firing at the beach crowded with men and machines. Omaha was shelled on June 7th, and so were the US Army Rangers were still battling on Pointe-du-Hoc.

The Rangers had destroyed the guns at Pointe-du-hoc, but they were barley holding on to the Pointe itself. They would fight for 48 hours after landing on D-Day. They would be counterattacked and shelled by the Germans until they were relieved by other US Army soldiers, including men of the 5th Ranger Battalion, infantrymen, and tanks arriving from Omaha Beach on June 8th. Where were these shells coming from? You may have surmised they were coming from the Maisy Batteries.

Three companies of the 5th Rangers: A, C, and F were chosen to lead the assault. They were chosen to attack the connected WN84 at Maisy-la-Martinière, and WN83 at Maisy-la-Perruque. The third battery at Maisy was put out of action on June 8th by US Navy guns just offshore at Omaha still protecting the unloading ships on the beach.

Elements of the 5th and 2nd Ranger Battalions spearheaded the assault. In overall command was Major Richard Sullivan, from Boston's tough Irish neighborhood in Dorchester. Sullivan started the War with the 101st Infantry Regiment. In 1943 he volunteered for the newly created 5th Rangers.

In his memoirs Captain Raaen noted: *"The Maisy Battery was a formidable location. It consisted of three batteries of artillery,* (and) *extensive minefields, major communications center, and a large medical complex…many troops* (defended) *such an important fortification…including Army* (German Army troops), *SS and Luftwaffe* (German Air Force) *Personnel."*

He further described the minefields they encountered as they began their attack: "*The minefields protecting the Maisy complex were extensive…*(measuring) *1,200 yards by more than 1,000 yards.*" Raaen then goes on an explanation of what type of mines were in these massive mine fields. Reading his words, I have an image of Captain Miller describing the minefield he encountered in *Saving Private Ryan*. It is eerily similar. [64]

The minefields at Maisy were so large and dangerous that they dictated the line of attack the rangers had to use. Before they attacked Maisy, it was shelled by US Army artillery and mortar units. The 2nd Rangers brought two half-tracks with 75 mm artillery pieces on-board. With the half-tracks firing, the Rangers advanced to silence Maisy once and for all.

Before long, they came under rifle and machine gun fire. They found trenches and started towards the bunkers. With the half-tracks rolling in and firing, the Rangers were right beside them advancing as quickly as they could. Some of the German resistance was as stiff you would expect, yet, others were captured, with less of a struggle needed. At times, the fighting was very personnel—as the Rangers and Germans came face to face in the trenches.

As the Rangers advanced around and then into the Maisy complex, they found paratroopers from the airborne assault that began in Normandy at 00:15 hours. They were men from the 101st Airborne. Ranger Jack Burke remembered, "*There were dead paratroopers in Maisy area…some in the flooded area… (and others) hanging in the trees.*"[65]

Another Ranger, Richard Hathaway remembered, "*They (the German defenders) folded up pretty fast initially. The battle took about 5 hours…simply because the size of the site…We were in a bayonet assault and there was no question we were taking the place…I did see the 155 mm howitzers…I saw no transport (of any type) to move them…but I did see a lot of 155 mm ammo…*"

US Army Ranger, Jack Burke said, "*I remember the big guns…the artillery emplacements all had painted charts on the walls…with objectives…and exact range for each place…there was no damage to the guns from the naval bombardments…*"[66]

---

[64] Raaen. Intact. Pp. 103–104.

[65] Sterne. Cover-Up at Omaha Beach. Page 255.

[66] Ibid. Pp. 259-261.

On 9 June 1944, Maisy was captured after bitter fighting between the American and Germans. The Rangers bagged over ninety German prisoners, and nearly 200 tons of ammunition for the big guns. As they captured the guns, the Rangers destroyed them forever silencing the Maisy Batteries.[67]

Lieutenant Charles H. "Ace" Parker was the commanding officer of A company 5th Rangers on D-Day. Lt. Parker was one of the first officers to fight across Omaha Beach and then breach the sea wall and continue inland. Parker and his A Company Rangers were the first to reach Pointe-du-Hoc in relief of Colonel Rudder and his beleaguered 2nd Rangers. Parker and his men were in the thick of the fight for Maisy, and years later, Parker recalled: "*...as far as he was concerned, the fight for Maisy was far worse than the Omaha Beach landings...*"[68]

And according to some of the Rangers that assaulted and captured the Maisy Batteries there was another prize in those bunkers. The German payroll for the area, and payday in Normandy was 6 June 1944. There were millions of French Francs liberated as the Maisy Battery fell silent.

Writing in a 2004 assessment, the same year Maisy Battery was discovered historian Joseph Baloski, author of, *Omaha Beach: D-Day June 6, 1944* addresses the US Army's casualty figures on the sand of Bloody Omaha Beach: "*...relevant documents yield the inescapable conclusion that Taylor's and Harrison's casualty figures are significantly underscored...*"

Citing available after-action reports, and unit histories for all the ground, naval and air units that participated in the assault at Omaha Beach, Baloski continues: "*A more realistic estimate of the killed, wounded, and missing of the Omaha Beach invasion...is about...4,700 men...*"[69]

Mr. Zaloga told us that, the Allies did not know the mobile artillery guns of the 352nd Infantry Division were positioned behind Omaha Beach. He said that the Allies did not know that those guns were there. They also had no idea that these large, deadly, field guns were well stocked with ammunition. The guns of the 352nd were the type easily towed by a prime mover such as a truck or a half-track. And that lends itself to further questioning of what the Allied leaders did not know on D-Day.

---

[67] Raaen. Intact. Page 108.

[68] Sterne. Cover-Up at Omaha Beach. Page 270.

[69] Baloski. Omaha Beach. P. 343

To that end, it is no surprise that the Allied leaders were surprised by Rommel's dummy battery on Pointe-du-Hoc and the size of his secretive deadly guns at Maisy. They knew Maisy was there, but they did not know to what strength, even though they tried with aerial and naval guns to knock it out.

Of the thousands of dead and wounded soldiers on Omaha Beach on D-Day, not a single telegram sent back to their loved ones included where the artillery shells were fired from. They were simply informed that the killed on Omaha Beach were forever lost.

Dead men, wounded men, broken men all deserve the truth. And I believe the truth is that the artillery fired on Omaha Beach was the *pièce de résistance* of Rommel's defense of the coast of France. He created obstacles to slow down and stop defenders creating his kill zones, which worked perfectly on Omaha.

To that confusion, he then added what none of those soldiers could be defended from—prolonged, accurate, deadly artillery fire. Rommel's final additive on the sands of Omaha Beach was a storm of violent, deadly artillery and mortar shells that further paralyzed his prey on Bloody Omaha Beach. The ceaseless shelling of those remarkable American heroes came from many, many guns, from many, many different locations. The dead would not argue that.

While *Chasing Rommel* in Normandy, I have found a very interesting place. It had artillery pieces that fired on Omaha Beach until it was captured by US Army Rangers on 9 June 1944—D-Day plus three. The attackers had to deal with deep mine fields containing a myriad of deadly mines that protected Rommel's mostly secret place. Those Rangers fought a bitter and difficult battle from German defenders who just didn't want to give up their guns.

It brings me back to, *Saving Private Ryan* and Captain Miller, as he describes the battle he had just fought. The references match the moment of the film most people do not understand. Those few minutes between Tom Hanks and Dennis Farina acting as a bridge between the surreal horror of Omaha Beach and the fantasy world of moving on and *Saving Private Ryan*.

Perhaps, the viewers of the film are glad that the scenes of carnage on Omaha Beach, and the brutal vengeance delivered by the Americans to the Germans has ended. The scene shifts and our Captain Miller is told of his next mission. He and his men will be *Saving Private Ryan*. Like the passing of the years dulled the memories of Maisy, so the passing of the movie's brief scene is not really remembered.

We know who buried Maisy, that would be the US Army Engineers and their big bulldozers. But who told them to bury this place? Who had that power? Those questions will probably never be answered, but we have learned why Maisy was buried. The guns of Maisy helped rain down death and destruction, while Pointe-du-Hoc was silenced.

The story of the guns at Pointe-du-Hoc not firing is the story. It is heroic, deliberate, and has an ending that was acceptable, and even embraced by the top brass in Normandy. Supreme Allied commander General Dwight Eisenhower visited the Pointe-du-Hoc site where he was shown one of the destroyed guns. That is where the seeds of the myths of our story grew from.

Eisenhower would never—could never acknowledge he fell for the ruse of a man the British labeled, *The Desert Fox* because he was so clever. Rommel's ruse needed to be erased, and so it was buried. As perfect an ending an imperfect story could have been given. Like the D-Day dead, Maisy was buried. That part of the story would have to wait for sixty years to be discovered.

US Army 5th Ranger Battalion, A Company veteran James Gabaree summed it up decades after the war while reflecting with other Ranger Veterans: *"Twenty-three Rangers* (5th Ranger Battalion) *fought their way from Bloody Omaha Beach to join the 2nd Rangers at Pointe-du-Hoc. To our dismay, the dreaded big guns were not in place."*

"I believe the Allied Intelligence missed the primary target at Maisy. We were subject to incoming fire (at Omaha Beach and Pointe-du-hoc) *from the Maisy fortification until the Rangers captured it on 9 June."* Ranger James Gabaree closes his comment with the question still asked, *"After the war, did the Allies intelligence bury their mistakes under tons of earth?"*[70]

---

[70] Sterne. Cover-Up at Omaha Beach. Page 301.

German gun on platform at Maisy Battery.

Part VI: Conclusion

"We shall not cease from exploration
And the end of all our exploring
Will be to arrive where we started
And know the place for the first time."

Little Gidding (1942)
T.S. Eliot (1888–1965)
American/British Poet, Nobel Laureate (1948)

Maisy is not unlike Eliot's words, as you cannot *cease from exploration* here. The story of Maisy is an argument for many authors, historians, researchers, and enthusiasts. But Maisy is also a reminder that our exploring, our questioning, our seeking the truth is what drives our examinations and considerations.

We arrive where we started—the water's edge at Bloody Omaha Beach. The now silent screams of America's dead soldiers at the blood red water's edge demands we explore, question, examine and reexamine.

My curiosity of Maisy, the beginning of my explorations, was ignited by Mr. Sterne's first book on the Maisy story. *The Cover-Up at Omaha Beach: D-Day, the Rangers and the Untold Story of Maisy Battery,* was the first of three books he has written on the Maisy story. All are well-researched, and well-written. I recommend you, at least, read the first book.

Some of his words pulled the curious like me into this place, and some of those words pushed others away. His story is a double-edged sword that cuts open a secret like Maisy and challenges the history of Pointe-du-Hoc. Sterne presents endless documents to support his opinions, but still, the monolith of the D-Day story at Pointe-du-Hoc and Bloody Omaha Beach does not crack, they are actions now legendary and seared into American history.

On 6 June 1964, America's Anchorman, Walter Cronkite returned to Normandy with then retired President Dwight Eisenhower. It was Eisenhower's only trip back to Normandy as a civilian. You can see the strain, the pain he carries in the American Cemetery above Omaha Beach.

The New York Times covered the visit, and near the end of the article this was written: "*Mr. Cronkite in his questions and the former President in his answers avoided possible areas of controversy.*" (New York Times 6 June 1964.) There would be no explanations from the Supreme Allied Commander. Leaving just the indictment of hearsay and Ghosts.

I see Maisy as an add-on to the D-Day Story. The dead of Omaha Beach are dead and will never speak to us, just as all the American commanders, and intelligence people are dead. But this cannot be denied, the dead of Omaha Beach, so many that the English Channel turned red from their blood, were killed by Rommel's well-hidden, well-supplied, well-located artillery.

I have visited Maisy, and it is very different than other of the historical sites in Normandy. It is, in a word, incomplete. It is still being unearthed and feels like a place waiting to be fully discovered. It pulls you into its mystery, daring you to decide its place in history. The soldiers are gone, the ground is no longer blood stained, the cannons are silent and still your heart will race as you walk in the footsteps of history.

The raw trenches leading from place-to-place leaves you unsatisfied and longing for the next stop. No one is there to tell you the history, you discover that with every step, every bend in the trench, every gun platform, every bunker.

The bunkers, some of which contain poorly made concrete, are a reminder that time was slipping away from the German builders. Tunnels that are dark and dank, like they were while the guns shelled Omaha Beach, lead you to the next trench. The endless trenches seem like a labyrinth pulling you to the next piece of history. You will find a large field gun sitting in its position, still aiming at the beach invaders. Quietly sitting under netting, it looks like the crew has just left for lunch.

The still but barely visible, painted references, marking out firing points that meant instant death to the American invaders of Omaha are still visible. Walking on you will find a Tobruk, a German small weapons bunker meant to protect gunners and soldiers at the battery. It is another empty place with its own story to tell.

Maisy is still alive. It is not like a marble statue, or memorial stone, Maisy still lives and breathes. Much of it is still buried, only partially excavated. It is an expanding site, with a story not fully told. As a researcher and frequent visitor to Normandy, it pulls me in, like a friend eager to share a secret.

Maisy is raw, in geography and history. That is the attraction of the place and the story. Maisy is out of place, in a place where the answers are as manicured as the monuments that line the Normandy coast.

The debate over the significance of Maisy Battery will go on for a very long time. D-Day's history is filled with old black and white photos, and time-honored books crammed with the opinions of noted historians and authors. And most importantly, there is the ever-fading voices of those brave men who fought on Omaha Beach. Only begrudgingly will history yield to our new discoveries allowing our curiosities to be satisfied.

At the end of my research, I find a component that is simple and uncomfortable to understand. Pointe-du-Hoc was a ruse. It was a brilliant diversionary installation that sat out on a promontory into the English Channel daring the Allies to attack.

Rommel understood that the Pointe could not be ignored. It was not. With the combined Allied: intelligence, air, naval, and ground forces, Eisenhower was all in on the attack at the Pointe. Rommel got his enemy to look away from where the real danger was, a battery of modern rapid firing field guns hidden under some netting in farm fields. Eisenhower had no choice but to attack Pointe-du-Hoc on D-Day.

You can dam him from your vantage point seventy-five years removed from the events. But that is unfair, he did what he had to do, Rommel's ruse made sure of that. The incredible daring, skill, and accomplishment of the US Army Rangers at Pointe-du-Hoc is military legend.

It should never be minimized, only respected and honored by we, who are its benefactors. And we must try to put into proper historical context the significance of the deadly Maisy Battery, *D-Day's Forgotten Place.*

Each year, I walk along the beach remembered as Omaha. Always in the fall when the tourists have disappeared. It is always quiet on my visits to Omaha, in stark contrast to that day many years ago. As I walk along, I remember I am on the same sands they fought and died for so long ago, sands that separated a world of tyranny from a world of freedom.

No longer soaked with the blood and dreams of boys who became broken men as they fought, suffered and died on Bloody Omaha. Those who fought here are no better off for being here on that fateful day of days. But we are better off that they were here. And if you walk off the beach and climb up the bluffs, you will find some of them are still here.

The men who fought in Normandy are fading from our collective memories, passing into history. Just like other places of historical significance, Normandy with all its purpose and remaining secrets, slowly fades into myth and legend.

In the American Cemetery at Normandy, take a moment and notice all the gravestones; they all forever face west, towards the home and lives they left. The beautiful white marble markers stand in defiance of nature and time.

Walking above the Beach gives you a clear view of the English Channel's rendezvous with the northwest coast of France. The land slopes down gently, as the dense green vegetation meets the sand. You can smell the sea, feel the wind and watch the waves relentlessly crash onto the beach.

If you get to Normandy in your travels, please take half a day and visit the Maisy Battery site. It is worth your time and will give you a different look at the events in Normandy and Omaha Beach. A rare opportunity to immerse yourself in what Normandy was in 1944, as you become a witness to history.

Bibliography

Adams, Stephen. *Amateur Historian Unearths Nazi Battery*, 04 Jan 2008 http://www.telegraph.co.uk/news/uknews/1574521/Amateur-historian-unearthsNazi-battery.html. Retrieved 13 January 2016.

Ambrose, Stephen. D-Day June 6, 1944" The Climatic Battle of World War II. Simon & Schuster: New York. 1994. Print.

Balkoski, Joseph. *Omaha Beach, June 6, 1944.* Stackpole: Mechanicsburg, PA 2004. Print

Bowman, Matin W. *Bloody Beaches.* Pen & Sword Aviation: South Yorkshire Print. 2013.

Butler, Daniel Allen. Field Marshall: the Life and Death of Erwin Rommel. Casemate Publishers: Oxford 2015. Print.

Conn, Stetson; Fairchild, Byron; Engleman, Rose. *Guarding United States Outposts: Attack on Pearl Harbor.* Center of Military History: Washington, D.C. 2000. http://www.history.army.mil/books/wwii/Guard-US/index.htm Retrieved 23 January 2016

Chant, Chris. *Artillery of World War II.* Zenith: Minneapolis, MN 2001. Print.

Callahan, Marion. "Recalling D-Day: "The High Ground Was Won", *The Intelligencer* (Doylestown, PA) 6 June 2014. Web. http://www.theintell.com Retrieved 8 January 2016

Cromwell, Sharon. *GI Joe in World War II.* Compass Point: Minneapolis, MN. 2009. Print.

Kershaw, Robert. *Landing on the Edge of Eternity,* Pegasus Books, Ltd.: New York. 2018. Print.

Lesjak, David. Historynet.com: *Does Point-du-hoc Still Matter?* History net.com. http://www.historynet.com/does-pointe-du-hoc-still-matter.htm n.d. Retrieved 14 January 2016.

Margaritis, Peter. *Countdown to D-Day: The German High Command in Occupied France, 1944.* Casemate Publishers: Havertown, PA USA. 2019. Print

Marshall, SLA. *First Wave at Omaha Beach, Atlantic Monthly,* Nov. 1960, http://www.theatlantic.com/magazine/archive/1960/11/first-wave-at-omaha beach Retrieved 5 January 2016

McManus, John. *The Dead and Those About to Die: D-Day: The Big Red One at Omaha Beach,* Penguin Books: New York. 2014. Print.

Milano, Vince and Conner, Bruce. *D-Day to Saint-Lô Through German Eyes Normandiefront.* History Press: Glouscestershire, UK. 2012. Print

Raaen, John C. Major General, US Army (Ret). *Intact: A First-Hand Account of the D-Day Invasion from A 5th Rangers Company Commander.* Reedy Press: St. Louis, MO USA. 2012. Print.

Ryan, Cornelius. *The Longest Day: 6 June 1944.* Simon & Schuster: New York. 1959. Print.

Sterne, Gary. *The Cover-Up at Omaha Beach: D-Day, the US Army Rangers, and the Untold Story of Maisy Battery.* Skyhorse Publishing: New York. 2013. Print

Sterne, Gary. *Allied Intelligence and The Cover up at Pointe-du-Hoc: The History of the 2nd and 5ht US Army Rangers 1943–30th April 1944*. UK. Pen & Sword Military Books Limited: South Yorkshire 2018 Print.

Sterne, Gary. *D-Day Cover up at Pointe-Du-Hoc: The History of the 2nd and 5th US army Rangers 1st May-10th June 1944*. UK. Pen & Sword Military Books Limited: South Yorkshire. 2018 Print.

Zaloga, Steven. *The Devil's Garden: Rommel's Desperate Defense of Omaha Beach on D-Day*. Stackpole: Mechanicsburg, PA 2013. Print.

Zaloga, Steven. D-Day Fortifications in Normandy. Osprey Publishing: Oxford. 2005. Print.

Saving Private Ryan. Dir. Steven Spielberg. Prod. Steven Spielberg. By Robert Rodat. Perf. Tom Hanks, Edward Burns, and Tom Sizemore. DreamWorks Pictures, 1998. DVD.

National World War II Museum, *D-Day June 6, 1944*, http://wwwnationalww2museum.org/learn/education/june-6-1944. n.a., n.d., Retrieved 10 January 2016.

Battle of Normandy: *Guns of Longues-sur-Mer.* http://www.normandy1944.org.uk/longues_sur_mer.htm. Retrieved 13 January 2016.

Battle of Normandy: *Azeville Battery*, http://www.normandy1944.org.uk/azeville.htm, n.a., n.d. Retrieved 13 January 2016.

Route of Liberation: *Crisbecq Battery* http://liberationroute.com/france/place-of-interest/the-crisbecq-battery n.a., n.d., Retrieved 13 January 2016

US Sherman Tank at Utah Beach.

Chapter 4
Utah Beach and D-Day's Old Man

Introduction

"It is not the critic who counts; not the man who points out how the strong man stumbles, or where the doer of deeds could have done them better. The credit belongs to the man who is actually in the arena..."

Theodore Roosevelt Sr. (1858–1919)

26th President of the United States of America (1901–1909)

Speech: Citizens in a Republic, Paris 23 April 1910

Only one General went ashore with the thousands of troops that landed in the first waves at Utah and Omaha Beaches. He was fifty-seven years old, older than most of the other soldiers landing on the beaches by three decades.

He was not well, and he knew it. He had heart problems and arthritis. He had a limp from being shot twenty-five years earlier, as well as numerous other pains from being wounded multiple times and gassed in World War I. Yet, he exited his landing craft leading the assault on Utah Beach with a walking stick in one hand, his pistol in a holster, and a book of poetry in one pocket.

The young soldiers ran by him, the few who saw he was a general were amazed he was taking the same risks as the ordinary infantry soldiers. While he was holding himself up with his walking stick and giving orders his son Quintin Roosevelt II (1919–1948) was landing with the 1st Infantry Division's first wave at Omaha Beach. No man was more aptly described by President Roosevelt's famed, *Man in the Area* speech than his remarkable oldest son, Theodore Roosevelt Jr.

I am standing on Utah beach it is an early autumn. It is a beautiful Normandy afternoon; the tide is low like it was on D-Day. I see tourists, fisherman, trotting horses pulling sulkies and horses galloping with riders bobbing in their saddles in syncopation with the horses splashing along the water's edge.

I am *Chasing Rommel* and find myself strolling along the sands of Utah Beach. I always think of General Roosevelt when I am here. Today, I pass one of the many tour guides telling their American customers of Roosevelt's heroics on this very beach, near this very spot. They tell the fascinating story of what could have been a beach-landing disaster—but was not.

They display an old black and white picture of General Roosevelt in protective film. Roosevelt is sitting on the bumper of his jeep which he named—*Rough Rider*. Pointing at him, they pronounce his name with a French accent that is hard and sounds like *Genn-er-al Roos-e-velt* the *here-ro* of Utah Beach.

They are correct, but it didn't start that way. When the first American soldiers stormed Utah beach, something was very wrong, and few knew it.

There was one man amongst them who knew it and made a difference. I know him as *D-Day's Old Man*, a man too often overlooked, he was the old man that made the big difference at Utah Beach on D-Day.

Utah and date written in the sand.

Part I: The Man in the Arena

"The credit belongs to the man who is actually in the arena,
whose face is marred by dust and sweat and blood;
who strives valiantly."

Theodore Roosevelt Sr. (1858–1919)

When he walked onto D-Day's Utah Beach, he was the eldest son of one of America's most beloved presidents. Ted's father was a man larger than life; he had been: a President, a Vice President, a Governor, and a NYC Police Commissioner.

He was a legendary war hero leading his *Rough Riders* up San Juan Hill in the Spanish American War, and the author of no less than forty published works. He was America's first Nobel Prize Peace Prize (1906) winner, a big game hunter, American rancher, avid adventurer, world explorer, and the creator of numerous national parks.

Ted's father achieved mythical status, and he is immortalized at the timeless memorial at Mt. Rushmore. He is forever beside America's founders, Washington and Jefferson and beside America's savior, Abraham Lincoln. Teddy Roosevelt was larger than life, and chosen for Rushmore because he represented a modern 20th century American President.

By 1939, when Rushmore was carved, President Roosevelt had been dead for twenty years, yet America was still fascinated by the man most called Teddy or TR.

This most famous of Americans nearly won the Spanish-American War in a single battle in Cuba. A fellow soldier described TR's ride into American legend as "...(He) *led his Rough Riders in two daring charges up Kettle Hill and the adjacent San Juan Hill...(a) pivotal battle of the Spanish-American War...No man, who saw Roosevelt take that ride expected he would finish it alive...the bravest thing he'd ever seen...*"[71]

Colonel Roosevelt rode into history as the leader of his *Rough Riders* and used that fame to become the Governor of New York and then Vice President under President William McKinley (1843–1901). The war with Spain ended, McKinley was assassinated in 1901, and the national spotlight now shown very brightly on Teddy Roosevelt who at 42 years old became 26th President of the United States. He was, and remains, the youngest President in US history.

Growing up with America's most famous soldier and politician taught young Ted Roosevelt Jr. that military service to his country was expected. But before he became a soldier, he followed his father's educational footsteps. First, it was one of the nation's most elite boarding schools, Groton School in Groton Massachusetts. Then onto Harvard College in Cambridge, Massachusetts, graduating in 1909.

When war in Europe broke out in 1914, Ted was twenty-seven years old and ready to fulfill the duty his father required from all four of his sons. Although he did not have a formal military school education, with the help of his famous father, Ted was placed with General "Black Jack" Pershing and shipped off to France to fight the Great War. Ted was commissioned a Major and then promoted to Lieutenant Colonel and made commander of the 26th Infantry Regiment assigned to the historic 1st Infantry Division.

---

[71] Renehan, Edward, Jr. The Lion's Pride: Theodore Roosevelt and His Family in Peace and War...New York: Oxford University Press. 1998. P. 199

Ted Roosevelt Jr and his three brothers: Quentin, Kermit, and Archibald, all went to fight in the Great War, World War I. Young Ted fought in many battles and was wounded and even gassed in 1918. War was remarkably painful for Theodore Roosevelt Jr. in other ways: "*...Heroic and tragic indeed. By the time of the Armistice* (11 November 1918)*, Theodore Roosevelt Jr.* (the eldest of Theodore Roosevelt's four boys) *and Archie Roosevelt* (the second-youngest) *were both gravely wounded...Quentin, the baby of the family, was dead.*"[72]

Returning from war, the still young Ted needed to make a living. Ted was suffering with painful war wounds and still grieving the death of his youngest brother Quentin. Before long, He was also grieving the sudden death of his father in January of 1919.

Despite these personal pains, Ted chose to serve again as he decided on politics like his father before him. In 1920, he was elected to the same body politic, the New York State Assembly his father served.

While in the New York State Assembly, in 1921, he was appointed by Republican President Warren G. Harding (1965–1923) to be Assistant Secretary of the Navy. The same post his father had held in 1897 under then President William McKinley. But here, the similarities ended.

Unlike his father who was famous for fighting corruption, Ted was falsely charged with corruption during the Teapot Dome oil leasing scandal. Ultimately, he was innocent of the charges, but it cost him his job and some of his legacy. To regain his position and standing, he decided to run for Governor of New York in 1924—as his father had done 26 years earlier as a republican.

Ted was ready to try to save his name and reputation by again following in his father's footsteps. In 1898, Theodore Roosevelt Sr. was elected Governor of New York. In a close and bitter political battle, the senior Roosevelt won by the slimmest of margins. Ted was not so lucky and he lost his race for the 1924 governorship of New York.

The campaign was hard fought, and it was believed that the presence of his first cousin, Eleanor the wife of Franklin Delano Roosevelt also a distant cousin had tipped the balance toward the victor, Al Smith. It was a very painful experience for the son of Teddy Roosevelt. In 1929, he accepted the post of

---

[72] Renehan. The Lion's Pride: Theodore Roosevelt... Page 3.

Governor of Puerto Rico from then Republican President Herbert Hoover, spending three years on the Island.

Next, he was appointed by Hoover as Governor of the Philippines. He was there briefly, as Hoover lost the election of 1932 to Ted's distant cousin FDR— Franklin Delano Roosevelt. Ted was done with politics and politicians, especially his first cousin Eleanor and her husband, the new President Franklin Delano Roosevelt. Ted was down but not out, and when asked after Franklin's election how he was related to the new President, he quipped, *"Fifth cousin about to be removed."*[73]

When he returned to the United States from the Philippines, he began a successful business career. He worked for Doubleday Publishing Co., and the American Express Company. He was also active with the Boy Scouts of America. Like his father before him, public and charitable service was a necessary part of life as a Roosevelt.

His peaceful life would not linger for long. In just a few short years, the sabers of war were rattling in Europe and Ted knew it was a matter of time before the United States went to war. This would be the second time he would volunteer in the service of his country at war.

Fifty-four-year-old Ted Roosevelt Jr. re-enlisted into the US Army in 1941, eight months before the attack on Pearl Harbor. Roosevelt took command of his old-World War I unit, the 26th Infantry Regiment. It was again attached to the most famous infantry division in the US Army, the 1st Infantry division, *The Big Red One*. Roosevelt was promoted to Assistant Division Commander, and to the rank of Brigadier General. A rank his famous father, Colonel Roosevelt never achieved.

With Commanding Officer Major General Terry Allen (1888–1969) and Assistant Commander Ted Roosevelt, the 1st Infantry Division began the war in French Algeria. They landed on 8 November 1942. They were off course from their landing zone, but undeterred, Ted led his troops to the edges of Oran, Algeria.

They fought against the Italians, Vichy French, and Rommel's famed *Afrika Korps* in the deserts of Northern Africa. Oran was not conquered; it was captured because Ted offered to drive into the hostile city under a white flag and persuade the Vichy French to surrender.

---

[73] Jeffers, Harry Paul. Theodore Roosevelt Jr: The Life of a War Hero. Presidio: Novato, CA. 2002. P. 198

Ted's actions spared Oran from being bombed and shelled into oblivion, as he persuaded the French to surrender. No more American or French blood was spilled for the African city. His success at Oran is little known in our military history.

Like much of Ted Roosevelt's wartime actions, it is little known because his name was *"Blacked Out"* in reports. The order originated in England and was called a *"Stop Order."* Ted's name was at the top of the three-man list for the European Theater of Operations. Therefore, Ted's name was censored in all the US and British news reports.

The reason offered seemed simple, Ted was the oldest son of former President Theodore Roosevelt, and it was important the Germans not know where he was. But is that the only reason? Then President FDR had sons who served during the war, their names were not blacked out, to the contrary, their exploits became very well known. The truth is, FDR did not want a heroic Ted Roosevelt returning to politics after the war ended. And this shadow, this blacked out existence because of politics, shamefully followed Ted for the rest of his life.

After the fight for Oran, the 1st Division continued towards their mission of defeating Field Marshal Rommel. They met Rommel's forces at El Guettar and battled to capture and hold the town.

General Roosevelt was instrumental in leading the attacking US Army troops into the contested town. He was also, leading the defense of El Guettar when the Germans counterattacked because Ted was always at the point of greatest danger—at the front.

After the battle of El Guettar, General Patton wrote of the 1st ID: *"For twenty-two days of relentless battle, you have never faltered...against a veteran enemy cunningly disposed, you have pressed on. Undeterred by cold, lack of sleep, and by continued losses, you have conquered..."*

The 1st's Commanding Officer General Allen wrote of his troops: *"You met and defeated the toughest units in the German Army with great credit to yourselves..."*[74]

General Allen recommended Ted for the Distinguished Service Cross, for his leadership under fire, but the award was denied, and instead he was

---

[74] Barren, Leo. Patton's First Victory. Stackpole: Gilford, CT, USA. https://www.google.com/books/edition/Patton_s_First_Victory/ digital version. 2018. Page 188. Retrieved February 2021.

awarded a Silver Star. This was the beginning of a pattern of overlooking and denying the blacked out heroic exploits of Ted Roosevelt. The credit he earned, and the respect and admiration of his fellow fighters followed Ted Roosevelt to every battlefield and ultimately into his grave.

In early July 1943, about one month after Ted learned his younger brother Kermit had killed himself, the Allies invaded Sicily. This was less than one year before the D-Day Normandy invasion, and the 1st ID with Allen and Roosevelt in command were at the tip of spear in Sicily. Roosevelt was everywhere he needed to be to keep the men moving.

He was always near the front, and never shied away from danger or battle. His presence was often what the men needed to get up and attack the Italians and Germans. The fighting was relentless and the 1st paid the price for attacking the enemy on a daily basis. After nearly thirty days of front-line action, the 1st was withdrawn, but not before it suffered almost two thousand casualties.

For his bravery and leadership under fire in Sicily, Ted Roosevelt was awarded another Silver Star. For his outstanding leadership of the 1st ID, General Allen made the cover of TIME magazine on 9 August 1943. Remarkably, TIME could not mention the exploits of General Roosevelt because of the blackout or stop order.

The two men who had led America's "fightingest" infantry division were near living legends as they directed the 1st ID to another victorious campaign. Beyond the accolades of the American public and the undying respect each man earned from the men of the 1st ID, Roosevelt and Allen were rewarded by their superiors by being relieved of command as soon as the Sicilian campaign ended.

They were to be sent home to train new soldiers, their beloved 1st ID would be commanded by General Clarence Huebner, who immediately installed the spit and polish the division lacked. That was very pleasing to Generals Eisenhower, Bradley, and Patton the men who selfishly wanted Allen and Roosevelt relieved.

After the war, General Bradley wrote in his memoirs, *A Soldier's Story*, the reasons he had demanded the firing of Allen and Roosevelt: "*To save Allen from both himself and his brilliant record and to save the division from the heady effects of too much success, I decided to separate them.*"

Bradley laments *the heady effects of too much success* which seems confusing to this writer because in war success saves lives. Bradley continued his self-sacrificing justification of the personal pain he endured in high command by explaining the failures of Generals Roosevelt and Allen:

Indeed, the whole unpleasant situation had been nurtured by a succession of excesses: too much brilliance, too much success, too much personality and too strong an attachment of two men to the 1st Division.

But General Bradley was not finished, he wrote his ending to this inglorious affair expressing his justification in firing two excellent generals. Explaining the latest serious breach precipitated on the war effort by Generals Allen and Roosevelt, Bradley wrote: *"To break the news as gently as I could— I called Allen and Roosevelt to my CP in Nicosia. En route they had been ticketed by a corps MP for violation of the uniform regulations."*

The two Generals who had valiantly commanded the 1st ID from the deadly sands of North Africa to the hills and valleys crawling with death in Sicily, were cited for not wearing a helmet in their jeep, behind the lines, on their way to meet Bradley. [75]

Ted Roosevelt served in combat in two world wars. He did not have a formal military education, never attending West Point as did his distractors: Generals Eisenhower, Bradley, and Patton. But Ted did something that neither of his three critics did as field commanders.

On the flagstaff of the 1st Infantry Division, you will find these battle streamers: *Lorraine, Aisne-Marne, Picardy, Montdidier-Noyone, St. Mihiel, and the Meuse-Argonne* (World War I); *and Algeria-French Morocco, Tunisia, and Sicily.*[76] One of the few things those nine steamers have in common is the presence of Theodore Roosevelt Jr., who was there as a combat leader in all those campaigns.

Of Roosevelt's dismissal, General Patton wrote in diary: *"...he* (Roosevelt) *has to go, brave but otherwise, no soldier."*[77] But the driving force that got them ultimately fired from their beloved 1st Infantry Division was General Omar Bradley.

---

[75] Bradley, Omar. A Soldier's Story. New York: Random House. https://www.google.com/books/edition/A_Soldier_s_Story/ Digital version. Page 155. Retrieved February 2021.

[76] Walker, Robert W. The Namesake: Biography of Theodore Roosevelt Jr. New York: Brick Tower Press. 2008. Print. Page 278.

[77] Blumenson, Martin. The Patton Papers, Vol. 2. Boston: Houghton Mifflin. 1974. Page 309

Bradley went to see his friend, old West Point Classmate, the overall commander General Eisenhower and complained, writing: "(Roosevelt and Allen were guilty of) *loving their division too much.*"[78] Fascinating that General Bradley who was christened, *The GI's General*, by famed war correspondent Ernie Pyle, for his care and support of the average GI, accused General Roosevelt of, "*loving* (his) *division.*" Again, think politics—envy and military politics and perhaps the men in Washington who did not want the United States to know how extraordinary a man Ted Roosevelt Jr was.

Ted Roosevelt never made it home to train troops. From Sicily, Roosevelt went back to North Africa assigned to General Mark Clark's 5th Army as a liaison officer working with newly attached French troops. But before long, it was Eisenhower who needed Roosevelt and his unflinching courage to go on a very secret mission.

Ted covertly travelled to the Island of Sardinia and met with the Italian commander of the troops still garrisoned on Sardinia and Corsica. These troops included some Italian soldiers who had fought with Rommel and the Germans against the Americans in North Africa.

When he met with the Italian commanders, he was unarmed, and that level of courage was said to persuade the Italian soldiers to join the Allied side and fight against the Germans. With his success, no Allied troops would have to invade the island. No Americans would have to fight and die to conquer Sardinia—it was a remarkable accomplishment by a remarkable man.

Ted returned to North Africa and was ordered to prepare French soldiers who were going to fight with the Allies in Italy. Ted did an outstanding job training the French soldiers, and accompanied them into some of their first action. The French soldiers respected and admired General Roosevelt and took the extraordinary step of inviting him to one of their awards ceremonies.

Unexpectedly, the French general asked Ted to fall into line with the French soldiers to be decorated. The General took his bayonet and slowly touched each of Ted's shoulders. In a word, Theodore Roosevelt Jr. was knighted, installed as an *Officer of the French Legion of Honor*. This honor had also been bestowed on Ted in World War I, and he was the only American to have been awarded such distinction in both World Wars. [79]

---

[78] Dawson, Joe. From Omaha Beach to Dawson's Ridge: The Combat Journal of Captain Joe Dawson. Annapolis, MD: Naval Institute Press. 2005. Print. Page 104
[79] Walker. The Namesake Page 290.

Roosevelt had suffered much in his life at the hands of America's political and military establishments. Somehow, lost as the years passed, was his unselfish sacrifice for his country. Ted never shrank from the family traditions of duty and service to one's country, and although hurt by his loss of command with the 1st ID, he accepted his firing in the summer of 1943 and rededicated himself to the mission at hand—to defeat Germany.

Before long, his extensive combat experience was sought as the Allied leaders planned the Normandy Invasion. By February of 1944, Theodore Roosevelt Jr. was helping with the preparations for the invasion of Normandy.

He was assigned to a new Division, the very green 4th Infantry Division who had a new commander, Major General Raymond O. Barton (1889–1963), a graduate of West Point, Class of 1912. Barton was also two years younger than Brigadier General Roosevelt. Ted is often referred to as the Assistant Division Commander of the 4th ID. He was not.

He was in military terms, *Supernumerary* General Officer attached to the 4th ID. He held his rank, Brigadier General, but he had no official capacity in the command structure of the division. Merriam-Webster on-line dictionary defines Supernumerary as, *"exceeding what is necessary, required, or desired."* The paltry, trifling, envious small minded military men of image exceeding substance had struck again, Ted had a place but no command. He would prove them all wrong.

In 1944, Ted was 57 years old and gladly accepted his new disparaging assignment with the 4th ID. Ted was not assigned to command a regiment but was expected to help train all the regiments in the 4th ID. The 4th ID needed Roosevelt as much as he needed them. Although the 4th fought in World War I, they had been deactivated in 1921.

With the sabers of war rattling, the 4th was reactivated in early 1940 but remained on American soil until January 1944. They were well-trained but had seen no combat as an infantry division when they were chosen to land on Utah Beach.

The experience and reputation he had earned with the 1st ID in North Africa and Sicily were needed and respected amongst the 4th ID troops. The 4th worked at their training for Utah Beach by having practice landings. One such practice was at a place called Slapton Sands on the English coast. It was during one of these practice landings, called *Exercise Tiger* that real trouble found the 4th ID.

Early on 28 April 1944, German patrol boats infiltrated the naval vessels gathered for the mock invasion. They began firing on the lightly armed landing ships. When it was over, there were lost ships, sailors, soldiers, and officers. The death toll according to the US Navy was over 700 men.[80]

Reports of more than twice that number of wounded has surfaced in the years since the attack. The entire incident was classified, and not revealed until after D-Day. It was a devastating blow to the invasion effort, but preparations continued as General Roosevelt worked with his new division.

By the end of May, the men were as ready as they could be with D-Day rapidly approaching. While gathered in their camps waiting to disembark onto the troop transport ships something happened that shocked nearly everyone who found out.

Roosevelt requested in conversation with his direct superior, General Barton, that he be allowed to land with the first wave of the troops at Utah Beach. These requests were denied by Barton, who citied Roosevelt's age and health problems when he quickly shut down Ted's requests.

Barton also understood who Ted was to the American people. He was the oldest son of a former beloved President, a member of a family that had created a political dynasty, and he was a cousin to the current US President. Barton would not, he could not be the man who guided Ted Roosevelt to his death.

Disappointed but undeterred, Ted put his request in writing, and it has been suggested he quietly mentioned his willingness to use his family's political influence to get what he wanted—be in the first wave of attacking troops on D-Day.

At the end of May, just a few days from the expected Allied Landings Ted Roosevelt wrote a six-point list and submitted his handwritten note to his superior. In it, he listed his reasons why he needed to be on that beach on D-Day at H-Hour:

---

[80] Bisno, Adam, PhD. Exercise Tiger: Disaster at Slapton Sands https://www.history.navy.mil/browse-by-topic/wars-conflicts-and-operations/world-war-ii/1944/exercise-tiger. April 2019. Retrieved February 2021.

1. *The force and skill with which the first elements hit the beach and proceed may determine the ultimate success of the operation.*
2. *The rapid advance inland of the assault companies is vital to our effort as the removal of underwater obstacles cannot be accomplished unless the beach is free from small arms fire.*
3. *With troops engaged for the first time behavior patterns* (will be set) *by those first engaged.*
4. *Considered, accurate information of the existing situation should be available for each succeeding element as it lands.*
5. *You* (Commanding General Barton) *should have* (accurate information) *when you get ashore an overall picture in which you can place confidence.*
6. *I believe, I can contribute materially on all of the above by going with the assault companies. Furthermore, I know personally both officers and men of those advance units and believe that it will steady them to know I am with them.*

Theodore Roosevelt
Brigadier General, U.S.A.[81]

Ted was correct on each of his reasons why he was needed up front when the 4th hit the beaches. It was a tough decision, but General Barton finally agreed that Ted could go in with the first wave at H-Hour. Barton understood that the chance Ted could be killed or wounded was very substantial. Roosevelt tried to assuage the fears of Barton and many others in the 4th ID as he humorously said: *"They'll figure that if a general is going in, it can't be that rough."*[82]

General Barton was reluctant to say the least, he needed a man like Roosevelt to stay alive and remain in command with him as the division went from the beaches to moving inland, chasing Rommel back to Germany.

He had known life's successes and failures. He had seen politicians at their best and in their frailest hours as ego driven selfish men. He had faced war,

---

[81] Walker, The Namesake. Page 300.
[82] Poe, Ted. The Tallest Warrior on the Longest Day. June 6. 2012. http://humanevents.com/2012/06/06/the-tallest-warrior-on-the-longest-day/ Retrieved February 2021.

been unjustly criticized and removed from the place he rightfully earned. He never complained as he suffered physical wounding, and the deepest of wars scars the death of a loved one.

Despite a full life lived in sacrifice to his country and in the shadow of an American legend, he never faltered. Ted Roosevelt strived valiantly to do his duty and earn his life of wealth and privilege. Once he lamented: "*I will always be known as the son of Theodore Roosevelt and never as…only myself.*"[83]

---

[83] Watson, Robert. Hidden History: Roosevelt's son a forgotten hero http://articles.sun-sentinel.com/2010-07-25/news/fl-rwcol-roosevelt-oped0725-20100725_1_teddy-roosevelt-franklin-roosevelt-hills
July 25, 2010. Retrieved February 10, 2016.

Part II: Who Strives Valiantly

"...who strives valiantly; who errs, who comes short again and again,
because there is no effort without error and shortcoming;
but who does actually strive to do the deeds..."

Theodore Roosevelt Sr. (1858–1919)

The assault at Utah Beach was very different than the assault at Omaha Beach. It required a complicated component that was not needed at Omaha Beach because each site had very different geography.

Where the ocean runs to the shore at Omaha, the land is a four-mile crescent shaped beach with a gentle incline that travels from the water's edge to large bluffs rising up to 100 feet into the sky. The bluffs are nearly sheer in places, and at the top of those bluffs, the Germans found a perfect place to defend a beach. The top of the bluffs are high ground and go inland at the same elevation.

The land became farm fields, pastures, houses, barns, orchards, and villages that rolled inland, as the land remained high and dry. But Utah was low country, with a beach that ended at the sand dunes and a short sea wall. On the dunes the Germans built their defense positions, many of them still in place and easy to view as you walk westerly from exit 2 at Utah Beach. Beyond the dunes, the land sloped down and was low, and Rommel had flooded the low areas. The only way from the beach inland was on the exits, or draws as some planners called them.

These narrow lanes leading from the beach inland were the only passable high ground to or from the beaches. Getting on the beaches was just part of the plan, the thousands of men, and hundreds of vehicles arriving at the beaches needed those roads intact, and passable.

The roads led inland to Sainte-Marie-du-Mont and Sainte-Mère-Église and other towns and villages with more roads that would allow the 4th ID to penetrate into the German lines. To insure those exits or draws were open for the 4th ID on D-Day morning, the 82nd and 101st Airborne were dropped beginning at 00:15 hours on D-Day. The assault on Utah Beach was an amphibious and airborne action.

(Author's Note: This chapter is centrally concerned with *Utah Beach* and General Ted Roosevelt, *D-Days Old Man*. In this chapter, we will not deeply examine the roles of the two American Airborne Divisions that were dropped into Normandy on D-Day. The stories of these remarkable men will be covered in the next book *Chasing Rommel-Again*. Together we will meet the 82nd Paratroopers at Sainte-Mère-Église and La Fière Bridge. We will meet the 101st at Brécourt Manor and the important crossroads town Carentan. We will also meet a group of US Paratroopers I call, *The Last to Fall* a remarkable story of men who faced Hitler's vaunted Waffen SS with odds longer than the Alamo.)

The 82nd Airborne's mission was called *Mission Boston*. They were expected to capture and secure the important road junction and communication hub at Sainte-Mère-Église. They were also charged with holding the only two bridges the Allies and the French resistance had not destroyed in the immediate area. These two vital bridges would allow the 4th ID troops advancing from the beaches to rapidly move inland, and cut the Cotentin Peninsular in half.

That would allow the Allied forces to advance on and capture Cherbourg, a deep-water port believed critical for the movement of supplies into the continent. The *Chef Du Pont Bridge*, and the *La Fière Bridge* and causeway that crossed the Merderet River just outside Sainte-Mère-Église were the most valuable bridges in the world on D-Day. They offered the US Army a way off the beaches, or they offered Rommel a way to push the US Army back into the sea.

The 82nd Airborne was commanded by General Mathew Ridgeway (1895–1993) a 1917 graduate of West Point. Ridgeway was posted to the US–Mexican border during World War I and never saw combat in Europe until World War II. The 82nd was a seasoned fighting division seeing action in Sicily and Italy before dropping into Normandy on D-Day.

The 82nd was tasked with one of D-Days most critical missions its importance is hard to overstate. They had no room for error, they had to capture their objectives for the invasion to be a success.

They were mostly dropped in their assigned drop zones and did not have the problems that the 101st had with their drop zones. Once on the ground, the 82nd troopers organized and attacked Sainte-Mère-Église, while others advanced to the critical bridges they were ordered to hold.

At Sainte-Mère-Église the residents and their German occupiers were trying to put out a roaring fire in the area of the town's square very early on D-Day morning. To the shock of the residents and the German soldiers in the square, the roar of low flying aircraft drowned out all other sounds. Suddenly, Americans started to fall from the skies. Many of the 82nd troopers descended directly upon Sainte-Mère-Église during the fire.

As the townspeople worked to stop the fire, the Americans and Germans killed each other all over the town in a battle that would determine who would control this important place. The US Paratroopers were well-trained and battled hardened.

Paratroopers were killed descending from the skies or the moment they hit the ground. The fight was fast and bloody, and before long, the men of the 82nd had captured their first prize, and in doing so, liberated the first French town on D-Day—Sainte-Mere-Église.

The 101st Airborne was charged with *Mission Albany*, and they dropped just ahead of the 82nd. The 101st was charged with securing the Beach exits and the roads that led inland. They arrived between the thin strip of land between Utah Beach and the towns that are just inland from the coast including, Sainte-Marie-du-Mont, La Madeleine, Pouppeville, and Saint-Martin-de-Varreville. Some of areas of these towns had been flooded by the Germans controlling the rivers, streams, and canals.

Only the existing roadways on high-ground offered any hope of movement inland from Utah Beach. Those roads, or exits were what would make the difference between getting ashore and fighting the war. The 101st was commanded by General Maxwell Taylor (1901–1987) a West point graduate in 1922.

Taylor saw combat with the 82nd in Sicily and Italy in 1943. He was chosen to lead the inexperienced, but highly trained new 101st Airborne Division because he was an experienced paratrooper leader.

The 101st were up against it from the start as they were dropped all over a twenty-mile area. They had three drop zones, or DZ's and were badly scattered as the C-47 troop planes took heavy anti-aircraft fire and often dropped the soldiers too early, too late, too fast and too high.

Despite their drops being badly scattered over a twenty-mile area, the paratroopers cobbled together small units and led by NCO's and junior officers advanced to their missions. The 101st has been immortalized by the 1992 book, *Band of Brothers* by Stephen Ambrose, and the HBO TV series of the same name from 2001.

The 101st was also used to assault known German Batteries that were firing on Utah Beach as the 4th ID began landing at H-hour, 06:30. But before the 4th ID landed on Utah Beach, the 9th US Army Air Force and US Navy warships attacked the German defenders of the French coastline. The results were devastating for the Germans defending the Beach.

The US Navy labeled them, *Force U* and they were just offshore on D-Day morning. The armed troop carrier, USS Bayfield was 12 miles offshore and was the command ship for the Navy and the Army, and in a rich irony, it was the ship that carried Ted Roosevelt and the 1st ID for the invasion of Sicily in 1943. The Navy's commander of *Force U* was Admiral Don Moon (1894–1944) and he was onboard the USS Bayfield.

So was General J. Lawton Collins (1896–1987), a West Point class of 1917 graduate, who was a short-tempered aggressive man who commanded *VII Corp*. General Collins held the distinction of being a veteran of the Pacific Theater where he participated in the battle on Guadalcanal and was now fighting in Europe.

He was the overall commander for the Army group assaulting Utah Beach including the ground, airborne and armored components. Also, on the USS Bayfield was Major General Raymond Barton and Brigadier General Ted Roosevelt, the team commanding the 4ID.

Only Ted would leave the USS Bayfield early, the rest stayed until the beach was secured. There was also a sailor on the Bayfield who would make a different kind of history. Gunner's Mate, Lawrence "*Yogi*" Berra was on the Bayfield for the D-Day Invasion. After the war, he would become one of the best players and a successful manger with the New York Yankees in Major League baseball.

There were 18 warships in *Force U* from the US Navy, British Royal Navy, and one old warship from the Netherlands. The Germans fired out to sea before the Americans began their bombardment. The German shells came up short of most of their targets. The American's answered when they were ready and began their shore bombardment earlier than planned.

Schedule for about 05:50 hours, the Navy opened fire at the German batteries twenty-five minutes early. That extended the planned naval bombardment time, nearly doubling the time of the naval shelling. Some of the first shots came from a near phantom of a ship, USS Nevada (BB-36) a survivor of Pearl Harbor.

USS Nevada was a World War I *Dreadnought* that was built in 1914. She saw continued service and was moored with the USS Arizona in Pearl Harbor on 7 December 1941. During the Japanese attack, she managed to get free of the pier and headed into the harbor running for the open seas.

She didn't make it. She was hit and badly damaged. Wisely, her skipper beached her rather than have her sink to the bottom and block Pearl Harbor. She was repaired and upgraded in early 1942, and on D-Day morning, she had a score to settle.

Nevada carried 10 massive 14" guns and 21 smaller 5" guns, "*Off Utah Beach battleship Nevada and the cruisers Tuscaloosa* (US)*, Quincy* (US) *and Black Prince* (Royal Navy) *seemed to lean back as they hurled salvo after* *salvo at the shore batteries...the destroyers pressed...*(and) *sent a saturating fire into targets all over the network of coastal fortifications...*"

One Navy man observed that he could not see how any army could possibly withstand the bombardment.[84]

The naval bombardment of Utah Beach was accurate and deadly. It destroyed some of the known German positions. The big guns on the USS Nevada were especially destructive. On the USS Nevada, they fired as fast as they could. The naval shore bombardment was planned to be limited to only thirty minutes and no time was to be wasted.

One gunnery officer recalled: "*...our 5" guns fired so much that the paint peeled off the guns...* (We halted firing) *the guns to clear the deck of empty shell casings...* (we dumped them) *over the sides they were hindering the movement of the gun turrets.*"

In the rush to keep firing the 5" guns, the gunnery officer failed to notice the massive 14" gun turret moved to line up a shot. Suddenly, the big guns and the smaller guns fired simultaneously: "(the gunnery officer) *lost the hearing in his right ear, and 50 percent of his left...* (the firing) *destroyed a small boat on deck, knocked the door off the mess hall...peeled all the insulation off the mess hall bulkhead, and broke almost every light bulb in the overhead fixtures on the port side* (of the battleship)."[85]

Raised from the dead on the shores of Pearl Harbor, she exacted a very heavy toll on the German coastal defenders. Nevada struck positions at Utah Beach, firing 337 rounds of 14-inch shells and nearly 2,700 rounds from her 5-inch guns.[86]

Not all the news for the US Navy was about success on Utah Beach. There was a price paid for having the ships close enough to shore that they were in range of German artillery. The Destroyer, USS Corry (DD-463) was used when the Allies invaded North Africa, and was also used on convoy duty in

---

[84] Ryan, Cornelius. The Longest Day. New York: Simon & Schuster. Print 1959. Page 198.

[85] Ambrose, Stephen E. D-Day June 6, 1944: The Climatic Battle of World War II. New York: Simon & Schuster. 1994. Print. Page 290.

[86] Nasuti, Guy, J. Operation Neptune The U.S. Navy on D-Day, 6 June 1944. NHHC Histories and Archives Division. May 2019. https://www.history.navy.mil/browse-by-topic/wars-conflicts-and-operations/world-war-ii/1944/overlord/operation-neptune.html Retrieved February 2021.

the Atlantic. She had four 5" guns, two stacks and could travel at nearly forty miles an hour in open seas.

The USS Corry was not far offshore and was pounding at the German batteries on 6 June 1944, (her guns): "...*were red-hot. (She was) firing so fast the sailors stood on the turrets...* (with water) *hoses on the barrels. Corry's guns had been slamming shells inland at a rate of eight 5-inchers* (sic) *a minute...Corry had ripped* (a German battery) *open with 110 well-placed rounds...*" The German battery at Saint-Marcouf, also known as Battery Crisbecq, answered with their big guns and the skipper knew it was time to pull the Corry away from sudden danger.

When she turned away, she could no longer fire on the Germans, and they opened with everything they had. The first shells missed, but the splashes got closer and closer, until BOOM! "*The shock was great...it seemed...the ship had been lifted by an earthquake.*" Some survivors claimed the USS Corry had hit a massive German sea mine, others said she was hit by the German guns.

The explosion was thunderous and ripped the Corry into two big pieces and lots of smaller ones. She settled back in water and her crew knew they had to abandon ship. But the sea was not deep where she was, and the Germans could still see her, and fired again "*...at least nine shells plowed into the wreck...*" Her crew continued to bail out, but even as she was settling on the sea floor, parts of this proud ship were still visible.

As navy ships moved in to rescue the survivors, what happen next no one could have imagined. One of the last men to leave noticed the ship's mast was above water but you could not see the flag "*...the sailor, shells still falling around him, calmly tied on the flag and ran it up the mast. It was just minutes after H-Hour, (of the) 294-man crew thirteen were dead or missing and thirty-three injured...*"[87]

The Navy guns continued to pound at the Germans until just five minutes before the assault troops landed at 06:30. While the Navy was pounding away at the Germans, the planes of the 9th US Army Air Force arrived.

The air assault on Utah Beach was one of D-Day's toughest assignments. They had a narrow band of identified German targets. On the south side of the Germans were the US ground forces coming in to assault the beaches, and on

[87] Ryan, Cornelius. The Longest Day. New York: Simon & Schuster. Print 1959. Pp. 233-235.

the north side, were the US paratroopers holding the roads and beach exits open and ready to use.

There was no room for error. And to complicate a complicated mission, the planes were approaching the beach at less than 4,000 feet. Before leaving their base in England, one group of flyers was told by their commander: "*I don't care if any of your aircraft are not one hundred percent. You'll fly them...and you'll get over that beach whatever happens, and you'll take any risk to get right on your targets...You will go in at any altitude necessary to get the job done.*"[88]

The 9th US Army Air Force arrived at Utah Beach 06:07 hours. The 9th was attacking with a two-engine airplane called, the "*Widow-Maker*" not for the soldiers it killed on the ground, but for the number of airmen who did not survive the vast number of crashes of these planes on takeoff and landings.

It is known as the B-26 Medium Bomber. It was designed to do exactly what it was being asked to do; attack a ground enemy in support of advancing friendly forces. The B-26 easily traveled at over two hundred miles per hour.

They were armed with a number of heavy .50 caliber machine guns that could be used in air to air, or air to ground combat. And it could carry a number of smaller 250-pound bombs, or a couple of massive 2,000-pound bombs, that would blow apart anything they landed on or nearby.

Lastly, these planes flew at much lower altitudes than the high-flying B-17's attacking Omaha Beach from above the clouds. The B-26 could get low, they attacked the enemy in a personal, in your face kind of way. The B-26 was so important to the story of Utah Beach that at the excellent museum on Utah Beach is a wing with a functional B-26 proudly displayed.

As the pilots of the 9th Army Air Force were crossing the English Channel in their B-26 Marauders, the clouds broke revealing the naval fleet off the coast of France. They descended lower until as one pilot said, "*...we approached the coast, we could see ships shelling the beach. One destroyer, half sunk, was still firing from the floating end. The beach was a bedlam of exploding bombs and shells...The water was just full of boats, like bunches of ants crawling around down there...I could see what they were headed into and I prayed for all those brave young men.*"

---

[88] Mayo, Jonathan. D-Day Minute by Minute. New York: Marble arch Press. 2014 Print. Page 144

The pilots of the B-26's dropped their altitude and began their run into the beach. One pilot remembered, "(The Germans could) *throw rocks at us.*" The men in the *Widow-Makers* could see "...*the first wave just a couple of hundred yards offshore...we were running right down* (Parallel with) *the shoreline...*"

One said: "*For a short second, I could look down the barrel of a* (German) *gun.*"[89]

The 9th US Army Air Force arrived as the naval bombardment was in full force. Over 340 B-26 Marauders with full bomb loads were sent from England to the French coast at Normandy. They flew down the Cotentin Peninsular along the eastern shore, putting them in perfect alignment with Utah Beach "...*from 06:07 to 06:27...* (with) *most aircraft armed with sixteen 250-pound bombs...* (and) *sixteen B-26s were loaded with two 2,000-pound 'blockbuster' bombs...*" were flying low and fast and as they passed over the Germans at Utah beach, the 9th US Army Air Force dropped, 4, 414 bombs on Utah Beach, totaling more than 1 million pounds of explosives.

The power unleashed on the dug-in Germans was inconceivable to soldiers who still used bicycles and horses to get around the area "...*16% were direct hits...fifty nine percent detonated within 500 feet of their targets...* (The bombers) *raised so much smoke and dust on Utah beach...that the bombarding warships momentarily lost sight of their targets* (on Utah Beach)."[90]

A US Navy sailor coming in on a LCT (Landing Craft Tank) observed as he got closer to the beach "...*all hell broke loose as the battleships, cruisers, destroyers and other ships opened up and shelled the shoreline.*"

The sailor on the deck of the LCT remembered: "*The concussions of these guns seemed to want to pull your clothes off.*" The ship carrying tanks and troops closed in on the beach, just before landing the sailor recalled: "*As we got closer to the beach, we could see the sand being kicked up by the exploding shells.*"

Arriving at the shoreline and driving itself into the sands of France, the ship stopped, and ramp immediately dropped "...*infantrymen and their equipment were discharged on French soil. The sounds of the shells exploding,*

---

[89] Ambrose. D-Day June 6, 1944: Pp. 244-5.

[90] Balkoski, Joseph. Utah Beach. Mechanicsburg, PA: Stackpole Books. 2005. Print. Pp. 88-91.

the machine guns firing, the airplanes overhead and all the other sounds of war was deafening."[91]

The aerial and naval bombardments of Utah Beach did exactly as they were asked to do. They were executed with astonishing accuracy delivering very destructive results. The Germans who lived there began to flee the destruction raining down on them. One German officer who stayed could not believe the ships at sea and the planes that seemed to be just over his head. He knew the American soldiers would be arriving shortly.

Years later, he mused: *"Here was a truly lunatic sight...I wondered if I were hallucinating as a result of the bombardment."* He lamented as he recalled: *"It looked as though God and the world had forsaken us."*[92]

The last act of the destruction of Utah Beach was when the US Navy fired over a thousand rockets at the defenders of the beach. It was closely followed by DD, for dual drive, swimming Sherman tanks that began to arrive at the water's edge. There were thirty-two tanks headed to Utah Beach with the first wave of invading liberators.

Although they were a few minutes late, 28 of the 32 tanks arrived just minutes after the 20-landing craft of the 8th Infantry Regiment of the 4th ID.[93] The Germans knew the American soldiers would arrive by landing crafts, they didn't expect them to bring their armored units in the initial assault wave. The tanks hit the beach and opened fire.

The first wave at Utah had something else no one had ever seen before. There was a general on one of the lead boats, and he was taking the same chances as the ordinary dog-faced infantry soldiers. In his landing craft, Brigadier General Ted Roosevelt observed: *"We heard the drown of the planes...silhouetted against the colored clouds of dawn, formations of planes swept by and passed towards shore. Flight after flight dropped its bombs on the German emplacements. There'd be a ripple of thunder, blazes of light, clouds of dust..."*[94]

---

[91] Bowman, Martin, W. Bloody Beaches. South Yorkshire: Pen & Sword Books Ltd. 2013 Print. Pp. 156-157.

[92] Ambrose. D-Day June 6, 1944. Page 277

[93] Harrison, Gordon. Cross Channel Attack. Washington, DC: Office of the Chief of Military History, Department of the Army. 1951. Print. Page 304.

[94] Balkoski. Utah Beach. Page 91.

Fifty-seven-year-old General Roosevelt was in a boat with thirty or so men, each man young enough to be his son. *D-Day's Old Man* was on his way to Utah Beach.

German Bunker at Utah Beach.

Part III: Daring Greatly

"who knows great enthusiasms, the great devotions;
who spends himself in a worthy cause;
who at the best knows in the end the
triumph of high achievement,
and who at the worst, if he fails,
at least fails while daring greatly."

Theodore Roosevelt Sr. (1858–1919)

The first wave of landing crafts contained 20 boats riding in on the rough seas. The wind, smoke, mist, and current tossed the little ships about in the Normandy surf. With their pilots doing the best they could to stay on course, they drifted off course—way off-course.

The soldiers bailed the water that came in over the sides when they weren't vomiting from the rough ride and the anxiety of facing death. As the sea water flooded the boats, it soaked the soldiers to the bone with icy cold-water barley 45 degrees. The calendar said it was June, but in the bone-cold water off the coast of France, it did not feel like it.

The boats got closer and the soldiers could hear and feel the naval shells fired at the beach. The velocity of the massive shells pulled the men up as they passed overhead. The soldiers also saw and heard the planes of the 9th Army Air Force diving down on their German prey. They were told the Germans would be pounded from the sea and sky, and they saw that was happening.

As the little boats came close to the shore, the pilots began slowing the diesel engines and announcing the arrival time in minutes. The minutes became seconds and then the boats slowed to a near stop, finally the power was cut, and the boats grounded on the beach. In a split second, the ramps went down, and the Americans rushed onto French soil.

The old man exited the landing craft with his walking stick in his hand. On the beach, exploding mortar and artillery shells, were interspersed among the advancing soldiers, some slowed, others stopped, and some kept moving towards the seawall.

The old man stopped and looked around, then looked around again. He quickly understood something was very wrong. He never panicked, he just studied the beach, shoreline, and the lone roadway off the beach. He understood he was not where he was supposed to be, and that meant everyone else on the beach and all those coming ashore were in the wrong place. Days later, Ted wrote: *"The moment I arrived on the beach I knew something was wrong."*[95]

Undaunted, he walked to the seawall and then over it. What he saw he should not have seen. Now, he really understood what was wrong. He and the Army destined to follow him were way off-course. He gathered his officers together and explained they were not where they should be and some of the officers agreed.

Roosevelt addressed Colonel Van Fleet, commanding officer of the first assault wave regiment. Ted said to the Colonel: *"Van, we're not where we should be."* Roosevelt used his walking stick and pointed to a building he could see. He quickly told the men that the building was on their right, when it should have been on their left.

"I figure we are more than a mile farther south," Roosevelt said. Ted was correct, they were just over a mile from where they were supposed to be. Roosevelt knew time was not on his side. He was ashore and that was the first

---

[95] Ibid. Page 180.

objective of D-Day. But getting off the beach and battling the Germans was the second objective, and he could only see one beach exit open to the road inland.

Had he been where he should have been, he would have had two or three exits available to his forces. But the exit in front of him was undamaged from the bombing and cleared of enemy resistance. It led straight into Saint-Marie-du-Mont. General Roosevelt had what he needed, an open beach and exit. While not knowing the conditions on the landing beaches elsewhere, Roosevelt instinctively told his men: "*Go straight inland...we've caught the enemy at a weak point, so let's take advantage of it.*"[96]

The quote above is what General Roosevelt said to his staff just a few minutes after landing on the sands of Utah Beach. What has come down through time is little different than that sentence. The popular quote was heard when millions of people saw the movie, *The Longest Day*. Actor Henry Fonda playing Ted said: "*We'll start the war from here.*"[97]

That is what is remembered, and Roosevelt did use that line as he limped from group to group of incoming men and equipment. It is pithy and delivers his clear message. Roosevelt used the short sentence as he drove men and equipment off the beach.

Making the decision was just the beginning of his problems. Next, he contacted the navy and told him where he was. He told the navy to bring all the men and material to his location. Roosevelt was a general and people tend to obey generals. Had General Roosevelt not been with the first wave, it is impossible to understate the confusion and delays that would have undoubtedly stalled the invasion of Utah Beach.

But his decision came with risks that he knew and understood better than anyone on the beach at H-Hour. With his forces concentrating in one spot, they became a large and excellent target for German machine guns, mortars, artillery shells or even a Luftwaffe attack.

Even with the German artillery shells falling around him, Roosevelt stayed on his feet and directed men and machinery to the open beach exit driving them off the beach and inland clearing the way for others.

---

[96] Ambrose. D-Day June 6, 1944. Page 279.

[97] Lacey, Jim. A Great and Terrible Day: D-Day Showed the Greatness of The American People, http://www.nationalreview.com/article/268846/great-and-terrible-day Retrieved February 2021.

It was risky, but *D-Day's Old Man* knew the secret was to get his troops on and off the beach very quickly. A General can do that, and General Roosevelt did. Next the tanks, tank dozers and demolition men were coming ashore, and the General informed them they were in the wrong place, they were at Exit 2 but it is OK: "*We'll start the war from here.*"

One demolition man remembered: "*...General Roosevelt was standing there...walking up and down the beach with his cane.*" The soldier called to another man closer to the General: "*Go knock that bastard down, he's going to get killed.*"

General Roosevelt just walked on, defying the German shells falling on the beach, and inspiring the green troops of the 4th ID to get up and move inland to fight.[98]

He looked out of place in the life and death struggle for a foothold on the continent of Europe. While others scrambled, his movements were intentional. The deliberate movements of a man who appeared to be driven by a force oblivious to others. General Roosevelt kept walking the beach and the dunes, inspiring others to move on.

"*...extremely accurate and heavy German artillery fire was plunging onto Utah Beach throughout D-Day...almost every GI who was there in the first hour of the attack witnessed German machine gun and sniper fire.*" He was a fearless old man standing mostly alone watching much younger men run and scatter from the seemingly undiminished dangers of Utah Beach.

One officer wrote after the battle: "*There was lots of small arms fire on Utah Beach—one of my first sergeants was killed by machine gun fire just as the leading waves of* (landing crafts) *touched down.*"[99]

On D-Day morning, General Roosevelt greeted each wave he could that was landing on the beach. Even with artillery rounds, mortar shell, and some sporadic machine gun fire he was undeterred. He went from group to group, exhibited calm to each man he encountered. He recited poetry and told stories of his famous father and used his cane to point to where the soldiers had to go.

Remarkably, he knew most of the officers in each regiment and could identify each group and tell them of their new plans to counter act the fact they had landed over a mile off-course. At 09:40 hours, just three hours after the first wave landed on the beach, Colonel Van Fleet radioed to General Barton

---

[98] Ambrose. D-Day June 6, 1944. Page 281.
[99] Balkoski. Utah Beach Page 184.

on the USS Bayfield: "*I am ashore with Colonel Simmons and General Roosevelt, advancing steadily.*"[100]

Roosevelt and his staff assigned men to clear the other exits as he continued to direct more men through exit two. The others exits opened as the men of the 4th ID attacked what remained of the dug-in Germans.

Before long Utah Beach offered enough relative safety that Ted's direct superior, General Barton, commanding officer of the 4th ID arrived by landing craft. He was followed by his staff and quickly drew as many conclusions as possible. He had never expected the landing to go so well. General Barton wrote: "*...Ted Roosevelt came up. He had landed with the first wave, had put my troops across the beach, and had a perfect picture of the entire situation. I loved Ted. When I finally agreed to his landing with the first wave of the assault, I felt sure he would be killed...*" When they met near a large sand dune, General Barton was overwhelmed to see his old friend alive. "*I embraced him and he me...*"[101]

About one year after the war ended, famed military historian SLA Marshall caught up with the man who was in overall command of the Utah Beach invasion. Major General J. Lawton Collins, who agreed to be interviewed by Col SLA Marshall, Chief Historian ETO (European Theater Operations).

Marshall was known by then to be a frank and controversial historian. He asked Collins: "*Did you feel you had to have two or more exits to insure success* (of the landing at Utah Beach)?"

Collins replied directly: "*Yes, we did; but the reports we had from shore indicated that everything was going very well* (we got across the beaches and the flooded areas) *at several points.*"[102]

It is not surprising that in his response General Collins never mentioned General Roosevelt and his mastery of the beach and the one lone exit. Yet, we know without Roosevelt being on that beach at H-Hour, Collins may have been asked what went wrong on his watch at Utah Beach.

On Utah Beach at H-Hour, an old man was one of the first men to step onto French soil. He was the only general to land with the first wave on any beach American or British on D-Day. As he landed on Utah Beach, his son, a captain, was landing with the first wave on *Bloody Omaha Beach* with the 1st ID.

---

[100] Ambrose. D-Day June 6, 1944. Page 285.

[101] Balkoski. Utah Beach Page 231.

[102] Ibid. Page 246.

Ted made one of D-Day's most critical decisions under fire on Utah Beach. The 4th Infantry Division landed way off-course, with thousands of men and hundreds of vehicles already on the water and arriving on a strict timetable, Roosevelt was under great pressure to make his decision.

He made the decision and that was the difference on Utah Beach. When the sun set on Utah Beach on D-Day, a large amount of men and material were ashore and moving inland. Some units had traveled as much as five miles into Hitler's *Fortress Europa*.

The casualties for Utah Beach, including the losses of the US Navy and 9th US Army Air Force was in total, 1,128 killed, wounded and missing (excluding all airborne casualties). When we examine the losses for just the 4th ID, Roosevelt's command, we find 311 total casualties.[103]

In comparison, in April of 1944, during one of the rehearsals for the assault on Utah Beach at Slapton Sands, over 700 deaths and many more casualties were not recorded because of the classified nature of the disaster. No one ever asked General J. Lawton Collins how *Exercise Tiger* could have gone so wrong on his watch.

Later in this book, reading about *Bloody Omaha Beach*, you will be shocked at the breathtaking differences in the losses between the Omaha and Utah assaults. One reason the casualties were kept low at Utah, was the presence of General Ted Roosevelt.

Ted's commanding officer General Barton fully understood the difference Ted made in those critical early moments on the Beach. Before the month of June was over, Barton recommended Ted for the Congressional Medal of Honor, America's highest military award. General Barton's recommendation was supported by men on the beach who had been eyewitnesses to what happened in those crucial first minutes and hours.

Lt. Colonel Carlton O. MacNeely wrote: *"With complete disregard for his own life and with utter contempt for heavy hostile artillery, machine gun, and small arms fire, he immediately went on a personal reconnaissance of the beach to determine the position of the troops in relation to previous designated points…strong enemy positions were firing at point blank range upon the assault troops and upon him from a distance of 100 yards…General Roosevelt's heroism, leadership, and presence in the very front of the*

---

[103] Ibid. Pp. 330-331.

attack...inspired the troops...under constant fire General Roosevelt moved from one locality to another...directed and personally led (the troops) *against the enemy. Under his seasoned, precise, calm, unfaltering leadership...*(the) *assault troops...rapidly moved inland with minimum casualties...General Roosevelt's actions...at the risk of his own life...sets him apart from his fellow officers and enlisted men of his command...*(his) *deep sense of responsibility to his men...during this decisive and vastly significant engagement, reflects great credit upon himself...*"[104]

On Tuesday morning, 6 June 1944 at 6:30 AM on a short stretch of unfamiliar sand on the coast of France, General Theodore Roosevelt Jr. stepped off a landing craft and walked out from under his father's long shadow and into his rightful place in American history.

---

[104] Walker. The Namesake. Page 312.

Grave of General Roosevelt above Omaha Beach.

Part IV: Conclusion
Victory — Not Defeat

"The credit belongs to the man who is actually in the arena...
who strives valiantly...whose face is marred by dust and sweat and blood
who spends himself in a worthy cause...while daring greatly,
so that his place shall never be with those cold and timid souls
who neither know victory nor defeat."

Theodore Roosevelt Sr. (1858–1919)

Long before the sun set late on Tuesday 6 June 1944, the entire 4th ID was onshore and moving inland to liberate occupied France. By D-Day's end, the entire 101st Airborne Division, and the 82nd Airborne Division plus their staffs were in France. Also, on the ground by D-Day's end were the many gliders caring additional troops and supplies for the airborne forces in Normandy.

When D-Day ended, the following was written into the record books: *"According to figures computed by the VII Corps staff, a total 21,328 men, 1,742 vehicles, and 1695 tons of supplies were conveyed across Utah Beach on June 6."*[105] But something was missing on the shores of Normandy when the sun set on D-Day.

The commander of VII Corps, Major General J. Lawton *"Lighting Joe"* Collins spent the night on the USS Bayfield 12 miles safely offshore. General Collins had earned the nickname, *Lighting Joe* because of his aggressive reputation. *Lighting Joe* Collins walked across Utah Beach on the morning of June 7, over 24 hours after Ted Roosevelt and the first wave hit the beach.

Lighting Joe Collins did not like Ted Roosevelt and took any opportunity to show his disapproval of General Roosevelt. In Normandy, *Lighting Joe* encountered General Roosevelt more than once as the 4th ID fought to defeat Rommel and the Germans. Once, *Lighting Joe* saw General Roosevelt, *not wearing his helmet*, and proceeded to gratuitously chew Ted out in front of his subordinates.

Lighting Joe also made it a point to berate General Roosevelt in front of his troops. He once told Ted that: *"...while everyone considers him to be the Assistant 4th Division Commander, he was only attached to the division* (as a supernumerary Officer) *rather than assigned to it and was really not in the chain of command."*

General Collins was a petty, jealous, small-minded rival of the man named for America's most beloved president. Not surprisingly, it was Collins who thwarted the efforts of 4th ID commander General Barton to see that Ted was awarded the Medal of Honor for his actions on Utah Beach on D-Day. Collins recommended that the award be reduced to the DSC (Distinguished Service Cross).

General Bradley agreed with *Lighting Joe* Collins that Ted's actions were best reflected by the DSC. But then, Bradley failed for some reason to forward

---

[105] Balkoski. Pp. 310-311.

the notice to Supreme Commander General Eisenhower's headquarters, or so claimed Eisenhower's staff.[106]

Despite not being properly recognized for his extraordinary contributions on D-Day, General Roosevelt continued to fight with his usual tenacity with the 4th ID in Normandy. For over a week, they slogged and fought their way up the Cotentin Peninsular and captured the important port city of Cherbourg.

The fighting was bitter all the way into the city. The Germans did not want to surrender a large port city. Ted was always where he wanted and needed to be—at the front. He kept the troops moving and attacking. When the city fell and was safely in the hands of the US Army, *Lighting Joe* showed up and gave a speech, and took his victory lap.

As D-Day's victory turned into the long struggle for Normandy, General Bradley needed help. Just about a month after D-Day and a few weeks after the battle for Cherbourg Bradley had a division that was performing poorly. The 90th Infantry Division was green when they landed in Normandy, and had been under the command of Brigadier General Jay W. MacKelvie since April 1944.

The 90th were nicknamed, *Tough Ombres*, but within a week of fighting in Normandy they need a new commander. General Collins fired MacKelvie, and replaced him with Major General Eugene M. Landrum. Collin's choice of General Landrum resulted in the 90th still underperforming. The 90th ID needed someone who could inspire a division of green troops to fight like veterans.

They needed a leader, and Bradley choose General Roosevelt. This was Theodore Roosevelt's dream come true. He would be promoted to Major General and assigned command of the 90th Infantry Division. In Normandy, when his country needed him most, Ted Roosevelt was being recognized for the man he was, not the son of President Teddy Roosevelt.

As June became July, Normandy was deemed safe for top commanders and politicians to visit Normandy. One of those men who visited was Secretary of War, Henry L. Stimson (1867–1950), Secretary Stimson was a man who had been in government nearly his entire life.

He began his service under Republican President Theodore Roosevelt, as a US Attorney, and continued to serve as Republican President Taft chose him to be Secretary of War. He became an emissary to countries in South America

---

[106] Walker. Pp. 314-315.

for Republican President Calvin Coolidge, and Secretary of state for Republican President Herbert Hoover.

After Hoover lost to Democrat President Franklin D. Roosevelt in 1932, Stimson quit government. But in 1940 FDR needed an experienced man to lead the War Department and nominated Stimson to be his as Secretary of War, a post he served until World War II ended.

While Stimson was in Normandy, he learned that General Roosevelt had been recommended for the Medal of Honor, but mysteriously it had never materialized, and neither had the recommended replacement of the DSC. Before he departed Normandy, Secretary Stimson was given the citation paperwork for Ted's Utah Beach, Medal of Honor.[107]

On D-Day, General Roosevelt and the 4th ID had got on the beach, secured the beachhead and had begun chasing Rommel in Normandy. Utah Beach had been a great success in great part to the *man in the arena*. Utah Beach would be an active landing zone for the US Army and Navy until November of 1944. It was in a word, indispensable to the war effort of the Allies.

When Ted Roosevelt finally found his rest at D-Day's end, you could state the following about Adolf Hitler and the Nazis. Hitler's promised Thousand Year Reich was no longer measurable in millennia, centuries, decades or even years. Hitler's Reich would end 335 days after D-Day.

General Theodore Roosevelt was one of only four generals awarded the Medal of Honor in World War II of the nearly five hundred remarkably courageous soldiers, sailors, and airmen that were awarded the nation's highest award for bravery in the Second World War.

On 11 July 1944, after having dinner with his son Quentin, time and his troubled heart, caught up with General Roosevelt. He suffered a fatal heart attack and died just outside, Sainte-Mère-Église, France. He had earned the promotion to Major General. He earned the promotion to Division Commander. He earned the Medal of Honor. Yet, he would die before being awarded any of those earned honors.

The next day, General Eisenhower's Chief of Staff General Walter Bedell Smith called General Bradley to tell him the Army headquarters in Washington, DC had approved Ted's promotion to Major General, and CO of the 90th ID. Bradley told Smith General, Ted Roosevelt had died.

---

[107] Ibid. Page 315.

With his death, the "Stop" order placed by the British Government, which created the blackout of any mention of Ted's name ended. Remarkably his exploits could not be reported, and in a stunning and cruel irony, his death could be reported. The political pettiness, vindictiveness and cynicism directed at such a fine man and soldier remains troubling even 75 years later.

American war correspondent Quentin Reynolds (1902–1965) of Colliers Magazine who was no longer bound by the blackout order wrote: *"Ted was the bravest man he ever saw."* Ted's commanding officer, General Barton wrote: *"He was the most gallant soldier and officer and gentleman that I have ever known, and I make no exception."*

With the blackout lifted, many correspondents and officers paid their public respects to General Roosevelt. As time passed and the war ended, the source of the blackout order was revealed to be not the British Government but from someone within the United States that had powerful influence over the leaders of Great Britain, someone who could ask/tell them to generate a "Stop" order.

The man in the US with the greatest political influence over the British was President Franklin Delano Roosevelt. No one had more politically to fear from a republican war hero named Theodore Roosevelt Jr. than aged democratic president FDR. Politics dispensed as trivial jealousy, and selfish vanities had followed Ted since his cousin was first elected President in 1932. Such paltry behavior followed Ted to the edge of grave. [108]

When General Theodore Roosevelt was laid to rest in Normandy, it was with his beloved soldiers. At his burial, which was held in a war zone, there were ten Generals present with six acting as pallbearers. Among them were George Patton, Omar Bradley, and *Lighting Joe* Collins.

When asked many years later, about acts of bravery in the Second World War, General Omar Bradley said, "(Roosevelt's actions on Utah beach were the) *single greatest act of courage he witnessed in the entire war."*[109] After receiving the news of Ted's death, General Patton wrote to his wife: *"He was the bravest soldier I ever knew."*[110]

---

[108] Ibid, Pp. 319-323.

[109] Poe, Ted. The Tallest Warrior.

[110] Morris, Seymour, Jr. American History Revised: 200 Startling Facts That Never Made It into the Text Books. New York: Penguin Publishing Group. 2010 P. 134.

On 28 September 1944, the US Army awarded the Medal of Honor to Brigadier General Theodore Roosevelt Jr. In part the citation reads,

"For gallantry and intrepidity at the risk of his life above and beyond the call of duty…He repeatedly led groups from the beach, over the seawall and established them inland. His valor, courage, and presence in the very front of the attack and his complete unconcern at being under heavy fire inspired the troops to heights of enthusiasm and self-sacrifice. Although the enemy had the beach under constant direct fire, Brig. Gen. Roosevelt moved from one locality to another, rallying men around him, directed and personally led them against the enemy…He thus contributed substantially to the successful establishment of the beachhead in France."[111]

General Theodore Roosevelt's widow was presented his Medal of Honor by his distant cousin, President Franklin Delano Roosevelt. Presenting the Medal of Honor to Ted's widow, FDR said quietly to Mrs. Roosevelt: *"His father would have been proudest."*[112]

Every year, I visit Utah Beach. It is easy enough to find as it is just outside the lovely village of Saint-Marie-du-Mont. I walk through the only cut in the tall sand dunes. It is not much more than a walking path, but on D-Day it was Beach Exit 2. That is where Ted Roosevelt made his decision and where he made all the difference.

It is a beautiful beach that is shared with tourists, beach goers, and fisherman. When I walk back through the path in the sand dunes I am at, *Le Roosevelt Cafe* at Utah Beach. It is a tradition to have a lunch there, enjoy the warm breezes from the beach, and listen to the languages different than my own. Utah Beach attracts people from all over the world. Sitting in the café, you first notice the walls are covered with old newspaper accounts of D-Day and World War II.

Next, you realize that properly uniformed mannequins dressed from World War II sit amongst the indoor visitors—it is so French and a perfect touch. Sections of walls are signed by men of a by-gone era. Thousands of signatures, dates, and unit numbers are scribbled and crowed together. They are the names and small stories of the men of D-Day.

---

[111] BG Theodore Roosevelt Jr. Military Hall of Honor.
https://militaryhallofhonor.com/honoree-record. Retrieved February 2021.
[112] Black, Conrad. Franklin Delano Roosevelt: Champion of Freedom. New York: Public Affairs. 2003. P. 912

The ones who did not or could not get here are remembered by their family members. Many of whom, made a pilgrimage to Utah Beach to memorialize the contribution of the loved and loss of their lives on the greatest of American days—D-Day.

General Ted Roosevelt is still in Normandy. His grave is a visited by thousands of grateful people every year in the Normandy American Cemetery and Memorial at Omaha Beach. We, who have gathered at his final resting place, are always respectful, and thankful to a great American, in a 172-acre field of great Americans.

When General Theodore Roosevelt stepped onto Utah Beach, he had a small book of poetry in one of his pockets. They were the words of English poet Winthrope Praed (1802–1839). This poem reminds me of Ted and how others failed him. Despite those failings, he took it in stride, with the devotion of a stoic hero, he became more authentic than any of those trifling souls who treated him so poorly.

> *"Good-night to the season! Another*
> *Will come with its trifles and toys,*
> *And hurry away, like its brother,*
> *In sunshine, and ardor, and noise.*
> *Will it come with a rose or a briar?*
> *Will it come with a blessing or a curse?*
> *Will its bonnets be lower or higher?*
> *Will its morals be better or worse?*
> *Will it find me grown thinner or fatter,*
> *Or fonder of wrong or of right,*
> *Or married, or buried?—no matter,*
> *Good night to the season, Good night."*

Good Night to the Season (1827)
Winthrop Praed (1802–1839)

D-Day's Old Man rests in the Normandy American Cemetery on the bluffs above Omaha Beach. After the war, his brother Quentin was removed from his World War I grave and reinterred in the Normandy Cemetery, beside *D-Day's Old Man*, and forgotten hero, General Theodore Roosevelt.

Bibliography

Ambrose, Stephen E. *D-Day June 6, 1944: The Climatic Battle of World War II*. Simon & Schuster: New York 1994. Print.

Balkoski, Joseph. Utah Beach. Stackpole: Mechanicsburg, PA PA: Stackpole Books. 2005. Print.

Barren, Leo. *Patton's First Victory*. Stackpole: Gilford, CT. USA https://www.google.com/books/edition/Patton_s_First_Victory/ digital version. 2018

Bisno, Adam, PhD. *Exercise Tiger: Disaster at Slapton Sands* https://www.history.navy.mil/browse-by-topic/wars-conflicts-and-operations/world-war-ii/1944/exercise-tiger. April 2019.

Black, Conrad. *Franklin Delano Roosevelt: Champion of Freedom*. Public Affairs: New York: 2003. Print.

Blumenson, Martin. *The Patton Papers, Vol. 2*. Boston: Houghton Mifflin. 1974. Print.

Bradley, Omar. *A Soldier's Story*. New York: Random House. https://www.google.com/books/edition/A_Soldier_s_Story/ Digital version.

Bowman, Martin, W. *Bloody Beaches*. South Yorkshire: Pen & Sword Books Ltd. 2013 Print.

Dawson, Joe. *From Omaha Beach to Dawson's Ridge: The Combat Journal of Captain Joe Dawson*. Annapolis, MD: Naval Institute Press. 2005. Print.

Harrison, Gordon. *Cross Channel Attack*. Washington, DC: Office of the Chief of Military History, Department of the Army. 1951. Print.

Jeffers, Harry Paul. *Theodore Roosevelt Jr: The Life of a War Hero*. Presidio: Novato, CA. 2002. Print

Lacey, Jim. *A Great and Terrible Day: D-Day Showed the Greatness of the American People*, http://www.nationalreview.com/article/268846/great-and-terrible-day. February 2021.

Mayo, Jonathan. *D-Day Minute by Minute*. New York: Marble Arch Press. 2014. Print.

Morris, Seymour, Jr. *American History Revised: 200 Startling Facts That Never Made It into the Text Books*. Penguin Publishing Group: New York 2010. Print.

Nasuti, Guy, J. *Operation Neptune The U.S. Navy on D-Day, 6 June 1944. NHHC Histories and Archives Division*. May 2019. https://www.history.navy.mil/browse-by-topic/wars-conflicts-and-operations/world-war-ii/1944/overlord/operation-neptune.html   Retrieved February 2021.

Poe, Ted. *The Tallest Warrior on the Longest Day*. http://humanevents.com/2012/06/06/the-tallest-warrior-on-the-longest-day/ Jun 6, 2012. retrieved February 9, 2016.

Renehan, Edward, Jr. *The Lion's Pride: Theodore Roosevelt and His Family in Peace and War...* Oxford University Press: New York: 1998. Print.

Ryan, Cornelius. The Longest Day. Simon & Schuster: New York. Print. 1959.

Walker, Robert W. *The Namesake: Biography of Theodore Roosevelt Jr*. Brick Tower Press: New York. 2008. Print.

Watson, Robert. *Hidden History: Roosevelt's son a forgotten hero*
http://articles.sun-sentinel.com/2010-07-25/news/fl-rwcol-roosevelt-oped0725-20100725_1_teddy-roosevelt-franklin-roosevelt-hills
25 July 2010. Retrieved 10 February 2016.

Looking over the edge where the Rangers climbed.

Chapter 5
Pointe-Du-Hoc—Hometown Hero

Introduction

"Here in Normandy, the rescue began. Here, the Allies stood
and fought against tyranny in a giant undertaking
unparalleled in human history."

US President Ronald Reagan (1911–2004)
D-Day 40th Anniversary Speech in France—6 June 1984

The cliffs offer a spectacular view of the English Channel. The expanse limitless as the cloud filled skies blend-in with the distant grey green waters leading to the coast of England, one hundred miles away. The water is rarely calm here and is always churning, looking cold and forbidding even from one hundred feet above.

The wind blows constantly, it only slows for a few deceiving moments, and then returns, sometimes, pushing you away from the cliffs they conquered. When you come here, nature's distractions are a necessary accompaniment to man's brutal and permanent destruction leaving behind massive bomb craters that dominate the landscape.

You must watch your step and stay on the defined paths as you walk around the bomb craters that seem to be everywhere. You have to get close to realize some of the chunks of concrete were parts of structures built to defend this place, structures reduced to jagged blocks with twisted rusty steel protruding from the wreckage.

These macabre pieces of man-made rocks were created by the extraordinary powerful aerial and naval gunfire. The broken German bunkers hold your gaze for their massive concrete construction, completely out of place as your eyes scan the surrounding cliffs.

The destruction here is so complete, with just a cursory glance, it is nearly inconceivable any German troops survived. What was here as the Allies approached the D-Day invasion, what demanded that such an effort was made to eradicate its very existence? Then you think of them—the men sent to capture or destroy what was remained after the bombardments.

Then you ask yourself, *how did they do it?*

When the sun rose on 6 June 1944, for some American soldiers the dangers were in the sky, or on the sea, and for others the dangers were where the sea crashed into the rocky, rugged Normandy coastline. And here on a small spit of land that neatly juts into the English Channel, the dangers getting to shore were only the beginning. Next they had to scale the 100-foot cliffs—while being fired on by the enemy.

But the American men exiting the British landing crafts were not just any soldiers, they were US Army Rangers. Men, who wrote history on a historic day, at a place where they were not expected to succeed. Theirs was an *Impossible Mission*, D-Day's most dangerous job, and General Eisenhower's number one objective on a day filled with important objectives, the deadliest day for Americans in the entire Second World War—6 June 1944.

I am where the land ends as rugged dramatic sheer cliffs drop to the sea. I am remembering her father, who was part of the legendary US Army Rangers, 2nd Battalion, D Company that assaulted the cliff-top gun batteries that Rommel had set to threaten both American beach landing sites. I am in Normandy; *Chasing Rommel*; at Pointe-du-Hoc.

To Tom Ruggiero
With best wishes,

President Ronald Reagan greets Tom Ruggiero at Pointe-du-Hoc, 1984.

Part I: Hometown Hero

"Ruggie, we're going to miss you"

Rich Harbert
Headline—Old Colony Memorial Newspaper, Plymouth, MA
Vol. 194. No 32—20 April 2016

It was to be a quick stop on a morning full of errands. I planned to give my PowerPoint presentation, The Americans On D-Day, later that day and needed something at the stationary store. As I was searching, I heard a voice from behind me: "*Can I help you find something?*"

I turned answering her: "*Yes, thank you—I need an easel to display a map.*"

She walked over to what I needed, and staring at my black tee shirt with Normandy Research Foundation in gold lettering she said: "*Normandy—like World War II Normandy?*"

"*Yes,*" I said while I studied the easels.

"*My father was there.*" I thought the easels suddenly meaningless. I looked at her, noticing she was timid, yet it was important she tell me of her dad.

"*Wow,*" I said. "*Do you know what he did in Normandy?*" I asked her, not expecting much of an answer. As the years pass and their sacrifices fade from our collective memories, even family members know little of the stories of their fathers, uncles, and grandfathers.

But her answer was different: "*He was in the Army. He was a Ranger.*"

I was shocked, I raised my brows and said, "*A US Army Ranger?*" I had run out of words, but she hadn't.

"*Yes. He was at Pointe-du-Hoc.*" My loss of words certainly must have shown on my face. I stared in disbelief, as she continued saying: "*He was in the 2nd Rangers, D Company at Point-du-Hoc—Sergeant Antonio Ruggiero.*"

I told her I would love to hear everything about her, Dad. I asked if we could meet sometime, she said yes. Her name is Karen Ruggiero, and she is the only child of Antonio, and I wanted to hear her tell his story.

I met Karen for coffee a few days later when her work schedule would allow. She brought me newspaper articles, a history of her father that she wrote for his funeral, and her memories of most remarkable man. "*He was my hero,*" she said guardedly with her characteristic humility. Her words were spoken quietly and with deep emotion.

Later, as I was reading the material she left for me, I came across a quote from Jack Williams a very popular Boston TV news anchor who had known Antonio Ruggiero for decades. Williams who was interviewed by a local newspaper, Old Colony Memorial, on 23 April 2016 said: "*What made him unique was his humility and his kind nature. I found out later there was much more to this man: an iron core and a fearless disposition.*"

I wanted to get to know this extraordinary man, who did extraordinary things at a most extraordinary place, on the most extraordinary day of the 20th century.

She told me her father was with President Ronald Reagan who addressed the surviving Rangers on Pointe-du-Hoc to mark D-Day's 40th anniversary. She gave me a copy of a photo with the President shaking her father's had.

On 6 June 1984, President Reagan delivered his famous, *Boys of Pointe-du-Hoc* speech. It was an era defining few minutes, as the President held those listening spellbound describing the little-known exploits of the US Army Rangers on D-Day.

He seemed to capture a part of the D-Day story most people were unfamiliar with, as he stood before the now aging heroes of Pointe-du-Hoc. He told their story with a short memorable speech, written by Peggy Noonan. With his dramatic and emotional delivery, he captured the determination of men like Antonio Ruggiero and his fellow US Army Rangers.

President Reagan said: *"And the American Rangers began to climb...to pull themselves up. When one Ranger fell, another would take his place. When one rope was cut, a Ranger would grab another and begin to climb again. They climbed, shot back, and held their footing. Soon, one by one the Rangers pulled themselves over the top...they began to seize back the continent of Europe."*

German Bunker at Pointe-du-Hoc.

Part II: The US Army Rangers

"The invasion of Normandy was a thunderously heroic blow
dealt the evil empire. Never again, it may be, would war
seem so impeachable, so necessary and just.
Never again, perhaps, would American power and morality
so perfectly coincide."

Lance Morrow
"D-Day 40 years after the Great Crusade"
Time Magazine, Volume 123, No. 22—28 May 1984

You have to volunteer to be a US Army Ranger, and soldiers have done so since the late 17th century, when the men of Massachusetts Bay Colony were fighting the native population. There were Rangers when the American

Colonies went to war with the British Empire against the French and Indians, and there were Rangers when the Colonies fought against the British Empire for their independence.

Rangers rode for the confederacy in the American Civil War, none more famous than the legendary, John Singleton Mosby. It seems Mosby was the prototypical Ranger as he was described in a letter from Major General J.E.B. Stuart to Commanding General Robert E. Lee, dated 9 February 1864: *"His exploits are not surpassed in daring and enterprise...in any age. Unswerving devotion to duty, self-abnegation, and unflinching courage...quick perception and appreciation of opportunity..."* That sounds a lot like the Rangers who assaulted Pointe-du-Hoc on D-Day.

In World War II, the US Army needed a group of highly trained and motivated soldiers like the British Commandos. The 1st Ranger Battalion was formed in May of 1942 and led by Captain William O. Darby. They were the first American combat troops in Europe, some of them participated in the disastrous 19 August 1942 Allied invasion of the French coastal city of Dieppe.

Undeterred, by the failure at Dieppe, the US Army Rangers went on to fight in North Africa, Sicily, and Italy. On 1 April 1943, the 2nd Ranger Battalion was formed and in just fourteen short months, Company D, E, and F of the 2nd Rangers, would pull off one of the most important missions on D-Day—silence the big guns at Pointe-du-Hoc.

The 2nd Ranger Battalion trained at the US Army Camp Forrest in Tennessee, named for Confederate Calvary legend Nathan Bedford Forrest. The camp was far from civilization, and because it was located deep in the Tennessee wilderness, it also housed German and Italian POWs.

The training of the Ranger volunteers at Camp Forrest was both mentally and physically difficult. The simple reason for such harsh training was the army would rather have you break under training than fail under the demands of a combat mission.

Years later, it was not uncommon for a 2nd Ranger Battalion soldier to say that the training was more difficult than mission or combat. The training assured that only the toughest, smartest, most dedicated men became US Army Rangers.

Plymouth, Massachusetts resident Antonio Ruggiero had a more difficult time than most volunteers for the Rangers. Ruggiero, or Ruggie as his buddies called him, was told he was too short for the Rangers. But, with the help of two friends that were also volunteering, the sergeant handing out applications was assured Ruggiero's size would not be an issue.

At his interview to be accepted as a Ranger, Ruggiero spoke with commanding officer Lt. Colonel Rudder, who noticed that on Ruggiero's service record, he was an excellent shot, he was very highly skilled with an M-1 rifle. Rudder knew he needed expert marksmen in his vaunted group— Ruggiero was in.

The 2nd Ranger Battalion left New York on November 23, 1943, and landed in Scotland seven days later. From Scotland, they traveled by train to the English village of Bude, on England's rough Atlantic Coast. It was at Bude that the Rangers learned to climb sheer rocky cliffs.

At Bude, they would also encounter the respected British Commandos, and one British Commando in particular, Lt. Colonel Thomas Trevor. Trevor would hone the climbing skills and introduce the Rangers to demolition by explosives. Lt. Colonel Trevor was a highly experienced British Commando, who became attached to the 2nd Rangers and would stay with them when they landed at Pointe-du-Hoc.

As his men were training hard on the rocky coast of southern England, Colonel Rudder traveled across the country to London. In London, Rudder met first with General Omar Bradley's staff, it was then he learned all about the missions his Rangers were expected to complete. On page 39 of his fine book, "Dog Company: The Boys of Pointe du Hoc," Author Patrick O' Donnell sets the scenario Rudder was facing,

"The Allied plans called for (2nd Rangers) *to land on a small beach, scale a cliff ten stories high under a torrent of enemy fire, and destroy the most lethal gun battery of the invasion—a suicide mission...casualties would top seventy percent."*

Some Allied leaders believed it was an impossible mission. Regardless, General Eisenhower believed that the silencing of the guns on Pointe-du-Hoc was the number one job to be done on D-Day. General Bradley, the man who commanded US ground troops on D-day, believed there was not a task more difficult in the entire D-Day operation than the job assigned Colonel Rudder and his 2nd Rangers.

Part III: Pointe-du-Hoc

"We have come to the hour for which we were born,
we go forth to meet the supreme test of our arms and our souls
...it is the cause of the God who created man free and equal."

New York Times Editorial
June 7, 1944

Understanding that the Allies needed flat beaches, with easy exit points leading inland, Field Marshal Rommel identified many such beaches on the Normandy coast Two of them fell into the American sphere of attack, Utah Beach was the code name given to the hard stretch of sand in the coastal town of La Madeleine.

Omaha Beach was the code name given to the flat hard sand that stretched over four miles and connected the three French villages of: Colleville-sur-Mer, Vierville-sur-Mer, and Saint-Laurent-sur-Mer. Half way between these flat hard sand beaches called Utah and Omaha, is a promontory of land with a dramatic pointed section sticking into the English Channel—Pointe du Hoc.

Pointe-du-Hoc was built before Rommel took command but he recognized the established gun battery on this elevated position exposing the Allies and their naval ships to deadly cannon fire. Six, French Built 155 mm World War I guns were installed in open concrete positions that allowed the guns to swivel east to Omaha Beach, or west to Utah Beach.

These were beasts of guns, weighing in at 14 tons with their carriages. The 155 mm gun barrel was twenty feet long and could fire a one-hundred-pound high explosive projectile accurately for over eleven miles. These remarkably destructive guns fired two shots per minute, or 120 rounds per hour, per gun. With six guns on Pointe-du-Hoc that translated into over seven hundred shots per hour. One quickly understands why General Eisenhower was obsessed with these guns.

Eisenhower had to attack and neutralize one of Rommel's most deadly gun batteries. He had bombed Pointe-du-Hoc months before the planned landing, but was unable to destroy the battery. It was just too threatening to ignore. By April of 1944, it was reported to Rommel at a meeting in the Normandy city of Honfleur that the German coastal gun batteries have been hit hard by Allied bombers.

Rommel was also informed that the dummy batteries he had ordered built had been bombed.[113] These dummy batteries drew attention away from the real batteries that Rommel had ordered to be well camouflaged.

Rommel ordered dummy batteries to be built to attract his enemy's attention, and, perhaps expose their intentions. Rommel had proven from his time as an infantry commander in World War I, and on modern armored battlefields in World War II, he was a master of the ruse.

First in France in 1940, then North Africa in 1941 and 1942, and now in Normandy, Rommel was implementing his latest version of a ruse. With the subterfuge of building artillery batteries that held dummy guns, Rommel understood he held his enemies attention. He could not defend all of France's coast; the German Army was too depleted by 1944. But his intentions were to make you think he could defend the French coast.

And as he prepared to fight his last battle, Rommel was using dummy gun batteries to draw Eisenhower to show his cards. Was it possible that Rommel's ruses in Normandy and elsewhere could expose the landing area? By the end of April, Rommel ordered the construction of more dummy batteries.[114]

He required that there be at least one dummy battery for every real gun position. His dummy batteries often contained real defensive positions including trenches, and machine gun emplacements. He believed his faints could be convincing and they were.

But the guns of Pointe-du Hoc were real and the destructive capabilities of the ferocious guns was most disturbing. Eisenhower would bomb Pointe-du-Hoc until H-Hour on D-Day. Walking the landscape today, one is reminded how often and strongly this place was bombed. It is bomb craters from one end to the other. It is only the carefully constructed paths that keep the modern-day invaders out of the massive crater holes.

The last aerial bombardment at the Pointe was just before 05:00 hours on D-Day, when bombers from the Royal Air Force dropped over 600 tons of

---

[113] Margaritas, Peter. Countdown to D-Day the German Perspective. Casemate: Havertown, PA. 2019. Print. Page 245

[114] Margaritis. Countdown to D-Day. Page 350.

bombs.[115] Then, in another massive bombardment, beginning at 05:50 hours, and lasting 34 minutes the US Navy destroyer, USS Satterlee (DD-626), with her five-inch guns, and HMS Talybont four-inch guns, opened fire.

The heaviest shelling came from the USS Texas (BB-35), a World War I era battleship, *"at 0550, against the site of six 155 mm gun, atop Point du Hoe(sic)...firing at the Point...255 14" shells...in 34 minutes."*[116] Those 14" naval guns, which were over fifty feet long and fired a shell weighing in at 1,500 pounds, left some of the biggest craters still visible at Pointe-du-Hoc. These final successful bombardments of Pointe-du-Hoc were the last things that went as planned.

---

[115] Steve Balestrieri. Rangers Storm The Cliffs Of Pointe Du Hoc On D-Day 75 Years Ago. SOFREP. "Special Operations Forces Report. Jun 6, 2017. https://sofrep.com/specialoperations/31021/ Retrieved September 2020.
[116] Moore, Charles. Battleship Texas (BB-35) https://web.archive.org/web/20060923092736/http://users3.ev1.net/~cfmoore/history /1944normandy.html. Retrieved September 2020.

Grave—Unknown Omaha Cemetery.

Part IV: The Assault of Pointe-du-Hoc

"In the fell clutch of circumstance
I have not winched nor cried aloud.
Under the bludgeonings of chance
my head is bloody but unbowed."

William Ernest Henley (1849–1903)
"Invictus" 1875

As D-Day approached Lt. Colonel Rudder was given command of the *Provisional Ranger Force*, which included the 2nd and 5th Ranger Battalions.

It was Rudder's responsibility to oversee the attack of **Force A** at Point-du-Hoc carried out by elements of the Second Ranger Battalion.

He was responsible as well for **Force B,** consisting of Company C of the 2nd Rangers, which was to attack the German radar installation at, *Pointe de la Percée,* the twin promissory just a mile or so east of Pointe-du-Hoc.

He was also in overall command of **Force C,** the largest body of assaulting Rangers consisting of companies A and B from 2nd Rangers, and Companies A, B, C, D, E, F of the 5th Rangers. **Force C** was to remain near their ships, waiting for the correct coded message from Pointe-du-Hoc.

If the signal did not arrive in time, **Force C** was to proceed to the western end of Omaha beach with the 29th Infantry Division. Rudder's job was to run these assaults from his command post on a US Navy invasion ship.

He was to coordinate these three deadly, dangerous, critical missions, where timing to the minute was planned. Rudder was the leader and the most important common thread between these three attacking forces.

If ever, *the fell clutches of circumstance,* had found a group of highly skilled and trained US Army soldiers it was the 2nd Rangers, Force A, Companies D, E, and F assigned to assault Pointe-du-Hoc. Problems first surfaced while the Rangers were at sea in the actions of the commander of Force A, Major Cleveland A. Lytle.

Major Lytle got himself drunk and proceeded to tell the Rangers with him that the guns on Pointe-du-Hoc had been moved. (The French Resistance forces in the area had told Allied commanders in London of this event. They were moved to avoid destruction from the continual aerial bombardments.)

He described the attack on the sheer cliffs, and the gun batteries located on the top as a suicide mission. Lt. Colonel Rudder had Major Lytle relieved of command and arrested immediately, while still on board the ship that carried the Provisional Ranger Force towards Normandy. Rudder decided at that moment, he would lead the attack on Pointe-du-Hoc himself.

In doing so, Rudder removed himself from his shipboard command post, and he failed to appoint anyone to coordinate the on-ship duties and responsibilities in his absence. This was a mistake that would haunt the Rangers on D-Day morning, because no one was in overall command. The three Ranger assault groups had lost their coherent thread.

At 04:05 hours, the Rangers were ordered into their landing crafts. By the time the Ranger got to Pointe-du-Hoc, the aerial and naval bombardments would lift and the cliffside assault would begin. The Rangers would arrive at H-Hour, 06:30 hours, the bombardment would end at 06:24 hours. So, it was planned, but it was not executed that way, *the fell clutches of circumstance* would have a say on this fateful and historic day.

The Rangers used British LCAs (Landing Craft Assault) with British sailors at the helms, and a few DUKWs (floating versions of the US Army 2 ½ ton truck). The LCAs headed for their targets, with **Force A headed to Pointe-du Hoc,** and **Force C headed to *Pointe de la Percée*,** and **Force B was held in a short reserve formation waiting for the signal** to follow Rudder into Pointe-du-Hoc.

Before long, some of the Rangers in Force A realized they were headed to the wrong point! They were accidentally following Force C towards *Point de la Percée,*

As the mist, smoke, and haze slowly lifted the error was clear. Rudder ordered the British sailors to quickly change course, they did, and Rudder understood his pinpoint timetable was irrevocably altered. With the LCAs changing course, they were no longer perpendicular to the coast, they were parallel, moving slowly through rough seas that threatened to fill the boats and capsize them.

To make matters worse, they were within range of German machine gunners and riflemen. This is where being in British LCAs made the difference. Unlike the American LCVP (Landing Craft Vehicles and Personnel) that was built from wood, the British LCA was built with steel covered sides and offered some insulation from the fire pouring in on the Rangers.

Before long, the seas began to accomplish what the Germans could not. As the LCAs and DUKWs were headed towards the Pointe, some were filling with water as the slow boats were now moving slower and slower as some filled with seawater and began to swamp. Soldiers were franticly bailing out the water with their helmets, as they were taking on fire from the Germans on the Pointe. Had the small landing crafts not traveled to the wrong point, they would not be in this trouble. They were traveling slower and losing time they could not afford to lose.

One of the LCA carrying the supplies filled with water and sank, and another LCA carrying supplies was in serious trouble. The crew had to start throwing supplies overboard just to stay afloat. Consequently, about three quarters of the supplies and additional ammo never made it to the shore. Things still yet got worse as the LCA carrying Sargent Antonio Ruggiero sank.

Ruggerio's LCA was nearly hit by a German artillery shell. But just being close to the explosion helped fill the slow-moving boat with water and it sank. Ruggiero would spend hours in the bitter cold English Channel. The water temperature was forty-two degrees, Ruggiero and his fellow Rangers were left to their fate, and many believed they would die in the water. The Rangers were mission centric and not even the sight of a capsized boat full of their fellow warriors could stop them from accomplishing the mission.

As the other boats were taking fire from the Germans on the clifftops, the US Navy noticed and intervened. The USS Texas, USS Satterlee and HMS Talybont opened fire and the Rangers could feel the shells that seemed to be barely over their heads. The USS Satterlee moved as close to the cliffs as it could and blasted away with her big guns.

USS Satterlee was also in range to use her machine guns, and the Navy men fired away at the stubborn German defenders. On the cliff tops, the Germans retreated for a brief spell as the naval gunfire tore apart the cliffs in some places, dropping huge piles of soil onto the cliff base. The naval gunfire lifted just after 07:00 hours as the Rangers were getting ready to land at the foot of the cliffs.

Rudder had planned to assault the Pointe from the east (E and F Companies) and west (D Company) sides. With the loss of time and his boats moving under constant enemy fire, he ordered all boats into the east side. Gone was the element of surprise and the plan of a two-sided assault. Rudder went all in on a single-sided frontal assault.

The ramps fell anywhere from 25–50 yards from the bottom of the cliffs as the British LCAs went in as far as they could. The Germans were back and raking the narrow shoreline beneath them with unrelenting machine gun and rifle fire as well as dropping grenades on top of Rudder's Rangers.

It was 07:10 hours, they were 40 minutes late. Rudder ordered his communication officer to contact the Rangers in reserve. The radios did not work, they were wet from the extra travel in the rough seas. The large reserve, Force C, companies A and B from 2nd Rangers, and companies A, B, C, D, E, F of the 5th Rangers, over 500 men who had trained to assault the cliffs at the Pointe, had been released to the assault on Omaha Beach. It was believed that the Rangers at Pointe-du-Hoc had failed. It appeared *the fell clutch of circumstance* were having their way with the 2nd Rangers at the Pointe.

The Rangers of companies D, E, and F fired their grappling ropes and ladders to the cliff tops. Some ropes were so wet they didn't make it to the top of the cliffs, falling back to the shoreline. Undeterred, with less ropes and ladders than they had planned to use, the Rangers began to climb.

While under enemy fire from above, and old artillery shells hanging by wires along the cliff face the first Rangers made it to the top in five minutes, the rest followed and nearly all the men who could climb, were on the cliff tops in fifteen minutes. Between the lost LCA carrying Ruggiero's group, and the casualties from landing and climbing, Rudder's force was reduced to less than 200 men.

Once over the top, the firing from German machine guns continued completely unabated as the Rangers ran for trenches and shell craters. As if the MG 42 machine guns were not a big enough problem, the Germans started firing their ant-aircraft guns at the Rangers. The German anti-aircraft gun was firing small 20 mm artillery shells, and they wreaked havoc on the aggressing Rangers.

Each Ranger knew his job and they all began to search for the big guns. They fought from crater to crater, jumped into trenches not knowing if Germans already there. They did what they did best, what they were trained to do—fire and maneuver, fire and maneuver, fire and maneuver.

Before long, they were attacking the concrete gun casements. The remarkably silent concrete big gun emplacements. None of the big guns were firing, yet the Rangers were there to silence the big guns atop the promontory.

There were no sounds other than rifles, machine guns, the moans of the wounded and dying, and the commands of attackers and defenders. Company D was responsible for the three-gun positions on the west side, facing Utah Beach, Companies E and F attacked the three-gun positions on the east side facing Omaha Beach.

First Sargent Lomell of D Company led the attackers who captured the first gun position. With the first gun platform secured, Lomell noted: *"When we got there, we found there were no guns…the big emplacements had telegraph poles looking like a big gun from the air…it startled and disappointed us…"*[117]

---

[117] Kershaw, Robert. LANDING ON THE EDGE OF ETERNITY: 24 hours at Omaha Beach. Pegasus Books: New York. 2018. Page 198.

169

All morning long, the Rangers had faced the longest odds of any American assaulting force on D-Day. And they could have never imagined: *the fell clutch of circumstance* were so stacked against them. They had lost: the element of surprise, lost men in sinking boats not combat, supplies lost with LCA's sunk into the unforgiving English Channel, time they needed was usurped by a simple navigation mistake, radios failing causing denial of needed reinforcements, an assault plan from two sides—which would split the enemy forces was scrapped for a shear daring frontal assault into the teeth of the enemies resistance, and now despite all they had overcome the fearsome guns of Pointe-du-Hoc were not on Pointe-du-Hoc.

The Rangers and their leaders quickly understood their mission had another objective, to cut the coastal road. Combined elements for the assaulting companies fought their way to the road, attacking enemy bunkers and trenches. They never stopped moving and did what they trained so well to do—attack.

Relentlessly, they pushed the Germans back and reached the coastal road that linked Utah and Omaha Beaches. It was vital to close that road and slow or stop any German reinforcement plans. Regardless of enemy strength, the roadblock was to be held until the defenders were relieved.

While his valiant Rangers were driving the German defenders from the Pointe, Colonel Rudder established a cliff top command post. Incredibly before long, it took a direct hit from a naval gun. Rudder's communication equipment that was working was destroyed.

But Rudders's communications officer, Lieutenant James Eikner, had brought a back-up. Eikner brought an old signal lamp which would allow him to communicate with the Navy. Using Morse Code signals through the old beacon light Eikner redirected their gun fire towards the German positions.

When Sargent Lomell reached the road, he and his fellow Rangers secured the roadblock. Lomell and another Sargent, Jack Kuhn moved down the road eyeballing all around their position, searching for Germans. Lomell noticed what looked like tracks in the mud on the side of the old Normandy road.

He cautiously followed the tracks into a wooded area where five of the guns of Point-du-Hoc, were sitting unattended in an apple orchard. The guns were elevated and appeared to be aimed at Utah Beach. First Sergeant Lomell knew what he had to do. He instructed Jack Kuhn to cover him.

Lomell slipped into the area where the guns were. He used thermite grenades on the metal mechanisms that control the guns. But he only had two thermite grenades. Lomell and Kuhn rushed back to roadblock and gathered as many thermite grenades as they could, they then rushed back to the still unattended guns.

Lomell finished off the other guns using the thermite, and further smashed the aiming mechanisms on each gun. The guns were inoperable. The two Rangers ran like hell towards the roadblock. Suddenly, a massive explosion knocked Lomell and Kuhn to the ground.

Other Rangers had found the ammo dump for the guns and detonated it causing a huge explosion. It was just past 08:30 hours, the Rangers had been on French soil for less than an hour and a half.

Lomell sent two runners who had to fight their way back to Colonel Rudder's position. They informed the Colonel the guns had been destroyed. Rudder informed Lieutenant Eikner to signal to Navy that the guns were destroyed using the code, "Blow6."

He also told Eikner to ask for reinforcements and additional supplies to replace those that had sunk on the way into the Pointe. The Navy responded they had no reinforcements available all forces sent to Omaha Beach. They would try to re-supply.

General Eisenhower's number one mission was to silence the guns on Pointe-du-Hoc, remarkably, it took the US Army Rangers less than an hour and half to fight ashore, climb the cliffs, fight across the gun batteries, create a vital road block, find the missing and guns and disable them.

With their mission partially fulfilled, the Rangers dug in on the coastal road to solidify the roadblock, while others dug in at Rudder's makeshift command post. They waited to be relieved, believing it would be a matter of hours.

Despite the challenges presented by *"the fell clutch of circumstance,"* determination driven by training centered the Rangers to accept any difficulty encountered on D-Day. Now, they just had to hold on until relieved, the Rangers dug in, not knowing the killing, wounding and dying had only just begun.

Part V: The Defense of Pointe-du-Hoc

"Out of the night that covers me,
Black as the pit from pole to pole,
I thank whatever gods may be
For my unconquerable soul."

Invictus (1888)
William Ernest Henley (1849–1903)

Hold on they were told; your relief will arrive in a matter of hours as the troops come off Omaha Beach. Rudder's men dug in at the command post, and the Rangers out on the coast road dug in, expecting to get the brunt of a German counter assault to drive the Americans into the sea from which they came. The three Ranger companies, D, E, and F shared the responsibilities of defending the coastal road creating a first line of defense for Pointe-du-Hoc.

In a reflection of the inability of the German Army to protect the guns and ammo inland from Pointe-du-Hoc, the Germans first counter assaults on Rudder's Rangers were weak and relatively ineffective. The initial assault against Rudder's CP was easily repelled. That would change.

Out at the blocked coastal road, things were starting to get very hot. The Rangers had placed some forward observation positions to alert the roadblock forces that an attack was coming. The forward positions were attacked by the Germans in what you could call a probing attack, designed to establish the strength of an enemy you plan to attack.

Like the initial assault at Rudder's CP, the probing attacks were repelled. But the larger gathering German forces now understood what was waiting for them. Good news came to Rudder as the sun was setting on D-Day, a platoon from Able company, 5th Ranger Battalion, led by a young Lieutenant Parker arrived from Omaha Beach.

Parker had about twenty soldiers, and Rudder sent them forward to help defend the roadblock. Currently, the bulk of Rudder's surviving men were defending the roadblock. His CP was staffed dangerously thin and some of defenders were already wounded. Rudder ordered a defensive perimeter established around the CP, to be manned by his scant force. The CP was being harassed by German snipers and that dam anti-aircraft gun was still firing.

The sun went down and enveloped those at Pointe-du-Hoc in a blanket of darkness and danger. All was quiet in the darkness for a few hours, until just after midnight when the Germans sent another probing attack into the Rangers at the roadblock. The attack was quick and did its damage, now the Germans knew exactly where the American lines were. Suddenly, it was quiet again.

Just about two hours later, the Germans dropped mortars shells on the Rangers, the next assault had begun. The Rangers had organized their defense with two lines that intersected at ninety degrees. The Germans crashed into the Rangers punching a hole in one of the lines.

In an effort not to get overwhelmed, a lieutenant ordered a retreat closer to the CP on the Pointe. He stopped and established a new line, but soon realized he had less than fifty soldiers remaining. The remnants of the three Ranger Companies defending the road had seemingly been cut in half.

Realizing their band of Rangers was rapidly shrinking, and that they had an acute shortage of ammunition, some of the Rangers headed back toward Rudder's CP. The battered Rangers reached Rudder's CP just before sunrise. It was Wednesday June 7, D-Day plus one, for Rudder and his men there was no relief in sight.

Rudder did not know how many Rangers were dead or alive out on the coastal road, and by now, some of his men who had ran out of ammunition were fighting with German weapons, Rudder ordered his troops to dig in as another assault was expected.

What Rudder did not know was a group of men from D Company was still out at the road. Led by First Sargent Lomell, they did not withdraw. Lomell was told to hold his position until relived, and that is what he and his fellow D Company stalwarts planned on doing, they were surrounded, and they dug in and waited.

Meanwhile, Rudder called in the Navy to blast away the Germans he was sure were gathering for the next assault. The Naval guns opened fire on the suspected German positions, and unbeknownst to Rudder some of the shells fell on D Company out on the coast road.

Rudder's luck changed on the afternoon of June 7; two American landing craft arrived at the bottom of the cliffs at Pointe-du-Hoc. They carried about thirty fresh troops including Antonio Ruggiero, food, medical supplies, and some ammunition. They evacuated some of the wounded Rangers, and a few German POWs. Rudder's men had not slept or eaten in nearly two days.

The US Navy guns pounded the German positions all afternoon and into the night. But at sunrise on June 8, the men of Dog Company, who had managed to survive the Naval shelling, heard the unmistakable sound of tracked vehicles on the road.

They knew the next battle was going to be against tanks, they wouldn't stand a chance. Suddenly, the Rangers could see they were American tanks, the battle was over. As the men of D-Company, out on the coastal road over a mile from Rudder's CP embraced their moments of relief as the tanks passed them continuing on towards the Pointe.

For one last, bitter, deadly moment, *"the fell clutch of circumstance"* found Rudder's Rangers. The tank commanders heard German weapons firing and assumed that the Germans were holding the Pointe, not Rudder. Several Rangers who had survived forty-eight hours of hell were killed by friendly fire.

It was not until a Ranger officer got on a tank, pulled his pistol out and told the tank commander that he was attacking Americans did the firing stop. The struggle for Pointe-du-Hoc was over. Rudder and his men had survived for two days, with little water and food, desperately fighting Germans, sometimes with German weapons.

Rudder led 225 Rangers in landing crafts to the Pointe and into battle at the clifftop gun batteries, he led barley ninety away.

President Obama speaking with Antonio Ruggiero.

Part VI: After Pointe-du-Hoc

"These are the men who took the cliffs.
These are the champions who helped free a continent.
These are the heroes who helped end a war."

U.S. President Ronald Reagan (1911–2004)
D-Day 40th Anniversary Speech, June 6, 1984

Sargent Antonio Ruggiero was in British LCA 860 when it went down. It sank because it was swamped by the rough seas, was full of Rangers each carrying some sixty pounds of gear, the boats were also burdened with the additional weight of the large mortars for firing the grapple ropes and ladders, and it was being shelled by German artillery. Yes, German artillery, not from Pointe-du-Hoc was shelling LCA 860.

The water-logged boat was moving slower when suddenly a German shell landed close enough to cause the boat to lurch violently to one side flooding the overloaded LCA, which began its decent to the bottom of the English Channel.

175

Those Rangers who were not pulled down with the weight of their gear tried to stay afloat. Time was not their friend as exhaustion and hypothermia were now the enemy of the Rangers in the 42-degree water.

As they clung to life in the frigid waters the drifting Rangers could see their fellow Rangers begin to assault the cliffs at the Pointe. After all their sacrifices, training and hard work, they could only watch until they drifted out of view.

Remarkably, most of them were picked up by a passing smaller ship. Ruggiero and the few survivors found themselves transferred on board the USS Texas. The ships doctor examined the men, and declared them unfit to return to duty, declaring that they need to rest and recover from hypothermia.

It was only their superb physical and mental condition that allowed them to survive in the deadly cold English Channel. Despite vigorous protestations, the Navy doctor had his way. Ruggiero and his comrades were stuck on the USS Texas.

Ruggiero and the other surviving Rangers from LCA 860 eventually made it to Pointe-du-Hoc, where Antonio Ruggiero insisted on climbing the ropes to the top—just like his comrades had done. Ruggiero's war lasted another year, his bravery would earn two Bronze Stars and two Purple Hearts.

When he was wounded, he kept arguing with medical staff that the job he was sent to do was not done. At one battle, he grabbed a crutch and hobbled back to the battlefield, back to his fellow Rangers. He served until Germany surrendered, and then returned to the States.

Ruggiero chose not to pursue the career in show business he had begun before the war, but to continue to serve his community. He got married, had a daughter, and became a Plymouth, Massachusetts firefighter where his courage and ability to lead under pressure served his fellow firefighters and community as he rose to the rank of captain.

The Rangers he served with became life-long friends. His daughter Karen told me of how she got to meet his Ranger buddies, at their frequent get-togethers. Antonio Ruggiero traveled back to Normandy with his remaining fellow Rangers in 1984 to join with President Reagan for the 40th Anniversary of D-Day.

Ruggiero and his comrades sat before the President as he memorably framed the *Boys of Pointe-du-Hoc* who were the men sitting before him. Reagan said,

"...We stand on a lonely, windswept point on the northern shore of France. The air is soft, but 40 years ago at this moment, the air was dense with smoke and the cries of men, and the air was filled with the crack of rifle fire and the roar of cannon...Forty summers have passed since the battle that you fought here.

You were young the day you took these cliffs; some of you were hardly more than boys, with the deepest joys of life before you. Yet, you risked everything here. Why? Why did you do it? What impelled you to put aside the instinct for self-preservation and risk your lives to take these cliffs? What inspired all the men of the armies that met here? We look at you, and somehow, we know the answer.

It was faith and belief; it was loyalty and love...We are bound today by what bound us 40 years ago, the same loyalties, traditions, and beliefs...Your hopes are our hopes, and your destiny is our destiny...Strengthened by their courage, heartened by their valor, and borne by their memory, let us continue to stand for the ideals for which they lived and died."[118]

The President's words moved many to tears, and he greeted the surviving Rangers with the appropriate humility and respect. The President shook Antonio Ruggiero's hand and said, *"it's an honor to shake your hand."*[119]

Ranger Ruggiero returned to Normandy one more time after that, in 2009 for the 65th Anniversary. In France, he was awarded, *Légion d'honneur*—The French Legion of Honor and in a word, he was Knighted. He got to shake the hand of another President in Normandy, President Obama, and was chosen as the escort of First Lady Michele Obama, as they listened to President Obama's speech at the Normandy American Memorial and Cemetery.

---

[118] Reagan, Ronald. Remarks at a Ceremony Commemorating the 40th Anniversary of the Normandy Invasion, D-day. June 6, 1984.
https://www.reaganfoundation.org/media/128809/normandy.pdf Retrieved September 2020.
[119] Harbert, Rich. Old Colony Memorial Newspaper, Plymouth, MA. Vol. 194. No 32 20 April 2016. Page A-7.

Antonio Ruggiero and First lady Michele Obama.

Sitting with his surviving veterans, and the First Lady, Mr. Ruggiero listened again as a US President spoke at Normandy. President Obama found instances of personal bravery and noted the sacrifices of some individual American soldiers whose actions still inspire us from all those years removed. President Obama spoke for less than twenty minutes and here is some of what he said,

"I'm not the first American President to come and mark this anniversary...This is an event that has long brought to this coast both heads of state and grateful citizens...And long after our time on this Earth has passed, one word will still bring forth the pride and awe of men and women who will never meet the heroes who sit before us: D-Day...Why is this?

Of all the battles in all the wars across the span of human history, why does this day hold such a revered place in our memory...Part of it, I think, is the size of the odds that weighed against success...And by the end of the day, against all odds, the ground on which we stand was free once more.

The sheer improbability of this victory is part of what makes D-Day so memorable...You're why we keep coming back...For you remind us that in the end, human destiny is not determined by forces beyond our control. You remind us that our future is not shaped by mere chance or circumstance.

Our history has always been the sum total of the choices made and the actions taken by each individual man and woman. It has always been up to us... (D-Day is) *a story written by men like Antonio Ruggiero, an Army Ranger who saw half the men on his landing craft drown when it was hit by shellfire just a thousand yards off this beach.*

He spent three hours in freezing water, and was one of only 90 Rangers to survive out of the 225 who were sent to scale the cliffs...To those men who achieved that victory 65 years ago, we thank you for your service. May God bless you, and may God bless the memory of all those who rest here. "[120]

[120] Obama, Barrack. Remarks by the President at D-Day 65th Anniversary Ceremony. Normandy American Cemetery and Memorial. Normandy, France. June 6, 2009. https://obamawhitehouse.archives.gov/the-press-office/remarks-president-d-day-65th-anniversary-ceremony. Retrieved September 2020.

Antonio Ruggiero's words carved into Pointe-du-hoc Visitors Center.

Part VII: Conclusion
Legends Never Die

"I say my prayers and ask the Good Lord
to help you end this mess in Iraq and Afghanistan...
get our boys home."

2009 Conversation—U.S. President Barrack Obama and Antonio
Ruggiero
Sergeant (Ret) Antonio Thomas Ruggiero (1920–2016)
US Army Rangers, 2nd Battalion, D Company (1943–1945)

I am on the craggy coast of France, where the wind is blowing, pushing the puffy colored clouds over the historic and battered landscape. The wind and rain are never far from me when I travel Normandy. For some reason, they particularly follow me to a dramatic spit of land hanging over 100 feet from the churning English Channel.

I am staring at the granite dagger monument to the Rangers who assaulted this place on D-Day. It dominates your attention jutting into the sky atop the old German command bunker. And it commands a most impressive view of the sea that brought the American liberators here so long ago.

On each side of the stone dagger are words carved into memoriam. On the right side the words are in French, on the left side the English words are carved:

TO THE HEROIC RANGER COMMANDOES
D 2 RN E 2 RN F 2 RN
OF THE 116th INFANTRY
WHO UNDER THE COMMAND OF
COLONEL JAMES E RUDDER
OF THE FIRST AMERICAN DIVISION
ATTACKED AND TOOK POSSESSION OF
THE POINTE DU HOC

My favorite visits to the Pointe are when it is cloudy, and the ocean is blanketed in a thin misty cool coastal fog. On the Pointe, the wind, chilled by the cold waters of the English Channel bites at you, and holds your attention.

That's when you look out to sea, standing atop the cliffs still so daunting and wonder how they did what they did. I imagine I see them, on D-Day morning, the men and boys of Company D, E, and F, 2nd Ranger Battalion. Theirs was *Mission Impossible*, to silence the guns of Pointe-du-Hoc. That was something Rommel thought would never happen, but Field Marshal Erwin Rommel never met a US Army Ranger.

On this visit, I think of Sargent Antonio Ruggiero and his daughter Karen. Standing with the wind whipping at me, I looked down at the cliffs, and out to the sea that brought him here. I remember his story as told in my dining room by his daughter before I left for France.

Karen brought an armful of memories. She passed me an old paper with small cursive handwritten lines filling the entire page. Then, I realized she had handed me three pages. She took a small bite of a cookie and watched my eyes scan the pages. It was night and hard to read the small print, but I kept reading. *May I copy this?*

I asked without my eyes leaving the paper. "*Oh, sure go ahead,*" she said in her amiable and friendly tone. She had other things to show me, but choose to start near the end, leaving newspaper clippings, and photos on the other side of the table. She chose to share her recollections from her handwritten eulogy of her father's extraordinary life.

"He was my hero," she said softly with a firm foundation of pride holding her short sentence together. If my eyes had not already teared over, I would have looked at her eyes.

"I know he was a hero to a lot of people, but I wanted him to know he was my hero." I had no response as I put down the handwritten pages as she passed the black and white photos of her young father. *"He dreamed of being a singer and dancer,"* she said with a loving smile.

I thought how foreign that sounded when you juxtaposed that to a decorated, fearless World War II US Army Ranger. But the old black and white photos of a well-lived life made me realize decades had passed since a world went to war.

When Pearl Harbor was attacked, Antonio Ruggiero, or Tommy as he was known to his friends and family, was in Hollywood trying to make it in show business. That was his dream, but he put aside his dreams, left Hollywood and came home to Plymouth, Massachusetts and volunteered to fight for his country. He tried to join the Marine Corps, but they said at 5' 3" he was not tall enough.

Undeterred, he joined the Army and then volunteered to be in the best trained, most highly skilled army outfit—the US Army Rangers. They could see he was short, but they could also see he was tough, hardworking, smart, and an excellent shot. He was accepted into the US Army Ranger and became a member of the legendary D Company, 2nd Ranger Battalion, a most extraordinary group of Warriors.

Antonio Ruggiero passed away on 14 April 2016, after a life full of unselfish service to his country and community. He was 95 years old. You can find him resting peacefully in Vine Hills Cemetery, in Plymouth, Massachusetts. There, at the top of a slight hill, his resting place is marked by a simple soldier's gravestone.

It is lovingly cared for and always has an American flag, and sometimes many of them, at the top of the stone. The top two lines are his name, and beneath that are carved the lines reminding us of his rank, service branch, when he served, and the date of life and death are also carved into the light-colored stone.

On this visit, I clear the leaves that the changing seasons have left on the ground and place a penny, a modern reminder of a visit. The last line on his stone reads, *French Legion of Honor*, and it is then when I am done reading, I reflect on his sacrifices—his many sacrifices.

The sounds of modern-day existence travel up the hill from the busy road beneath, and as they find me, I think he is gone but not forgotten. He, like the other veterans of World War II, lifted a world from the dangerous dark shadows into the light of life. Their war was a war of clearly defined morality and injustice.

The peaceful world of his youth in Plymouth was intersected with unbridled hate and cruelty in the war he fought in Europe. He, like so many others, were more than equal to their nearly impossible task. Turning to leave, I remember my many visits to Pointe-du-Hoc and ask him silently—*"How did you do that, Ranger?"*

Antonio Thomas Ruggiero was a perfect representative of the men who have become known as, *The Greatest Generation.*

Karen Ruggiero visited Normandy in June of 2019, seventy-five years after her dad fought and nearly died there. She got to see Pointe-du-Hoc, and get a glimpse of her father's world when he was a young man. She called it a *Dream come true* and spent time in Normandy where he would have been in 1944. But of all the things she saw, it was the visitors' center that held a special reminder of her gallant dad.

When the US Government expanded the visitors' center at Pointe-du-Hoc, it included a beautiful brown wall, made of flawless cut and fitted stone. The beautiful light brown stones are representative of the local native French stones and remind me of the cliffs located just a short walk away at Pointe-du-Hoc.

But it is the words carved with perfect precision on the wall that are striking. They express the spirit that liberated this part of France and began the struggle to crush the tyranny and oppression of the Nazis. The words were spoken by a foreign soldier, 3,000 miles from his home. He was on a foreign shore, sent to liberate a foreign people, from a foreign oppressor, the words chiseled into the stone were spoken by a US Army Ranger on 6 June 1944.

He was struggling for his life in freezing cold waters off Pointe-du-Hoc when he asked God for help. The words of our hometown hero, the words of *her hero*, greet every visitor who comes to Pointe-du-Hoc:

*"Dear God, don't let me drown. I want to get in
and do what I am supposed to do."*

Sargent Antonio Ruggiero, 2nd Ranger Battalion 6 June 1944

Legends never die.

Bibliography

Ambrose, Stephen E. *D-DAY 6 June 1944: The Climatic Battle of World War II.* Simon & Schuster: New York. 1994. Print.

Balestrieri, Steve. *Rangers Storm the Cliffs of Pointe du Hoc on D-Day 75 Years Ago.* SOFREP. "Special Operations Forces Report. Jun 6, 2017. https://sofrep.com/specialoperations/31021/ Retrieved September 2020.

Brinkley, Douglas. *The Boys of Pointe du Hoc.* HarperCollins: New York. 2005. Print.

Kershaw, Robert. *Landing on the Edge of Eternity: 24 Hours at Omaha Beach.* Pegasus Books: New York. 2018. Print.

Margaritas, Peter. *Countdown to D-Day the German Perspective.* Casemate: Havertown, PA. 2019. Print.

Moore, Charles. *Battleship Texas (BB-35).* https://web.archive.org/web/20060923092736/http://users3.ev1.net/~cfmoore /history/1944normandy.html retrieved September 2020.

O'Donnell, Patrick K. *Dog Company:* The Boys of Pointe-du-Hoc. De Capo: Boston. 2012. Print.

Ruane, Michael E. *'The Boys of Pointe du Hoc': The Reagan D-Day Speech That Moved a Nation* Peggy Noonan wrote it. Ronald Reagan delivered it. And in 1984, dozens of the aging 'boys 'were there to hear it. https://www.washingtonpost.com/history/2019/06/05/boys-pointe-du-hoc-reagan-d-day-speech-that-moved-nation/ Washington Post, 5 June 2019. Retrieved September 2020.

Sterne, Gary. *The Cover-up at Omaha Beach:* D-Day, the US Rangers, and the untold story of Maisy Battery. Skyhorse Publishing: New York. 2014. Print.

Chapter 6
Oradour-Sur-Glane

Introduction

*"I have wanted to go to Oradour-sur-Glane for a long time.
I have feared going to Oradour-sur-Glane even longer."*

Amelia McNutt
Oradour-sur-Glane, France
September 2016

The human darkness in the story of Oradour-sur-Glane hits you hard as you walk through the ruins, you quickly realize something extraordinarily evil, unnatural happened here. Oradour's destruction was thorough and orderly, it was in a word—complete. It lacks the random chaotic damage brought by the forces of nature like tornados and hurricanes.

The barns and the bank—the markets and the manufacturers—the schools and the church—none were exempted from the unbridled destruction of monsters masquerading as men. No place or no one was spared. At Oradour, the destruction is so complete that even to this very day the haunting brutality surrounds the visitors, who become prisoners more than visitors.

Decades in the past, soulless monsters once filled this place with such a horror that we can easily imagine the screams filling the silence as we come face to face with our unimaginable yet very palpable imagined visions. Our frightened imaginations walk with us, deeper and deeper into man's darkness—this is Hell, this is Oradour-sur-Glane.

On a peaceful, sun filled, summer's day in early June 1944, lives ended in minutes, forever incomplete, in a horrific brutality that defines the Nazis of World War II. As civilized people, the events that occurred here are rightfully beyond our comprehension, certainly beyond our explanation and our understanding of humanity. They are not beyond our acceptance as they still surround you, they exist in nearly all their brutality, and seventy-five years later it is a shocking place.

At Oradour-sur-Glane, time is frozen into twisted steel, collapsed buildings, and black soot strained stones. It is a place locked in time even as the shadows of unforgettable lingering memories continue to inevitably lengthen. As time passes, the emotions conjured in this place fade like the blackened fire-stained stones that are washed by natures cleansing rains. Still, not all forget, or forgive as time passes here.

Although this is a place and story I want to omit—I can't. I am on the road to Normandy, *Chasing Rommel*. I am going to Oradour, a place that peacefully ages beside the gentle River Glane. Its existence exchanged in a lasting historical example of mass murder by the Nazis.

Oradour-sur-Glane is not in Normandy. But it has a place in the Normandy narrative and as we share this horrific story, we will discover why the story of Oradour must be remembered with the sacrifices of amazing American soldiers in Normandy. This is my journey to Oradour-sur-Glane. Come with me, and together we will—*remember*.

Ruins of a building in Oradour.

Part I: My Journey to Oradour

"No one ever told me that grief felt so much like fear…"

C.S. Lewis (1898–1963)

It is an early October morning in France, the hotel door opened to a chilly breeze. Not cold, but brisk enough to disturb my concentration. Getting into the car, I noticed the sun was very bright with strong rays of light passing through the trees.

Some of the leaves had fallen, yet my eyes were attracted to the warm yellow and rusting red leaves hanging on to the increasingly barren trees. Gone were their vibrant greens as the French summer faded into early autumn. Autumn in France always reminds me of my New England roots, colorful and cold.

I entered my GPS destination and realized—*"It was time."* I had traveled so far, in time and distance and now Oradour was just a car ride away. It had been decades since my youthful introduction to Oradour, now I crossed an ocean, and many time zones, and I was getting ever closer. I could feel the building tension.

I backed out of my parking space listening as the GPS announced I would be there in four hours. I could feel my pulse rise, my heartbeat jump, I breathed deeply and shifted my small rental car forward, and began the end of my long-awaited journey.

The village of Oradour-Sur-Glane is nestled beside the peaceful River Glane, it was a suburb of the French city of Limoges. A place that mixed the old and the new, with large stone buildings seemingly standing for centuries, beside old barns with horses and carts, juxtaposed with modern automobiles and an electric streetcar on rails.

It had old chateaus, hotels, cafes, and it had bakers, butchers, blacksmiths, and mechanics. It was as modern as it was old world French. Over two hundred and fifty homes and businesses were located in this idyllic place.

By June 1944, the German's had occupied France for four long years. The Allied Armies had just landed in Normandy on *D-Day*, 6 June 1944 and a foreign army—Germany, was in a foreign country—France, fighting a foreign enemy—America, to save a foreign people—the French.

It was quite simply and an event history had never witnessed. Oradour-Sur-Glane is only 550 kilometers from the historic landing beaches in Normandy, and the residents of Oradour, like all the residents of conquered France held their collective breaths hoping the hated Germans would be defeated—soon.

My ride is comfortable and as the time passes, the sun warms me and the windows are opened. The warm breeze, now a welcome companion, replacing the morning chill. Looking to my right and left the farm fields are empty, already harvested.

The remains have been plowed under as tranquil brown rows appearing neatly arranged for the winter. I am on a country road, and I think—*"Were they on this road?"* Was this the road the *Monsters* used to find Oradour? Continuing with my thoughts, I recall how I came to know of Oradour.

I met Oradour-sur-Glane on my television screen in 1974. The Boston PBS channel carried the show which was made in England and was accompanied by the voice of Sir Lawrence Olivier. The show "The World at War" began its first of twenty-six episodes with the images of a rusted deserted car, on a deserted street, lined with deserted buildings which caught my attention. Olivier said: *"They* (The soldiers) *stayed only a few hours. When they had gone, a community which had lived 1,000 years was dead. This is Oradour-sur-Glane."* He had my attention.

The images and the words he spoke with his graceful British accent, underpinned by a wave of tense symphonic music drew me to learn more. At first glance, the completed destruction shown from an arial view looked like a Nazi destroyed Russian town. I quickly realized he was speaking of a town in France and was drawn to learn more: What and where was this place? And why?

Later, as I researched Oradour, my recollections were shifted to the limitations of World War II history books containing old black and white photos. Images and words that freeze that fateful day of 10 June 1944.

"...the day the soldiers came..." as Olivier said.

Olivier described a perfect summer's day in the French countryside when everything stopped, everything changed, and nearly everything died. A place reduced to broken and fire-stained stones, rusting steel contorted by the heat of gasoline induced flames that consumed a place, a way of life, and its people that had lasted a millennium.

I am close to Oradour. The signs reassuring me that I am on the road to the martyred village, I shut off my GPS, its voice now out of place as I feel I am traveling back into time. My heart races. I am closer now to Oradour than I have ever been. The breeze from the open window reduced to a disruption, interfering as I concentrate and prepare to come face to face with the most evil of mankind.

I guide my car into a shade covered parking spot. My senses are heightening, and the closing of a car door sounds like a gunshot. The asphalt reflects the sun, and I am hotter than I have been all day—perhaps, more anxiety than weather.

It would take me over forty years to reach Oradour, my thoughts are a mixture of curiosity and wholesale fear. I stop, and make sure I have my camera. I slowly walk to the visitor's center, guided by the signs.

Hell, I am here.

Sign greeting visitors at Oradour.

Part II: The Place

"This place (Oradour) *is pervaded by a classic tranquility in which one can live as a human being should."*

Michael Forest, Poet, diarist, law student.
Resident of Oradour-sur-Glane,
victim of the massacre of 10 June 1944.

Entering the visitors center, I am struck by the quiet. People whisper, like those barley speaking at a funeral. My ticket in hand, I walked out of the visitor's center through the glass doors and into the warm air. I am mixed with a small group, and although we are strangers, we are on a momentary common journey.

A few steps together and we all stop as if we were told to halt. Before us is a sign that looks as old as Oradour, it is white with red letters. The capitalized French words on top, *SOUVIENS-TOI*, below a lone English word, *REMEMBER*. A few more steps and we pass by another white sign, we again stop, as if ordered.

It is instructional and issues its demand with blue letters on a white background. No French is scripted on this plaque. It is only in English, and instructs us in the manor we are to respect Oradour-sur-Glane. With one word, its message is delivered, and we stand silently and understand. The old sign imperatively reads—*SILENCE*.

As I walk the path into the town, the first ruins immediately remind me that Oradour-sur-Glane reflects its violent past. Slowing my already slow pace, my vista includes the convulsions of burned-out disintegrated homes and buildings. The disintegrating roads, rusting railroad tracks, and spasmed twisted steel structures. Oradour is home to the past, shrouded in a silence that you struggle to bear in this town with no residents, only relics.

The violence inflicted upon this place surrounds you. The blackened charred stone walls hold your gaze. In your imagination, you can see the flames belching from the opening, roaring and red-hot consuming everything combustible, and tormenting steel and iron articles, changing their shapes into nearly unrecognizable hulks.

The fires stopped burning over 70 years ago, yet, the soot remains like an old faded tattoo that reminds its bearer of another time. I got the feeling something was looking out as I was looking in, something I could not see only feel. That feeling followed me all day at Oradour.

The emptiness seems to have a life of its own, and stares back at you in a profound silence. What stories the tattooed stones hold, stories, I think of overwhelming terror. I notice there is no wood, no doors, no windows, just openings that pull you towards them but not through them.

The world inside these places reserved for ghostly artifacts of a fierce, abusive, inhuman event. I do not see any roofs, only the charred stone walls that once supported the burned away wooden tops that were reduced to smoke and ash. The same fiery fate consumed the furniture, now there is little reminder that people lived here.

Attached to these fossilized building remains are steel brackets that once carried electric and telephone cables. The cables' insulation burnt off and the soft copper metals easily melted in the intense heat. I think for a moment: the destruction is so complete, it seems staged like a Hollywood movie set, the wreckage perfect in its abhorrence.

The only signs of life in the gutted, roofless buildings are the growing trees, weeds, and grasses thriving where people once walked on floors. Green shades filling in the spaces between life and death, growing around rusted artifacts, and broken, blackened stones. Life has found the lifeless in this horrid place.

The old street that ushers you into and through this hell, is broken, and yet, it still frames the rusty old railroad tracks that carried the modern electric tram from Limoges. Above hangs its twisted steel rigid power cables. The insulation burned away, but the steel unlike the softer copper cables remains. Today, they are silhouetted against a blue sunny sky, and I remember that the "...*day the soldiers came*..." it was an equally sunny day.

The rails below, and the contorted steel cables above guide you down Oradour's main street, framing the view like an apparition wanting to be revealed on a still life canvas. For now, the imperfect image pulls one perfectly into this hell.

Silently walking along the quiet streets is eerie as visitors try to take the unimaginable into our 21st century lives. I walk along and hear only my slow steps crunching the small broken stones that rest on the sidewalk and road. There are small green signs attached to some of the ruins.

The signs are in French, yet some are easy to understand. Modest signs tell us who lived in these buildings and of a places' purpose. Some, I managed to translate: *Courtier* was a broker, *Cafe* was a coffee shop, *Epicier* was a grocer, and *Boulangerie* was a bakery.

Most of the ruins are indistinguishable, hollowed out places with a few metal pieces scattered about. Except the bakery you notice, the bakery is different. It is obvious as you can still see the standing ovens, with red brick construction contrasting the otherwise tan blackened wall stones.

The metal oven doors are bleak and rusted and all remain closed except one. One is partially opened like the baker was checking his work when the Nazis came. Staring at the ovens and thinking of Nazis, the parallel to other heinous events quickly materialize. I turn away full of sadness and shame in a place already overburdened with sadness and shame.

Other buildings are littered with warped bed frames, misshapen buckets, and bicycles in tense contorted forms, unrecognizable for only the spoked wheels. Of all the rusted forms of steel, it is the many automobiles in various states of disintegration that remind me of the people that lived in Oradour.

That lives stopped so quickly and brutally, you could not drive away. Rather what would have been your escape was to remain as a reminder of your swift, brutal execution.

Some were in garages and grouped together. None alike except they share a common color—rusted steel red. Some are barely recognizable as autos, crushed by falling flaming roof timbers, and reduced to piles of rubble with fenders, headlights, or a grille. Otherworldly, like some modern art piece that draws your curiosity.

Others are in, what seems to have been, barns. They are aligned in their destruction with other devises that were pulled by horses on Oradour's farms. But it is one car in particular that grabs my attention as I slowly walk toward a car the has its own history, in a place full of history.

It rests where the operator stopped on 10 June 1944, like the owner was in a hurry to attend to something. The doors are now closed and strangely some door handles are intact. Everything that could burn is gone as the interior has been reduced to just metal. Tireless rims resting on the ground, windowless openings, the interior and exterior rusting together in a pale faded nearly uniform, burned red. A ghost of a car, in a most ghostly place.

The still life canvases that are the streets of Oradour pulls me along until I am face to face with a burned and rusted, steel structure. It stands slightly less tall than I, and it takes a human form to me. It is wider on the top half and narrower at the bottom half, like legs standing straightly together.

It remains like a mute sentry, standing at attention. Glancing from top to bottom, I see it has been dutifully anchored to the sidewalk. It was a spectator and victim through the best and worst of this place. Unable to move, it had to bear witness to that which was unwitnessable. If it could speak, what would it say about its time here in Oradour? What had it seen?

What had it heard or smelled? My gaze returns to the present and I realize it was a French mailbox. As I turn away from the valiant mailbox, I wonder what stories were within its now rusted exterior on 10 June 1944. Perhaps, it held news of the recent invasion of the Normandy Beaches by the liberating Allies.

Maybe letters of happiness filled with words to be shared by those who longed for peace during the awful war. Possibly, greetings from relatives in other parts of occupied France sharing common stories of shortages, and words of hope for an end to what must have seemed like a never-ending German presence. Lost forever are its contents and yet its macabre existence holds my attention as I think—*letters to and from the dead.*

The mailbox reminds me that this empty, silent place was so alive one day and utterly dead the next. I question myself amid the silence and peace of this place. Who would do such a thing to such a place? Who could, who would do such a thing?

Why? Always why? A suitable answer is never found, because this cannot under any human terms be explained beyond just the known facts.

In your mind's eye, you witness vicious cold-blooded killers masking themselves as soldiers as they pitilessly ended the existence of 642 innocent men, women, and children. The SS reduced this place from a vibrant piece of France to a cold and hollow grave the size of a village. It is a lasting signature, a warning to we who dare visit this place. This is what hatred becomes.

Oradour-sur-Glane was left standing after World War II as a city-sized memorial. It is shocking in its sobering, ghastly demeanor. At every intersection, every building, every moment, I am reminded of the depravities of war and the unmeasurable brutality of monsters who looked like men.

Burned-out building remains in Oradour-sur-Glane.

Part III: 2nd SS Panzer Division Monsters Masquerading As Men

"Hell is empty and all the devils are here."

The Tempest, Act 1 Scene 2
William Shakespeare (1564–1616)

Early on the morning of 10 June 1944, 29-year-old Waffen SS *Strumbannfuhrer* (Major) Adolf Otto Deikmann, commander of the 1st Battalion, 4th SS Panzer Grenadier Regiment, 2nd SS Panzer Division, known as *Das Reich* Division rapidly entered Headquarters and stated he knew that his missing friend and comrade *Strumbannfuhrer* (Major) Kampfe was alive. He also claimed he knew where Kampfe was being held.

The 29-year-old was a rising star in a falling empire. He was described as tall, handsome, athletic, the embodiment of the fictitious Nazi Aryan race. He was also a cold-blooded killer, a perfect Nazi. A member of Hitler's *Waffen-SS*, he had honed his killing skills fighting on the *Eastern Front*, the battleground of annihilation between the Nazis and the Soviets.

He did not sleep overnight, worried for the fate of his friend who was missing and believed kidnapped. He and his missing friend were occupiers of a foreign country, and not just any occupiers, they were part of a notorious group of killers.

And this morning his quick pace was driven by the encouraging news that he knew where his friend was being held prisoner by the French Resistance. He could feel his hope, believing his friend alive and the possible rescue and deadly revenge was within his grasp. The perfect scenario for the Nazi killer, as the killer could now kill more.

As found on Page 162 of Max Hastings, *Das Reich—The March of the 2nd Panzer Division Through France*, Deikmann told his commanding officer that,

...two French civilians...told him that a high German official (Kampfe) *was being held by the Maquisards* (French Resistance) *in Oradour...That day* (10 June 1944) *he was to be executed and publicly burnt...In his opinion, it must be Strumbannfuhrer Kampfe...*

Deikmann was immediately given permission to go to Oradour and rescue Strumbannfuhrer Kampfe. He was further instructed to capture the leaders of the local French Resistance who had committed the crime. By 1:30 that afternoon, Deikmann and his convoy of 120 soldiers using: motorcycles, trucks, half-tracks, and staff cars departed St. Junien and headed to Oradour-sur-Glane.

Before arriving in Oradour, according to Hastings in *Das Reich* page 163 Deikmann pulled over his troops, gathered them together and stated the following:

...(this is) *a search and destroy operation...*

On the very same day that Deikmann raced towards Oradour, an order was issued to all soldiers in the 2nd SS Panzer Division. SS General Heinz Lammerding, commander of the division issued the following orders,

"In the course of its advance, the division has already dealt with several Resistance groups...(and) has succeeded, in carrying out a knife stroke— "coup de filet"...The division is now proceeding to a rapid and lasting clean-up..."

Hastings, Das Reich
Page 159.

General Lammerding's idea of a, *rapid and lasting clean-up* was death and destruction. Oradour's fate was sealed. With the blessing of his superior officers, 29-year-old Waffen SS *Strumbannfuhrer* Adolf Otto Deikmann, commander of the 1st Battalion, 4th SS Panzer Grenadier Regiment, 2nd SS Panzer Division had made his plan. He was motivated, determined, and an experienced killer who was about to write history with the blood of over six hundred men women and children.

The fast moving, rumbling, out of place convoy entered Oradour as a loud, large, frightening armed beast descending on its unsuspecting, unarmed prey. Exiting the vehicles, the disciplined soldiers were shouting harsh, fragmentary instructions in staccato German. A place that had never seen battle was embattled as all exits were blocked, peaceful Oradour was besieged.

All residents were instructed to gather on the *Champ de Foire* (town common) with their identification papers. The residents were quickly pushed and shoved into place, and families were pulled apart by force as men and women were separated.

Above the visceral fear, and cries of the women and children came instructions delivered from German soldiers that were natural French speakers. They looked like beastly German SS soldiers but sounded like Frenchmen. It was as if space aliens had landed.

The local baker asked if he could go back to attend to his ovens which were full of bread and pastry. The response in French was,

As the tension filled residents were gathered and separated, a car pulled onto the *Champs de Foire*. It was Dr. Jacques Desourteaux returning to Oradour after finishing his house calls. The Germans halted his car and demanded he exit and leave his car there—and there it still sits seventy-five years later.

Next, the monsters led the terrified women and children to the church at the end of town near the tranquil river Glane. There they were told to enter the church.

A loud German addressed the men, shouting in abrasive German,

The shouting German stopped occasionally so his words could be translated by the German soldiers who spoke like Frenchmen. The men of Oradour offered no information, for they had no information to give. Oradour was not a base of resistance supply or organization.

The German continued shouting, and the Germans who spoke French issued instructions to all the men and boys. They were divided into six groups and led away to garages, barns, and a warehouse. They offered no resistance, and like the women and children were unaware of what was waiting for them in their own barns, garages, and warehouse.

As Deikmann's convoy arrived in Oradour, and rounded up the innocents, a few hundred miles away, the Allied forces were fighting hard in Normandy. On 10 June 1944, the US 101st Airborne, including the famous *Band of Brothers* were fighting and holding the very important French city of Carentan.

Men of the 82nd Airborne were fighting and dying with odds longer than the *Alamo*, at a little-known village named *Graignes*. Bravely, and greatly outnumbered, they were holding up SS troops headed to Carentan, and from there to the landing beaches, they hoped. They made it to neither place.

Other 82nd paratroopers, and 325th Glider Infantry were desperately fighting for a priceless stone bridge and causeway two miles outside Sainte-Mere Église. So violent was the battle that 569 US soldiers were killed, wounded, missing. Military historian S.L.A. Marshal called the struggle for the bridge and causeway at La Fiere "...*probably the bloodiest small unit struggle in the history of American arms*..." (Author's Note: All three of these US Paratrooper stories are contained in the next volume of *Chasing Rommel*.)

By Saturday 10 June 1944, it is estimated the Allied Forces had suffered over 15,000 casualties battling Hitler's once mighty army in Normandy. Field Marshal Rommel was in command of the German forces. By 10 June, he had suffered extraordinary losses in men, equipment, and supplies. Rommel needed units like the 2nd SS Panzer to stop the Allied gains.

The events that the Germans committed in Oradour-sur-Glane and the sacrifices American soldiers in Normandy are a perfect contrast. Illustrating for eternity the incompatible, inconceivable, irreconcilable difference between Hitler's Nazis and America's valiant army of liberation.

On 10 June 1944, the 2nd SS Panzer Division was killing unarmed men, and helpless women and children. Although they were ordered to proceed to Normandy, the 2nd SS division was taking the time to massacre the innocent.

Already suffering from the lack of railroad transportation, the entire division had to move over dangerous roads where French Resistance fighters were waiting in roadside ambushes blowing up bridges, and causing any disruption they possibly could.

The Resistance fighters hit the Germans fast and often, causing 2nd Panzer great delays and significant damage to the tanks and trucks. On 10 June 1944, the day men from the 2nd SS Panzer Division were massacring Oradour their commanding officer, a very frustrated General Heinz Lammerding had to answer to his superiors as to why he was not in Normandy. The following is his message defining the state of 2nd SS Panzer,

"...lack of adequate transport...(covering) *substantial distances over unfavorable terrain...lack of preparation for operational and supply measures...has weakened the strength of the division... Unserviceability amongst tanks is 60%...*(trucks) *and half-tracks 30%...Adequate fuel supplies...are nowhere in sight. The paralysis of the German posts is quite disgraceful... "*

Hitler's shrinking Third Reich was in great danger in the summer of 1944, it was exhausted of quality fighting men and low on materials like rubber, oil, gasoline, medical supplies, food, and ammunition of all types. Yet, Adolf Deikmann and his 120 men took the time they did not have, expended resources they could not expend, and began the extermination of the small idyllic village beside the river Glane. They used their time and weapons to kill the innocent, and hide from the advancing armies. These men were never soldiers—Never.

The bells of Oradour's church rang out 3:30, and in a mere two hours the vengeful, motivated Deikmann and his charges had traveled to Oradour, and subdued the doomed inhabitants. And as the old bell tower tolled out the time with its aged bells, the shooting of the men began, accompanied by the terrified shrieks of the women and children below that very bell tower.

They had been locked in the church by the river, listening in unimaginable horror as the German machine guns fired on their unarmed fathers, husbands, brothers, sons, and friends. The doors of Hell had been flung wide open. They knew their world was ending, and they would be next.

They were locked in the church and forced into the area of the alter of God. As they prayed, cried, and lost hope, the Germans set the church on fire with hundreds of innocent people inside. The flames got so hot that the bells that had tolled the fate of the men, the same bells that had tolled for hundreds of years measuring the hours of the days of the village, fell into the doomed sanctuary and died with the women and children.

The SS had murdered Oradour-sur-Glane. On a near perfect summer's day *"...the day the soldiers came..."*

Hollowed-out building remains—Oradour.

Part IV: The Victims

"For the dead and the living, we must bear witness."

Elie Wiesel (1928–2016)
Nobel Laureate, Holocaust survivor, Author.

It had rained overnight in Oradour-sur-Glane. And as the morning of Saturday 10 June 1944 broke the clouds floated away, sanctioning just the warm sun and the blue skies to create a near perfect summer's day. The very last hours, of a community that had lived a thousand years, was suddenly fixed in Hell's long dark shadow.

In 1944, French children had no school on Thursdays, rather they attended classes on Saturday. As the day began, one of the local schoolteachers, Denise Bardet, who turned 24 on 10 June, was with her students. Denise was recently engaged, and could dream of teaching her own children in the beautiful town beside the River Glane.

Professor Forest was in Oradour that morning. He was a philosophy professor who lost his job when the Nazis closed the university where he taught. He had moved to Oradour to escape the bombings and dangers of the war—a war that seemed a world away from Oradour-sur-Glane before June of 1944.

On 10 June, he was going by tram to Limoges with his three youngest sons. His two oldest sons stayed in Oradour that Saturday. His eldest son Michel was a student, poet, diarist, and dreamed of becoming a lawyer. Michel's younger brother was Dominque, by all accounts, a young happy boy. He remained with Michel in Oradour so he could get a haircut. Dominque was looking forward to the next day, Sunday, 11 June, the day he would celebrate his First Holy Communion.

Oradour was crowded by June of 1944. Many refugees arrived from Paris, and many more from the region of France that borders Germany—Alsace-Lorraine. Also, among the refugees were Jewish and Spanish families that sought peaceful sanctuary in the quiet village of Oradour.

Dozens of Spaniards had found refuge and hope in Oradour as they tried to rebuild their lives far from Franco's tyranny in Spain. They worked the fields, and did what odd jobs were obtainable in the village.

So many refugees from the Alsace-Lorraine region arrived in Oradour that a special school was set up specifically for Alsace-Lorraine children. Known as Alsatians, some spoke German, some spoke French, and many spoke both languages.

Some had noticeable accents and spoke French with a German accent, or spoke German with a French accent, and others spoke French perfectly well. Alsace was on the German French frontier and had been hotly contested in the Franco-Prussian War (1870), World War I (1914–1918), and World War II (1940).

Jacqueline Pinède was a Jewish refugee, and part of a three-generation family that resettled in Oradour. Surprisingly, Jacqueline and her family had found safety in a country that worked with the Nazis to round up Jews. From

1940–1944 the Nazis, with the aid of the French Vichy government, deported over 75,000 French Jewish citizens, mostly in the vicinity of Paris. It is imperceivable and breathtaking that 97% of French Jews would never return, murdered in Auschwitz.

Jacqueline's father Robert, mother Carmen and elderly grandmother were taken by the rampaging Nazis in Oradour. But long before they were taken, Robert Pinède drilled into his son's head that if he saw the Nazis,

"Take your brother and sister and hide…"
Hawes, Page 57.

Robert Hébras was a 19-year-old mechanic and lifelong resident of Oradour. His father Jean worked as an electrician on the lines that powered the tram between Oradour and Limoges. Robert was not needed at Schmitt's Garage on this Saturday, so he was helping a neighbor fix an electrical problem.

When he finished, he found his friend, Martial Machefer and they walked down the main street talking about the upcoming soccer game. As Robert reached his house, the German convoy appeared in all its terrifying suddenness. It was 1:45, Robert Hébras, his friend Martial, and Robert's family were rounded up by the Germans.

It was about 2:00 on Saturday and seven-year-old Roger Godfrin was at school with his two older sisters. They were among the nearly 50 children that attended the new school for Alsatian refugee children. They had found a new home in Oradour, but their life in Alsace made them very familiar with the brutality of the Germans. Roger's father was Arthur, he was a baker and a supporter of the fallen French Republic.

He disliked the Nazis and the Vichy Government currently ruling southern France. Young Roger and his fellow pupils did not hear the convoy. But they did hear shots being fired as the round up was beginning. Roger told his sisters to come with him, they were too frightened and did not move. Roger did what he had been told by his parents,

"If you see the Boshes (Germans) *hide in the woods…"*
Hawes, Page 59.

Marguerite Rouffanche was the married mother of three grown children: Jean, Amélie, and Andrée. She and her husband Simon lived on their farm, at the southern edge of Oradour just over the bridge that crosses the River Glane. Marguerite was forty-six years old and a grandmother, when the Germans found her and her family, they were taken to the *Champs de Foire* with the rest of the residents.

On the afternoon of 10 June 1944, School teacher Denise Bardet was murdered on her 24th birthday. Eighteen other residents with the surname Bardet died that day as well. Denise died with many of her young school students in the horror of the burning *Église D' Oradour-Our Glane*—The catholic church at the River Glane.

Early on the evening of 10 June Professor Forest and his three youngest sons returned by tram from Limoges to Oradour. By then, Oradour was burning, and his older sons Michel Forest, the young student and poet, and Dominque were dead. The Germans told the Professor and his children to get back on the tram and leave Oradour. They did.

The young Jewish immigrant Jacqueline Pinède escaped before the round up. Her father, mother and grandmother did not. Seven-year-old immigrant Roger Godfrin ran towards the woods. He was shot and fell to the ground playing dead.

When he could, he got up and ran towards the River Glane, he swam the river and hid in the woods. Roger survived his day in Hell, but his father, mother, three sisters and brother were all murdered by the Nazis in Oradour.

Robert Hébras was led down the road that leads to the Cemetery. He was with the largest group of men, they walked to *Laudy Barn*. In front of the barn were placed German machine gunners. Once the men were inside, the guns opened fire on the unarmed innocent men. The first rounds were brutally directed at the men's legs so they could not escape.

When the shooting ended, the Germans finished off some of the wounded with pistols and took pitch forks to others. Then they stacked anything that would burn on the dead and dying and set Laudy's barn on fire. Robert was underneath the dead and dying men, he could feel the blood of men he knew dripping on him.

He was shot in the arm, and still managed to get himself free. In the blinding smoke and having difficulty breathing, Robert searched frantically for an exit. He eventually climbed through a hole in the wall and hid in a rabbit cage, before running into the woods and escaping the massacre. While Robert was running to save his life, his mother and sisters were being marched towards the church.

The Nazis brutally forced all the woman and children into the church. They stacked anything that would burn into the church, including a large wooden crate full of combustible material that made enormous amounts of smoke. They sprayed the women with machine guns, tossed hand grenades into the church and shut and locked the doors, and started the fire.

Marguerite Rouffanche remarkably managed to climb out a broken window behind the alter. Exiting the window, she fell nine feet, and was shot and wounded. Still, she managed to escape her cold-blooded executioners to a garden where she hid for the next 24 hours.

The SS monsters had sealed the fate of 250 women and 200 children. It was the flames and smoke that suffocated the cries and screams of over 450 dying human voices, murdered in the church by the peaceful River.

When it was over, 642 men, women and children were gone.

Ruins of the Catholic Church at Oradour.

Part V: Conclusion
Injustice

"Those who can make you believe absurdities,
can make you commit atrocities."

Voltaire (1864–1778)
Ou Extrait de Diverses Lettres de M. de Voltaire
(Extract from Various Letters of M. de Voltaire)

The following words on the aftermath of the massacre at Oradour have haunted me since I closed the book that contained them. British author, and historian Max Hastings relays a conversation between two old SS officers long after the war. After living in plain sight and not facing retribution for their heinous acts, one Nazi monster says to another Nazi monster, concerning the massacre of 642 men women and children in Oradour,

"Herr Muller, (Oradour) *was nothing"*
Hastings, Das Reich
Page 224

At 2:10 PM on 12 January 1953, a military tribunal opened in Bordeaux nearly ten years after the massacre of Oradour-Our-Glane. After nearly a decade of justice delayed, the families and the victims of Oradour would only find justice denied.

The President of the military tribunal was Marcel Nussy-Saint-Saëns. His father was an orchestra conductor, and his uncle was the celebrated French composer and musician, Camille Saint-Saëns. Camille had written *Danse Macabre* (Dance of Death) where a violinist representing Death, summons the dead to rise and dance as he plays.

The tribunal opened with the following statement from President Marcel Nussy-Saint-Saëns,

*"The real issue on trial here is Hitlerism…*He continued and closed saying, *I am certain, and I do not say this without emotion, that the victims of Oradour are present here, present and we hear them."*
Hawes, Page 104.

The *Danse Macabre* had begun.

Twenty-one SS soldiers went on trial in Bordeaux, amazingly fourteen were French Alsatians. These fourteen men were all involved in the horror that was Oradour. All of these men were participants, none exempt from the savagery perpetrated that day at Oradour.

They slaughtered innocent women and children, many burning alive in a man-made hell that been a church. They killed unarmed men, shooting first at their legs, so escape was impossible. They killed their countrymen. They were the monsters who looked like Germans and spoke like Frenchmen.

The outcries for the defense for the French Alsatians on trial began immediately. And it was the French residents of Alsace-Lorraine that offered an unbelievable premise, a statement that even decades later, is shocking in its contempt towards the victims of Oradour-sur-Glane.

"They (the Alsatian SS soldiers) *were all victims of the Nazis."*
Beck, Page 137.

The foundation of this grotesque logic was that the fourteen Alsatians were forcibly conscripted into the German army and beyond that were also "forced" into the *Waffen-SS*. If these Alsatian Frenchmen resisted entry into the German Army, they and their families would be exported to concentration camps like Dachau and Auschwitz. That is a difficult decision to have to face.

But the men on trial for the murders at Oradour declared they did not choose to become members of the notorious Nazi SS. They were forced into that elite Nazi political and military organization, the most vicious killers in the Nazi arsenal—the SS. If they were so destitute and bereft of hope that they accepted the German offer, once armed, why would they not attack their enslavers?

Why would they not attack those that had threatened their families with certain death? Why did they turn their automatic weapons on people as innocent as they proclaimed they were? Their conundrum is no mystery at all. They lacked courage; they were soulless men who aided other soulless men in a massacre civilized people cannot comprehend.

If you accept their argument, then they became German SS soldiers, but they really became much more than that. These men became heartless cold-blooded killers. They were never soldiers, they were monsters, the executioners of the men, women, and children of Oradour. On 10 June 1944, they were not victims.

They exchanged their humanity in a deal with an inhuman devil, its contract written in the blood, bone and ashes of the 642 victims. The Germans and Alsatians tried in Bordeaux included dozens of soldiers and officers tried in absentia.

Cooperation between the French, British, American, and Soviet occupiers of Germany was not always concerned with justice, and extradition by 1953 was rare, and reserved for monsters more significant than the SS Monsters of Oradour. That is a remarkably feeble statement, and as I write it, I still cannot process how these monsters were lesser than other monsters. The judgements of those who rendered such a betrayal are criminal.

The trial included testimony of some of the victims of Oradour, eyewitnesses who managed to escape the fury and flames of the SS. Yet, their escapes offered no relief and insured that theirs would be the mantle of a lifelong death sentence.

They suffered intolerable days of grief, months of unendurable anguish, years of unendurable guilt. Their memories included a lifetime of seeing the unseeable, of listening to the unlistenable, of bearing the unbearable. They had to *REMEMBER*.

They lost everyone they knew and loved, everything they had including their families, homes, and village. The ruins of Oradour were never rebuilt, it has been a memorial since the fires went out. French President Charles de Gaulle ordered it never to be rebuilt. The Village of Oradour was itself a victim. A martyred place.

The testimony of the survivors was not enough for the French Court, justice was sequestered and the *Dance Macabre* was ready for its final act.

The trail ended and the verdicts were read on Friday, 13 February 1953. In a word, the sentences were incomplete. The Germans and Alsatians were given prison sentences of 7–12 years. One sergeant was given a death sentence that would remain unfulfilled. Those tried in absentia were also given unfulfilled death sentences.

Death sentences that ended with the peaceful deaths of those never accountable for their crimes. 2nd SS Panzer Division General Heinz Lammerding died peacefully in Dusseldorf, Germany.

In 1971, he was 65 years old, he had lived a very comfortable life after the war. All of the accused were released in a few years. The political climate in Europe had shifted, and it was time to forget, time to forge new relationships, time to find a lasting peace.

SS Major Adolf Deikmann never stood trial. Battlefield justice found him in Normandy where a piece of shrapnel from an Allied artillery shell hit his head, killing him instantly.

Remarkably, the French Parliament voted an amnesty to all the conscripted Frenchmen into the German Army during the Second World War. The Germans who spoke like Frenchman were effectively liberated from the brutal, inexcusable murders they perpetrated onto their own countryman.

The victims, survivors, and France as a nation would never know justice. An act of remarkable brutality was usurped by an act of extraordinary injustice, delivered by French Politicians.

Even those who served sentences were freed by 1958. In protest, the residents of the new village of Oradour did not cooperate with the French Government. They would routinely block any attempt of the French Government to participate in memorial services. It was not criminal enough they were massacred by the Nazis, but their own government had betrayed them.

They kept the injustice alive for decades, French government officials were routinely pushed away from the martyred village and its smoldering memory. It was not until French President François Mitterrand visited in the 1980s that the French government was welcomed into Oradour-sur-Glane. Reconciliation had been found, but not justice.

It would take forty years for the last act to be played out in this breathtaking human drama of death and betrayal. The first act began on 10 June 1944 at the peaceful village beside the river Glane, "...*the day the soldiers came...*" The second act was macabrely danced in a courtroom full of injustice for those who could no longer speak for themselves.

The Dance Macabre had not ended, it plays out for all who dare visit this place. The legacy of Oradour-sur-Glane follows humanity to his very day. Nietzsche wrote in his 1886 book, Beyond Good And Evil: "*And if you gaze for long into an abyss, the abyss gazes also into you.*"

Visiting Oradour and thinking of the victims, I believe the emptiness is very much alive in this place, and it stares back at you. You need not take my word for it, go to Oradour, the dead village by the peaceful river Glane, you will never again be the same.

Date marker at Cemetery—Oradour

Part VI: Epilogue
Remember

"Je prends la résolution de ne jamais faire de mal aux antres."

(I resolve never to do ill to others)
School room blackboard, Oradour-sur-Glane, 10 June 1944
Beck *Oradour,* Page 38

What makes Oradour-sur-Glane unique is only its location on a map—its geography. The massacre there, was not the first, not the worst, not the last, and its place in an amnesic history is a timeless reminder of the unbridled hatred, and damming violence that follows mankind. Man has committed, and continues to commit acts of unspeakable violence, and always offering inexcusable excuses.

Chasing Rommel in Normandy is full of special moments. Each visit, I watch the sun rise over Omaha Beach at H-Hour—06:30. I walk accompanied by my visions of young American men dying on the sands of what is now a peaceful place.

Each visit, I sit in Ste-Mere-Église square at midnight and remember the remarkable young American Paratroopers who fell from the skies over occupied France, to liberate a foreign people, in a foreign land, from a foreign oppressor.

And this visit was like all the others, except my Omaha sunrise, and Ste-Mere-Église vigil came after my time in Oradour-sur-Glane. In both places I lamented that some died for freedom, others were massacred—each in their own ways martyred by monsters.

As I walked away from the village of Oradour-sur-Glane I was filled with heart rendering sorrow, albeit in vain to reconcile such a place. I walked slowly, the sun still strong, my steps labored. I felt I was carrying a tremendous weight. Before I started the car, I looked at my traveling companion and told her I have no words for Oradour—neither did she.

Sitting motionless, I stare straight ahead at the colorful early autumn trees. My mind races, and it is the victims that I see, but cannot hear, their cries forever lost, they reduced to images of lives unfinished, whose legacies must include more than broken buildings, heaped rubble, twisted steel, doorless, windowless openings framed by blackened stones, and the never-ending silence that lives in the old village by the gentle river Glane.

I follow the signs for the exit, *sortie* in French. Suddenly, the words find me,

"You can leave Oradour-sur-Glane,
but Oradour-sur-Glane will never leave you."

Amelia McNutt

Bibliography

Beck, Phillip. *Oradour: The Massacre and Aftermath*. Print. Pen & Sword: South Yorkshire, UK. 2011. Print.

Chrisafis, Angelique. *Nazi Massacre Village Oradour-sur-Glane: where Ghosts Must Live on*. 2013 The Guardian. London. Retrieved 2019.

Farmer, Sarah. *Martyred Village: Commemorating the Massacre at Oradour-sur-Glane*. University of California Press: Los Angeles. 1999. Print.

Harris, Shane. *The Massacre at Oradour-sur-Glane*. https://foreignpolicy.com/2014/06/05/the-massacre-at-oradour-sur-glane. 2014. retrieved July 2019

Hawes, Douglas W. *Oradour: The Final Verdict*. Author House, LLC.: Bloomington, IN. 2014. Print.

Hastings, Max. *Das Reich the March of the 2nd Panzer Division Through France*. Holt, Reinhard, & Winston: New York. 1982. Print.

Mackness, Robin. *Massacre at Oradour*. Random House: New York. 1988. Print.

Malm, Sarah. Sparks, Ian. Finan, Tim. *Prosecutors charge 88-year-old man over 1944 Nazi massacre at Oradour-Sur-Glane*. 2014. Daily Mail. London. retrieved 2019.

Peregrine Anthony. *Oradour-sur-Glane, France: Moments of Nazi massacre frozen in time*. 2013. The Telegraph. London. Retrieved July 2019.

Reid, Donald M. *Teaching in Tragedy by Teaching the History of Its Remembrance: Oradour-sur-Glane and American Students in September 2001.* The History Teacher Vol. 35, No. 4 (Aug. 2002), pp. 441–454.

"A New Germany (1933–1939)" Episode 1. *The World at War* (1973–74) 26-episode British TV Documentary. Produced by Jeremy Isaacs. Narrated by Sir Laurence Olivier.

Place and date written in the sands by author.

Chapter 7
Bloody Omaha

Introduction

"Half a league, half a league,
Half a league onward,
All in the valley of Death
Rode the six hundred."

Alfred, Lord Tennyson (1809–1892)
Charge of the Light Brigade (1854)

The D-Day planners gave it the code name, *Omaha Beach*. The American soldiers who fought, suffered, and watched their comrades die on those sands called it, *Bloody Omaha*.

General Omar Bradley, the overall commander of the troops on Omaha Beach, wrote in his memoirs: *"Every man who set foot on Omaha Beach was a hero."* He also wrote: *"Omaha Beach was a nightmare."*[121] General Bradley was correct on each count because the men who fought on Omaha Beach were the *heroes* of Bradley's avoidable *nightmare*.

The long dark shadows of those remarkably bloody hours, hidden in the feigning specter of what was not the truth, has only recently been established. Decades removed; the degree of truth we find in the Omaha Beach story vacillates from unacceptable to shocking.

Every year, I travel to Omaha Beach and walk the sands at the edge of the surf watching the sun rise. As the years pass, the feelings and questions never abate as I continue to struggle with what happened here. On this morning, the rolling waves quietly break just a few yards from where I am standing.

My walk is always un-rushed, slow moving. I lament what happened here, and while looking down on the sand, my grief always finds itself framed in questions.

Questions linger and follow me like the relentless driving wind coming off the cold English Channel trying to push me off the beach. I feel like the wind is blowing me away from the truth this hallowed place holds for many of us. And then I realize, the driving winds push me to where the sea ends and the land begins, where the truth still lies buried.

My gaze captures the raise in the land that is where you will find the immense American cemetery on the bluff above. There, thousands of Americans find eternal rest in a massive graveyard, covering 172 acres. I reflect on why was the struggle for Omaha Beach was so deadly, and why this story is still mostly unknown?

General S.L.A. Marshall, the official US Army historian for the European Theater of Operations wrote a decade and a half after the war: *"The story of*

---

[121] Mayo, Jonathan. D-Day: Minute by Minute Marble Arch Press: New York. Print. 2014. Page 267.

Omaha (Beach) *is an epic human tragedy which in the early hours bordered on total disaster.*"[122]

I am *Chasing Rommel* to a most hallowed place. I am alone, it is low tide and very quiet at the shoreline still called Omaha. The waves are mesmerizing. In my mind's eye, I labor to see them, to hear them, to know them—the men who died here. The sun is rising, it is H-Hour, D-Day plus 74 years. I am at once filled with a sense of immense pride repressed by profound heartbreaking sorrow.

---

[122] Marshal, S.L.A. General US Army. First wave at Omaha Beach. The Atlantic. November 1960. Digital Version.
https://www.theatlantic.com/magazine/archive/1960/11/first-wave-at-omaha-beach/303365/ Retrieved January 2021.

Exhibit at Normandy American Cemetery—
photographed with added text by author.

Part I: A Human Tragedy

"Forward, the Light Brigade!
Charge for the guns! He said.
Into the valley of Death Rode the six hundred."
Charge of the Light Brigade (1854)

Lieutenant General Omar Bradley, US Ground Forces Commander, was in charge of the US Army landings at Omaha Beach, Utah Beach, and Pointe-du-Hoc. It is only 08:30 hours, just two hours after H-Hour when suddenly, Bradley issues an immediate halt to all landing craft headed to Omaha Beach.

He suspends the landing of American troops, and begins to ponder how he can evacuate Omaha Beach.

The landing crafts at sea began to circle, and some of the Germans noticed the landing crafts were no longer headed towards the beach, leading some Germans to believe they had won the battle for the deadly sands at Omaha. Observing the carnage on the beach, in men and in material, the Germans draw an accurate, yet premature assessment of the struggle for Bloody Omaha.

It was not over.

General Bradley was aboard the US Navy cruiser, USS Augusta, he was safely 12 miles off the Normandy coast and well behind the Omaha Beach battlefield. Bradley could not see the shoreline from his command ship, and relied on early and sporadic reports from the beach landing forces. They were not good. They were frightful, even to an old soldier like Omar Bradley.

The US Navy destroyers were much closer to the beach than Bradley's position out in the English Channel. Some destroyers, which are much smaller than cruisers and battleships got as close as a few thousand yards from the beach.

All the early reports arriving at Bradley's command ship carried the same ominous message, that the landings were a disaster. The sporadic reports claimed the men were pinned down at the water's edge, stuck on a beach full of obstacles that should have been blown to bits.

The men were facing countless machine gun positions that created layers of overlapping deadly fire tearing apart the troops floundering at the water's edge. The reports from the navy also claimed mortar and artillery rounds were raining down with unencumbered accuracy, finding men, tanks, and landing crafts alike.

This was not what Bradley had anticipated as he and others planned the invasion at Normandy. It was Bradley's nightmare, and for those unlucky soldiers on Omaha Beach, it was Hell.

On the planning tables Omaha Beach was four miles wide, with hard packed sands that were perfect for men, trucks, and tanks to cross. Omaha Beach has a gentle incline rising from the water's edge to the natural seawall of rocks that the locals call the *Shingle*.

The seawall in some places is at the base of the natural sheer elevations where the land ascends over 100 feet high. At low tide, all the landing zones offered at least 400 yards or more of nearly flat open beaches, without natural impediments like rock formations.

The beaches were wide open expanses, and the Americans landed at low tide, and were exposed to a maelstrom of German weapons that promised to sow death and destruction.

It was a perfect place to land troops, so it follows, it was a perfect place to kill those landing troops. The well dug-in German defenders, and their commander, Field Marshal Rommel had anticipated the Allied invaders would need beaches with hard packed sand, and roadways, or exits that led inland.

Omaha Beach was seen as one of many beaches that fit that description, and Rommel was determined to trap the invaders at the water's edge where he believed they were most vulnerable.

Of all the military and political leaders in Germany, Field Marshal Erwin Rommel had the best grasp of what was facing Germany in the spring of 1944. Simply stated, the Germans had never repelled an Allied amphibious invasion. Rommel had been defeated in North Africa when the Americans had conducted amphibious landings.

Those landings put Rommel and his legendary *Afrika Korps*, in an inescapable position as the British were chasing Rommel across the North African desert and into the arms of the invading Americans.

Rommel understood by studying the successful Allied invasions of North Africa, Sicily, and Italy what he was up against. He knew the Allies would follow the same successful patterns they had established with all their amphibious assaults. Rommel found striking similarities in the previous Allied invasions.

Firstly, he noticed that the weather needed to be clear for air cover and paratroop drops. He also understood that the Allies needed a near full, or full moon to offer some light to the air components bombing and paratroop dropping at night.

Rommel noticed that the Allies only invaded areas where their smaller attack aircraft could reach easily on their limited fuel supplies. Lastly, Rommel also noticed that the Allies came at night and on a rising or high tide.

But at Normandy, those would be incorrect observations as Eisenhower was coming not only at low tide, but in daylight at a very low tide. Rommel drew only one conceivable conclusion as he prepared for the invasion—to meet the Allied armies at the water's edge.

Rommel wanted mines to greet the invaders. He ordered his engineers to make "...*anti-personal mines, antitank mines, anti-paratroop mines...mines to sink ships and mines to sink landing craft...mines that detonate when a wire is tripped...explode when a wire is cut...mines...remotely detonated.*"

Rommel ordered some beaches lined with belts of obstacles including, "*concrete tetrahedrons...jagged steel hedgehogs...rails welded at right angles, wooden stakes...with artillery shells attached...*"[123]

Rommel backed up the beaches with riflemen, machine gunners, mortar pits, and artillery positions all within easy reach of a fully mapped shoreline with coded names to ensure artillery accuracy. Lastly, Rommel wanted his Panzers units, or tank forces just slightly inland but within striking distance of the invasion beaches.

That was the reason Rommel was not in Normandy when the Allies invaded, he was trying to meet with Hitler and get control over more Panzer units and to move them forward behind the beaches.

Rommel summed it all up to his staff: "*When the invasion begins...our own supply lines won't be able to bring forward any aircraft, gasoline, rockets, tanks, guns, or shells because of the enemy air attacks. That alone* (Allied air power) *will rule out any sweeping land battles. Our only possible defense will be at the beaches—that's where the enemy is always weakest.*"[124]

He wanted to slow or stop the invaders making them stationary targets, trapped in his kill zones, they would be wounded, dying, or dead in the same water that led them to France.

For Bradley and his D-Day planners, to counter Field Marshal Rommel's plans, it was decided that a massive aerial bombardment would destroy the German gun positions, resistance nests, beach obstacles, and trenches on the bluffs. Also, the aerial bombardment was designed to create craters on the beach offering cover for the assaulting forces.

Bradley believed that the 8th US Army Air Force would all but eradicate the Germans defending the beaches in front of the small French towns of *Colleville-sur-mer* on the eastern end, *Saint-Laurent-sur-Mer* in the center, and *Vierville-sur-Mer* on the western end.

---

[123] Butler, Daniel Allen. Field Marshal: The Life and Death of Erwin Rommel. Havertown, PA: Casemate. Print 2015. Pp. 459-460.

[124] Butler. Field Marshal: The Life and Death of Erwin Rommel. Pp. 460-461.

Bradley thought it would be a slam-dunk, telling some of soldiers, months earlier: *"You men should consider yourself lucky. You're going to have ringside seats for the greatest show on Earth."*[125] General Bradley was wrong. He was breathtakingly wrong. How could Bradley have been so wrong?

On D-Day, just before first light many of the sailors and soldiers heard the bombers fly overhead towards the coast, but not many saw those bombers. The bombers were strategic, high altitude, four engine B-17, and B-24 bombers. At 05:50 hours, 40 minutes before H-Hour the roar of 448 heavy bombers could be heard above the warships sitting off the coast of Omaha Beach.

For the sailors and soldiers below, it was a welcome sound of uncontested American might. For General Omar Bradley, it was the sound of his US Army Air Force arriving to do the job he would not entrust to the US Navy.

Bradley held the opinion that the US Army was superior to the US Navy. In 1944, the Air Force was part of the US Army, Bradley's Army—US Army Air Force. Whether an old inter-service rivalry, or a real acetic opinion Bradley all but dismissed naval gunfire support, he believed air power would win the day in Normandy.

Remarkably, Bradley ignored a messenger sent to England to help plan the assaults at Omaha and Utah Beaches. US Army Major General Charles Corlett (1889–1971), was transferred to Europe in early 1943, making him one of the few commanders who had experience in the Pacific, where the US Army and US Marines invaded islands on a regular basis.

Once in Europe, General Corlett tried to pass along to Bradley, the success the Army and Marines were finding when they invaded Pacific islands, pummeled by accurate destructive naval gunfire. Bradley was not interested, and according to General Corlett, General Bradley believed: *"The Pacific was strictly bush-league stuff..."*[126]

---

[125] Bowman, Martin W. Air War D-Day: Bloody Beaches. Pen & Sword Books: South Yorkshire, England Print. 2013. Pp. 23-24.

[126] Penrose, Jane. Editor. The D-Day Companion: leading historians explore history's greatest assault. Osprey Publishing: Oxford, UK. Print. Page 155.

Omaha Beach from American Cemetery.

Part II: "The Longest Day"

"Forward, the Light Brigade! Was there a man dismayed?
Not though the soldier knew. Someone had blundered,
Theirs not to make reply, Theirs not to reason why,
Theirs but to do and die: Into the valley of Death
Rode the six hundred."

Alfred, Lord Tennyson, Poet Laureate (1809–1892)

Just before the sun was able to rise on a cloudy, cold French day the droning sound of the bombers could be heard. The naval transports and warships had been in place for just a few short hours. Soldiers were already in landing crafts, and others, still on the decks were praying for deliverance as their turn to climb down the ropes and into history approached.

Every man must have wondered if he was experiencing his last sunrise. As D-Day began, the words of the German commander spoken just a few weeks earlier on a French beach seemed the most appropriate of all prognostications:

"...the first 24 hours of the invasion will be decisive...the fate of Germany depends on the outcome...for the Allies, as well as Germany, it will be the longest day."[127]

German Field Marshal Erwin Rommel had been at war since 1939, he was the famed, Desert Fox, a name he was given by his British enemy in North Africa. Rommel knew instinctively, that when the sun set on the day of the invasion the fate of Hitler's Empire would be solidly cast.

D-Day on Omaha Beach began just as General Omar Bradley had planned it, with hundreds of high-flying American bombers headed to Omaha Beach to obliterate Rommel's dug-in defenders.

The commander of 8th US Army Air Force, Lieutenant General James Doolittle, chose to approach Omaha Beach perpendicular to the shoreline. That narrowed the distance and time of the arial bombardment and required Doolittle's flyers to do something they could not do in 1944.

The Army Air Force had been the subject of an article written in 1939 where it was claimed that with their new *Norden Bombsite* they could, *"drop a bomb in a pickle barrel from 18,000 feet."* That quote is on the webpage for the, National Museum of the United States Air Force (https://www.nationalmuseum.af.mil/Visit/Museum-Exhibits/Fact-Sheets/) and it is a museum exhibit labeled as a *Fact Sheet*.

It was a gross exaggeration and was never close to being true. American bombers, flying thousands of feet in the air, moving at over two hundred miles per hour, were not very accurate, Norden Bombsite or not.

General Doolittle's high-flying bombers were not designed for pin point accuracy, they were better suited for carpet, or saturation bombing. They bombed factories, and at times entire cities to destroy a factory. Bombing a narrow slice of beach, just a few hundred yards wide from high altitude, while smoke, clouds, and mist obscured their view created a recipe for disaster on D-Day.

As they approached the coast running into Omaha Beach, the lead bomber pilots looked beneath and could see the landing crafts approaching the Normandy shoreline. They held the release of their bombs, as to not accidentally drop them on the landing craft below.

---

[127] Ryan, Cornelius. The Longest Day: June 6, 1944. Simon & Schuster: New York. 1959. Print. Epigraph at Preface.

This was a predetermined fact when the bombardment was planned. A fact that Eisenhower himself supported. He did not want any accidental loss of American life from friendly fire. The brief delay of the big bombers flying over 200 MPH, translated to a result no planner expected, because a few seconds meant a great deal of distance.

The 8th US Army Air Force sent to obliterate the Germans at Omaha Beach deferred to caution waiting up to an extra 30 seconds to release the over 13,000 tons of bombs that had been destined to destroy the Germans. The results destroyed pastures, orchards, farms, barns, and livestock two miles inland from the shoreline.

But the beach, the obstacles, the German defenders, the trenches, the resistance nests, machine gun installations, and mortar positions that lined the top of the bluffs were intact.

One German soldier on the bluffs overlooking Omaha Beach recalled,

"They were missing us…the bombs hit inland areas behind us…This was a great relief, and we laughed in a nervous apprehensive manner as the planes moved away inland…"[128]

Amazingly, and unknown at this time to General Bradley, the Germans were relativity untouched by the massive aerial assault. Bradley had bet on a first-round knock-out punch that failed.

As the sounds of the high-flying bombers of the 8th US Army Air Force faded another round of destruction was beginning on Omaha Beach. This second act was intended to soften up the remaining resistance after the destructive rain of bombs from the Army Air Force. It was the US Navy's turn to attack the Germans at Omaha.

The Navy attacked with heavily armed ships. One of the first to fire was the Battleships *USS Arkansas* BB-33 (1912–1946), a remarkable World War I era *Dreadnought* that was retrofitted in 1942 and boasted 12 x 12," 50' long guns that could fire a projectile weighing nearly 900 pounds, a distance of 13 miles.

Arkansas was anchored thousands of yards off Omaha Beach, and just past 05:50 hours, the USS Arkansas opened fire on the known German gun

---

[128] Kershaw, Robert. Landing On The Edge Of Eternity: Twenty-Four hours at Omaha Beach. Pegasus Books: New York. 2018. Print. Page 104.

positions at Omaha. Arkansas fired for only 30 minutes and there is no record of the number of shells she fired for those first thirty minutes, but historian Mark L. Evans wrote: *"Arkansas fired 163 armor piercing and 656 high explosive 12-inch rounds* (totaling 819 shells), *along with 94 5-inch and 104 3-inch shells on D-Day."*[129]

Evans' account was based on Arkansas firing for over seven hours, so we do not know exactly how many shells Arkansas fired in the opening thirty-minute naval bombardment. But we do know how many one of her sister ships fired in the opening naval bombardment.

USS Texas BB-35 (1914–1948) like the Arkansas was a World War I era *Dreadnought*. But Texas was built with 10 x 14" guns as her main armament. Her 14-inch guns were truly massive, each weighing about 70 tons, firing a 1,400-pound projectile up to 23,000 yards at two and half times the speed of sound.[130]

Just passed 05:50, Texas opened fire on Pointe-du-Hoc, and Omaha Beach simultaneously from about 12,000 yards away. The Texas was the flagship for the Omaha Beach shore bombardment on D-Day *"...over the period of 34 minutes she fired over 250 rounds of 14-inch shells from her large guns..."*[131]

Along with The Texas, and Arkansas, the Omaha Bombardment Group included four light cruisers, two British ships: HMS Glasgow, and HMS Bellona, and two French ships: *FFL Georges Leygues* (1937–1957), *FFL Montcalm* (1937–1957). The French cruisers each carried, nine-six-inch diameter high velocity guns. The British and French warships fired away at known or suspected German gun positions and resistance nests.

The US Navy also supplied nine destroyers to the Omaha Bombardment Group: USS Baldwin DD 624 (1943–1946), USS Carmick DD 493 (1942–

---

[129] Evans, Mark L. Arkansas III (Battleship No. 33)1912–1946. Naval History and Heritage Command. June 2020. https://www.history.navy.mil/research/histories/ship-histories/danfs/a/arkansas-battleship-no-33-iii.html Retrieved January 2021.

[130] NavWeaps: Naval Weapons, Naval Technology and Naval Reunions. http://www.navweaps.com/Weapons/WNUS_14-45_mk1.php Retrieved January 2021.

[131] The Battleship Texas BB35. Invasion of Normandy, France 16 April to 18 June 1944. History. https://web.archive.org/web/20060923092736/http://users3.ev1.net/~cfmoore/history/1944normandy.html Retrieved January 2021.

1954), USS Doyle DD 494 (1943–1955), USS Thompson DD 627 (1943–1954), USS Satterlee DD 626 (1943–1946), USS Emmons DD 457 (1941–1945) USS McCook DD 496 (1943–1949) USS Frankford DD 497 (1943–1946) and USS Harding DD 625 (1943–1945). These smaller ships went in closer than the battleships and cruisers, and they too were limited to a paltry thirty minutes of gunfire. [132]

The British Royal Navy also contributed three smaller ships called, escort destroyers. For D-Day, it was the British Royal Navy who was tasked with suppling most warships for the attack on Normandy because, during World War II, the United States Navy was spread very thin across the Atlantic Ocean on convoy duty that supplied North Africa, Sicily, and Italy in the Mediterranean Sea, and the massive war zone encompassing the Pacific Ocean.

The warships of the Omaha naval gunfire group were given just 30 minutes time to shell the beach and known German gun batteries. Between 05:50 and 06:00 hours, they began a precise bombardment of Omaha Beach.

Some of the planners believed that the US Army Air Force would deliver a devastating knockout punch. Therefore, a naval bombardment of short duration was all that was needed, and the planners felt that prolonged naval gunfire would compromise the element of surprise.

It was well understood by the D-Day planners, and the military personnel involved in the assault at Omaha Beach that heavy, accurate naval gunfire was the surest way to alter, or destroy an enemy defending a coastline. Yet, Bradley and his direct superior, British General Bernard Montgomery, went all in on the massive aerial bombings of the shorelines.

They were not ignorant to the damage naval gunfire could do to a dug-in enemy but chose to limit the naval gun fire to a cursory role. General Bradley should have known better. He had seen the US Navy at work in support of the amphibious landings in North Africa and Sicily.

Bradley had been involved in the successful invasions in North Africa in 1942, code named *Operation Torch*, and in Sicily in 1943, code named *Operation Husky*. Both those amphibious assaults used naval gunfire very

---

[132] Tillman, Barrett. Brassey's D-Day Encyclopedia: The Normandy Invasion A-Z. Internet Archive. Pp. 170-171. Digital version. https://archive.org/details/unset0000unse_v2r2/page/170/mode/2up 2004. Retrieved January 2021.

effectively. But for Bradley, Normandy in 1944 was different than the earlier landings.

Close to the home bases of the US 8th and 9th US Army Air Forces in England the Normandy beaches were just a short flight across the English Channel. He, like others, felt that the Allies' air superiority, which was more like air supremacy in 1944, had to be exploited to the fullest. After all, air power was a game changer.

The 1944 Normandy invasion was the world's largest amphibious invasion, but unlike all the other European seaborne invasions to that point, it was headed directly into an enemy that had been digging in and building points of resistance for four long years. There was no easy avenue for the Allied attack; the Germans knew they were coming and were prepared.

For experienced naval officers this only illustrated their belief that a short duration bombardment was a grave mistake. The Navy argued for a longer duration, heavier and more precise naval gunfire option, explaining that the lost element of surprise was offset by the devastation the naval guns could inflict.

Although he was not chosen to command the naval assault forces in Normandy, the Americans had a keenly experienced, highly decorated US Navy admiral who had led the naval assaults at North Africa, Sicily, and the September 9, 1943, landings at Salerno, Italy—*Operation Avalanche*. Admiral Henry Hewitt (1887–1972) was the Navy's version of General George S. Patton.

Admiral Hewitt was a resourceful, daring naval commander. It was Admiral Hewitt who got General Patton ashore at Casablanca, North Africa. While he was getting Patton and his troops to shore, he also engaged in a powerful, violent naval battle against the French Vichy Navy working with the Germans to protect the port of Casablanca.

It was Admiral Hewitt's naval gunfire that made a tremendous difference in North Africa, as they silenced the French guns. For his actions on sea and land, Admiral Hewitt was awarded the United States Army and United States Navy Distinguished Service medals for his command in November of 1942, at the invasion of North Africa. Of his experience, Admiral Hewitt wrote,

"...fire support destroyers were effectively used against tanks, shore batteries, and personnel. If some Army commanders had failed to appreciate

*the capabilities of Naval gunfire in supporting landing operations, their doubts
were dispelled in this operation."[133]*

In his memoirs, Admiral Hewitt has a photo from 1943 of Secretary of War, Henry Stimson personally awarding him his distinguished service medals, as General George C. Marshall, US Army Chief of Staff, and Admiral Ernest King, Chief of Naval Operations look on. That was the level of respect Admiral Hewitt commanded.[134]

Admiral Hewitt was involved in the July 1943 amphibious landings in Sicily. In an eerie parallel with the Normandy Landings just eleven months away, the army attacked the beaches with their preferred aerial bombardments. Admiral Hewitt was disappointed in the Army having such a one-track approach to these landings.

Even in 1943, they were still dismissive of the effectiveness of naval bombardments. The Army still claimed naval bombardment negates any element of surprise, and that is correct, but the naval bombardment delivers a destructive, demoralizing effect of those surprised defenders.

In Sicily, the Americans landed on beaches weakly defended by Italians, but before long the Germans counterattacked the American invasion forces. Up against a formidable enemy, the Army called in the naval guns. Of the US Naval gunfire called in to support the troops in Sicily Admiral Hewitt wrote,

"...the Seventh Army began to appreciate the true effectiveness of naval gunfire...He further commented...Dazed (German) survivors...had never experienced anything like the rapid fire of (the 6") 15-gun battery...they had no idea what had hit them..."[135]

Admiral Hewitt also earned the Navy Cross—twice. First, he was awarded the Navy Cross for his bravery in World War I, and again for bravery during World War II at the Allied landings in Salerno, Italy.

---

[133] Lewis, Adrian R. Omaha Beach: A Flawed Victory. University of North Carolina Press: Chapel Hill, NC. 2001. Print. Page 73.

[134] Hewitt, Henry Admiral. The Memoirs of Admiral H. Kent Hewitt. Edited by Evelyn M. Cherpak. Naval War College Press: Newport, Rhode Island. 2004.
Digital Version. http://www.ibiblio.org/anrs/docs/C/1004hewitt_memoirs.pdf retrieved January 2021.

[135] Lewis, Omaha Beach: A Flawed Victory. Page 82.

Just nine months before the Normandy landings, on 9 September 1943, at Salerno, the Allied invasion of Italy suddenly went terribly wrong. In a precursor to what would occur on Omaha Beach on D-Day, the Germans had the Americans trapped on the beach and were pouring fire on the soldiers.

Admiral Hewitt took a landing craft and landed on the beach during the battle. He personally located the German strong points, and while still under fire returned to his flagship. Then, he personally directed the US Naval firepower at sea until the German resistance was broken.

Admiral Hewitt was recognized by many for his fearlessness at the Salerno Landings. Hewitt gave credit to his well-trained staff for their fast and successful reactions. One of those subordinates would lead the naval assault at Omaha Beach on D-Day. Admiral John Hall (1891–1978) was every bit the believer in naval gunfire as was his hard charging mentor, Admiral Henry Hewitt.

Admiral Hall was a well experienced, fearless naval warrior. Hall was chosen to lead the naval transport and fire support component at Omaha Beach. In the spring of 1944, just a few months before the planned invasion, Admiral Hall was being told by the US Navy planners what he would have available to him for naval gunfire at Omaha Beach.

During the explanation, Admiral Hall interrupted the Navy D-Day planner and angrily stated: "*It's a crime to send me on the biggest amphibious attack in history with such inadequate* (naval) *gunfire support...*" Hall was then interrupted by the D-Day planner trying to defend the plans. Hall cut him off.

"*I didn't give a dam what they'd agreed on in conference. I wanted to give my troops the proper support.*"

The US Navy planner fired back at Admiral Hall claiming he was out of line. Hall held his ground: "*All I am asking you* (is for some destroyers) *...give me a chance to train them in gunfire support for the American Army at the Omaha Beaches.*"[136] Admiral Hall's outbursts got him a few more destroyers, but he still knew he was going in with a slight force, not the overwhelming force the job required.

---

[136] Astor, Gerald. June 6, 1944: The Voices of D-Day. Random House: New York. Digital Version.
https://www.google.com/books/edition/June_6_1944/krV85AufvzAC?hl Page 125.

Omaha was ill-fated from the start, as the table-top Generals and Admirals decided what would happen, and staff officers inserted economy into the D-Day attack.

On D-Day morning from the German perspective, they were soon aware that the aerial bombardment missed them, but they could see the ships at sea firing and they held out little hope they would escape again. They could see the muzzles of the massive guns as they spewed fire and smoke.

Appearing as fire breathing medieval angry dragons, the ships seemed to expel an unrelenting yellow and red fire followed by clouds of thick dense black smoke. The ships never moved but the black smoke slowly blew away only to expose more lethal fire breathing bombs being hurled at the surprised Germans.

Even from thousands of yards out at sea they knew they were in trouble. One German POW told his captors of his experiences being bombed by the US Navy: "(He) *had a very bad feeling...the warships...were lighting up...with flash of their guns...the intensity of that bombardment was more than anything I had known on the eastern front...When one of these naval shells exploded near us, the shock wave...felt like a punch in the stomach. These blows came again and again...*"[137]

At the other end of Omaha Beach, another German soldier had a similar experience, as the deadly accurate naval bombardment slammed against the unsurprised Germans in their concrete gun batteries.

"The intensity was astonishing...heavier and more accurate than the bomber planes...The power of the explosions...made the concrete...ripple and fracture... (knocked the) *air out of our lungs...made our eyes bleed...It went on and on...salvo after salvo...no pause in between...*"[138]

After the battle, many unsurprised Germans spoke of losing their hearing and bleeding from their eyes, and ears as a result of the concussions from the massive navy shells.

The Naval bombardments were precise and destructive, they were doing the job that so badly needed to be done. Then, like you shut off a water spigot, the big guns from the ships at sea went silent. The thirty minutes of hell raining

---

[137] Kershaw. Landing on the Edge of Eternity. Page 106.
[138] Ibid. Pp. 107-108.

down on the Germans was over. Before long, the Germans returned to their positions ready to defend their beach.

The closing act of the bombardment at Omaha Beach began when nine ships carrying thousands of rockets opened fire on the beaches. Using modified LCT (Landing Craft Tank) ships built by the Royal Navy, and specifically positioned nearer the beach for maximum effect, the rockets were fired when the landing crafts carrying the troops, were about 500 yards from the beach.

The Navy fired thousands of rockets right on schedule. Through the clouds and mist, the sailors fired at what they could not see—Omaha Beach. Salvo after salvo was released one behind the other, each screaming towards the Normandy shoreline. Some rockets burst and exploded in midair, others landed in the surf short of the beach obstacles and defenders.

Others overflew the beaches and still others landed in grassy areas causing fires, sending smoke out to sea obscuring the job of navigating the landing crafts. It was great theater as some of the troops in the landing crafts could see and hear the rockets fly over their heads seemingly leading the way to the beaches they had been assured would be destroyed.

The rockets were a new, relatively untested, and ineffective final act in the attempted destruction of the Germans defending Omaha. The Germans had survived all three bombardments relatively unscathed. They understood as the firing from the ships and rockets stopped, the next step was for thousands of American soldiers to arrive on the beach.

The failures to eradicate, destroy, disrupt, or interfere with Rommel's dug-in troops on one of his most heavily defended beaches, was about to be measured in the blood of American soldiers.

It would exact an unimaginable price.

A German howitzer in museum in Normandy.

Part III: Broken Plans

"Cannon to right of them, Cannon to left of them,
Cannon in front of them Volleyed and thundered;
Stormed at with shot and shell."

Alfred, Lord Tennyson, Poet Laureate (1809–1992)

It was all planned to the minute, from H-Hour–5 minutes until H-Hour +225 minutes. Like the aerial and naval bombardments, everything had a schedule and everything was expected to go as planned—nothing did.

236

As the landing crafts arrived so should have another layer of fire support. Floating tanks, called DD, short for dual drive, were Sherman tanks that had an inflatable canvas skirting for flotation, and raised air inlet and exhaust pipes to prevent water from killing the engines, while propellers were driven off the drive mechanism for the tracks. They were slow speed floating, or swimming tanks that would go in with the first wave of invaders all along the beaches.

Behind the swimming tanks were over a dozen LCT (Landing Craft Tank) that had 105 mm howitzers on the top deck to offer more local fire support. First, as the LCT were headed towards the shore the 105s fired effectively, but as they got closer the elevation of the 105 mm howitzers could not be lowered.

The result was they could not fire at the bluffs where the Germans were, they could only fire over them. The LCTs were also large and attractive targets for the Germans, and before long the German guns, mines, and beach obstacles found the LCTs and left many in ruins. Other 105 mm Howitzers tried to get ashore on DUKW, floating trucks.

The 111th Field Artillery Battalion lost all but one of its howitzers at sea. The 7th Field Artillery Battalion suffered a similar fate as they lost five of six guns. [139]

The DD tanks which would have made a difference on the beach in the opening moments of the invasion fared worse than the howitzers. Their mobility and firepower were needed as the first infantry wave arrived.

The soldiers landing on the beaches were told that tanks were there to blow away the last remaining vestiges of German resistance. It was a well-intended promise, as was the aerial bombardment, shortened naval bombardment, and the rockets. Like the other plans it was a grave, costly failure.

First, they were released far from shore, the sea was just too rough to float a tank weighing over thirty tons. Many went down like boxes of rocks, in some cases taking most or some of the crew.

The D-Day planners fully understood that the DD tanks required calm seas. On D-Day the Normandy coast was anything but calm. Rough seas with four- and six-foot swells were tossing large ships about, those tanks never stood a chance.

---

[139] Harrison, A. Gordon. Cross Channel Attack. The Center of Military History, United States Army: Washington, D.C. Digital Version. https://www.google.com/books/edition/Cross_Channel_Attack/STU35Lza2mIC?hl= en&gbpv=1&printsec=frontcover Pp 309-313. Retrieved January 2021

The 741st Tank Battalion had two companies of DD tanks launched at H-Hour minus one hour. That would give the very slow swimming tanks the time to get ashore as the first soldiers arrived. Thirty-two tanks were released into the angry ocean swells. Twenty seven of the thirty-two only had only enough time to find the bottom of the Channel.

Over 130 men from the 741st Tank Battalion entered the water with their tanks, over thirty drowned. Beyond the loss of life, over 84% of the DD tanks from the 741st were on the bottom of the English Channel, where they still are to this day.[140] With such a disaster unfolding before their eyes, the rest of the tanks remained on the LCTs and would be released at the water's edge.

The assumption was the tanks would cross the beach with their guns blazing in support of the landed infantry soldiers. But, because the aerial bombardment was such a failure, Omaha Beach was still covered in beach obstacles that blocked or limited the advances of many tanks. When the tanks stopped moving, they became perfect fixed targets for the zeroed in German artillery. It was another bitter failure.

H-Hour was 06:30 hours, and the arrivals to Omaha Beach were scheduled like a busy train station—right down to the minute. Between H-Hour–5 minutes and H-Hour the DD tanks would be crawling onto the beaches. At H-Hour +1–3 minutes it was the infantry of the 1st and the 29th Infantry Divisions that would begin to splash ashore.

After the first wave, the second wave arrived just minutes behind the initial invaders. The unrelenting schedule expanded beyond the infantry soldiers as the planners brought more men and material by the minute: demolition specialist, engineers, navy gun spotters, beach masters, headquarters personnel, weapons specialists, medical personnel, and even more tanks and more infantry. It was all planned to the minute until H-Hour +225 minutes, all to be neatly wrapped up in three hours and forty-five minutes.

The extra-long days of early summer allowed the planners a window of over 15 hours of some degree of daylight. They needed it all, because when the sun did set on D-Day at Omaha Beach, the planners imaged landing nearly 40,000 troop and 3,000 wheeled and tracked vehicles.

The unyielding schedule with its strict timing of arrivals was hinged on the ability of men and machines to move off the beaches and onto the exits leading

---

[140] Harrison. Cross Channel Attack. Page 309.

inland. In order to unload the second wave, the first wave had to unload and aggressively move off the beach, making way for the in-coming waves already at sea.

The entire timetable required that personnel as well as vehicles arrived, unloaded, and advanced clearing the landing zones. It all looked good on paper. Before long, the shoreline at Omaha Beach was a traffic jam of boats, uncleared obstacles, tanks, wounded, dying, and dead men. In minutes, the well-planned schedule was an exercise in futility that added to the profoundly grave, growing problems on the Omaha Beaches.

Earlier, on D-Day, while the plans were still intact, all began right on schedule.

For the infantry soldiers of the first wave the day began early, as some started boarding the landing crafts at 04:15 hours—two hour plus before H-Hour. The seas were rough, and the small, flat-bottomed landing crafts, with a big flat bow made of steel, like a bulldozer, had to be preloaded so they could arrive onetime by the developed schedule. The soldiers gathered by their units, and slowly mustered on deck and into their assigned areas, it was a slow process.

The hours passed as they assembled on the decks. The rough seas tossed the landing craft against the sides of the much larger troop ships. Down the nets, they slowly descended clinging for their lives as the ships heaved and tossed. When they reached, the landing craft things only got worse for them as the light, mostly wooden, flat bottom little ships violently raised and lowered in the angry English Channel.

The little boats could barely remain attached to the larger navy troop carriers, waves splattered against the boats and the soldiers got easily and quickly soaked with very cold seawater barely forty-five degrees. Each landing craft had about 30–32 soldiers and most of them shivered, and some got sick, as the endless motion was too much to bear by men who understood they could be facing death.

Some men vomited from the motion, others vomited from the sounds, sight and smells they were sharing. But the unstable boats full of seasick soldiers eventually moved towards the beaches and their appointment with a destiny they could not have foreseen in the months, weeks, and days of their training. No one trains to be slaughtered.

Hours became minutes as they heard the navy shells fly over their heads, reassuring some of them they were not alone on their one-way boat ride. Then they heard and saw the rockets, another relief as their desperate boat ride was nearing its end. One can imagine the questions, fears, doubts, and ghastly images that pervaded their minds.

Minutes ticked down, and soon US Navy, British Royal Navy, and American Coast Guard personnel commanding the flotilla of landing crafts announced the landing time in minutes and seconds. The pilots yelled out the anticipated arrival times at the shoreline. Like a conductor on a loud train, they counted down; *"Three minutes! Two minutes!"*

Then it was measured in seconds, *"Sixty seconds!"* was shouted. The soldiers heard the drowning of the diesel engines powering the boats. Now, officers and NCOs quickly offered last minute instructions to the young men who stood shivering cold, soaking wet, seasick, and weak from vomiting. Their leaders drove home the training and experiences they had shared.

They shouted over the sound of the engines powering the small boat that floated on top of the water, not so much in the water. The engine was pulled back as they neared their destination, allowing them to float onto the beach. They were told, *"Get off the beach, Get to the seawall, Advance and attack any German resistance, Make way for others, and remember to keep your weapons clean and dry."*

When the NCO's and officers finished shouting, it was mostly silence, except for those whispering prayers for God's mercy. The Germans would be destroyed, they had been assured. They were nearly on French soil and an uneasy silence descended upon the liberating invaders. The flat-bottomed landing crafts slowed as the engines were pulled back.

As the landing crafts made their way to shore, they were easily spotted by the Germans. The Germans could hardly believe their eyes as the Americans got closer and closer. One German said: "(they are) *Right under our muzzles.*"[141] Experienced German officers and NCOs warned the eager beach defenders to hold their fire. Most of the German guns: rifles, machine guns, mortars, and artillery had a finite amount of ammunition, all shots had to count.

"Thirty seconds!" shouted the navy skipper piloting the land craft. Silence for just the briefest of moments. Then the silence was broken by the cables

---

[141] Ambrose, Stephen E. D-Day June 6, 1944: The Climatic Battle of World War II. Simon and Schuster: New York. Print 1994. Page 322.

being released and loudly running over the pulleys that raised and lowered the ramp. In an instant, the ramps splashed down and silence was replaced by unfathomable violence, as machine gun bullets tore into man and boat alike.

As the ramp lowered there was no defense. Suddenly and violently men were being pushed into the boat as the force of the bullets entered the bodies of the men who had been closest to the ramp. The experience was overwhelming for some, as they and their comrades were shot to bloody pieces.

In a vain attempt to survive, some tried to crawl over or around the dead to cross the ramp, only exposing themselves to the cruel inhuman machine gun fire. Other desperate men went over the sides to escape the massacre. Many of them were shot in the water or drowned as their heavy packs filled with water and pulled them to the sea floor, sparing them the horrendous fate of their comrades being ripped apart by machine guns.

German machine guns fired relentlessly, so did the trained riflemen, and soon the mortar and artillery shells landed. Many soldiers never knew what hit them. They never stood a chance. The crisis at Omaha Beach was just beginning. Many of the commanders, sitting aboard naval vessels offshore received scattered, scrambled, at times incoherent messages from the troops landing.

Before long, those commanders understood they had a much different invasion than they had planned. As the reports were passed along to the senior commanders of the American landing forces, some realized they had a potential disaster unfolding on the Omaha Beaches.

General Clarence Huebner (1888–1972) was in command of the 1st Infantry Division, which was charged with landing at east end of Omaha. Huebner was a Bradley appointee to command the 1st during the Normandy Landings. The 1st had been commanded in 1942 through 1943 by Generals Terry Allen and Ted Roosevelt, but Bradley thought they were poor commanders and had them relieved.

As he was being updated on the crisis on Omaha, Huebner later recalled, *"I had not had very many good reports. Most of these reports were rather fragmentary in character but they informed me that the fighting was heavy and we were still confined to the beach itself."*[142]

---

[142] Kershaw. Landing on the Edge of Eternity. Page 249.

When news arrived on the bridge of the USS Augusta, it found a stunned General Omar Bradley. Bradley was surprised by the news that his plans seemed to be failing. Not trusting the errant and scattered reports, he eventually sent his trusted aid, Major Hansen to the beach to see first-hand what was going on twelve miles in front of him on the French coast he planned to easily conquer.

When Major Hanson returned, it was with news Bradley did not want to hear. The reports of a crisis on the beach were real. Bradley's staff now understood the battle for Omaha Beach was not a cake walk, and at this point, the victory that Bradley had planned was tenuous at best, and perhaps, rapidly fading out of reach.

When the seriousness of the failures at Omaha Beach sank into his mind, Bradley was so overwhelmed that years later, he wrote: "*I reluctantly contemplated the diversion of Omaha follow-up forces to Utah and the British Beaches.*"[143]

The battle was not over but it was out of the hands of General Omar Bradley. The men who had already landed on Omaha Beach would now answer to each other, not to the voices of those table-top battle planners. Observing the landings from the sea, US Navy Admiral Cooke observed;

> *"The landings are a complete disaster…*
> *The troops are pinned to the beach…"[144]*

---

[143] Bradley, Omar Nelson. Omar N. Bradley; A Soldier's Story. Edited by Caleb Carr. New York: Random House. 1999 Print Page 271.
[144] Ambrose. D-Day June 6, 1944… Page 386.

Part IV: The Unplanned Crisis

"Boldly they rode and well,
Into the jaws of Death,
Into the mouth of hell."

Alfred, Lord Tennyson, Poet Laureate (1809–1992)

While General Bradley pondered the fate of the men he sent to Omaha Beach, from twelve miles offshore, the furthest distance of any D-Day commander, he also considered his own legacy. Bradley realized: *"He had no control of the battle on the beaches…"*

But he had been informed: *"There were reports of progression on the British Beaches and Utah…"* And abroad his command ship, Bradley's reports from Omaha Beach were getting worse: *"From these messages we could piece together only an incoherent account of the sinking, swamping, heavy enemy fire, and chaos on the beaches."*[145]

At the eastern end of Omaha Beach, where the American Memorial and Cemetery are positioned atop the bluffs overlooking Omaha Beach. The 1st Infantry division landed. They were the only American infantry division that had combat experience before they landed on the beaches on D-Day.

The 1st ID, was also known as the *Big Red One*, because of large number 1 insignia on their uniform shoulder patch, had the experience Bradley needed

---

[145] Kershaw. Landing on the Edge of Eternity. Page 242.

for landings in Normandy. Interestingly, the battle experiences of the Big Red One, were gained while they were under the very successful command of Generals Allen and Roosevelt.

In a rich irony, after Bradley had Roosevelt removed, Ted Roosevelt was placed with the 4th ID and would land nearly perfectly at Utah Beach. General Roosevelt was the only general officer to land with the first wave in either the British or American Armies. He was also the father of a son landing in the first wave. His son, Captain Quentin Roosevelt II was in the 1st ID and went in with the first wave at Omaha Beach.

Under Generals Allen and Roosevelt, the Big Red One participated in the amphibious landings at Algeria in November of 1942. The Big Red One and Roosevelt helped chase Rommel out of North Africa. In 1943, they were part of the amphibious landings at Sicily, chasing Hitler's Nazis off the Island and onto the Italian peninsular.

The commander of the Big Red One, Terry Allen was a successful and beloved commander who made the cover of Time Magazine on 9 August 1943. It was after the Sicilian campaign that General Bradley, going behind the back of General Patton asked his old West Point classmate, General Eisenhower to relieve Generals Allen and Roosevelt. Eisenhower had them both relieved.

With a new commander, the veteran 1st ID was chosen to spearhead the American amphibious landings in Normandy and chase Rommel back to Germany. And as they rode their landing crafts towards Omaha Beach, the men of the Big Red One had already lost over five thousand comrades, and two beloved commanders battling the Germans in North Africa and Sicily.[146]

The air was full of sea spray and low clouds so you could not see much once in your landing craft. Before they got to the Normandy shoreline the soldiers had to fight the rough seas that slowed them down, and filled the landing crafts with seawater. The boats and the heavily armed, weighted down soldiers inside were being swamped, and as the boats filled with water they slowed.

The soldiers used their helmets and bailed as much water out as they could. As they bailed the water out of the boats, they were unaware that another problem had found them on this day of problems. The strong winds and rough

---

[146] Army Battle Casualties and Non-battle Deaths in World War II. Final Report. 1941-1946. https://apps.dtic.mil/dtic/tr/fulltext/u2/a438106.pdf Retrieved January 2021. Page 86.

seas were pushing them off course and that was just the latest in a day full of broken promises and broken plans.

The Navy boat pilots could not see they were off course. Their vision of Omaha Beach was obscured until it was too late to change course, and by then some of the landing craft were taking fire. Being out of place broke the chain of command, companies were not always near their company commanders, and being out of place interfered with the strict timetable that applied to all the landings on the beach.

The junior officers and NCO's that survived the landings would have to lead their troops off the beaches. One by one, the first boats arrived at a beach full of obstacles, and German gun fire. They were running straight into Rommel's Kill Zones.

On the eastern end of Omaha beach, the Germans had built a series of *Widerstandsnestern*, which means, resistance nest in German. Where the 1st landed, there was five known resistance nest positions: WN61, 62, 63, 64, 65. They held troops, and all manner of arms, including the deadly German machine gun, MG42.

The MG-42 was introduced by the German Army in 1942 to replace an older, slower, less effective machine gun. The German World War II MG 42 was so advanced that it is still in use to this very day. It was so modern and distinctive that the US troops sent to Europe were schooled in this killing machine; learning to identify it by the specific sound it makes—like canvas being quickly torn.

It could fire 1200 bullets per minute, or 20 bullets per second, yes 20 bullets per second. It fired a bullet equal to the US 30 caliber, and the effective range, or the killing range of this weapon was 2,300 yards. When the soldiers started exiting the landing crafts, they were only 400–500 or so yards away from the Germans.

On Omaha Beach when an MG42 was fired at you the bullets were traveling at 2.7 times the speed of sound. It was the speed of the bullet that was devastating to the human body. Traveling at supersonic speeds gave it devastating hitting power as it smashed into flesh and bone, easily tearing apart a soldier. You were dead before you heard the shots. [147]

---

[147] Collections, Small Arms, Light Machine Guns MG 42
https://norfolktankmuseum.co.uk/mg-42/ Retrieved January 2021.

If more than one MG 42 was trained on your landing craft, and when the first wave was landing that was entirely possible, you could have faced anywhere from 20, 40, 60, 80 bullets per second when that ramp fell down. In the time it takes to count, "One" the 32 soldiers in a landing craft could have had eighty bullets fired into the boat.

As the first wave arrived where the English Channel washes onto French soil, some were out of place and some were out of time. All along the coast the German artillery spotters could not believe what they saw, the American landing crafts arriving at the beaches were unprotected and very vulnerable.

The boats slowed, and almost stopped, as a German officer on the bluffs overlooking the arriving Americans muttered: *"But that's not possible, that's not possible."* The officer called his gun battery, and forwarded the precise coordinates of the beached boats: *"Dora,* (The Germans sited or zeroed the entirety of Omaha Beach using German female names) *all guns, range four-eight-five-zero, basic direction twenty plus, impact fuse."*

Then he told his gunners to, *"Wait."*[148] The boats stopped where the sea ended and the land began and then the lethal artillery shells fell like rain. When Cornelius Ryan wrote his influential book, *The Longest Day*, he was able to talk to the hundreds of veterans of D-Day all within just a handful of years after the World War II ended.

Many veterans were still young and could remember well that June morning on Omaha Beach. Ryan's account after talking to American and German veterans alike was *"Artillery roared. Mortar shells rained down…All along the four miles of Omaha Beach German guns flayed the assault craft."*[149]

They didn't have a chance, as they had no cover, and no answer for the hell they had been led into. They could not retreat, behind them was only ocean, they had to advance to the seawall, that was the only cover they could find. They huddled by Rommel's beach obstacles, and behind destroyed tanks.

Some quickly understood the water's edge held only the promise of death. They had to defy the German onslaught and move across the sands to the seawall. They moved slowly as lone survivors or as small groups from obstacle

---

[148] McManus, John C. The Dead And Those About To Die: D-Day: The Big Red One At Omaha Beach. New York: NAL Caliber. 2014. Print. Page 74.
[149] Ryan, Cornelius. The Longest Day: June 6, 1944. New York: Simon and Schuster, 1959. P. 207.

to obstacle. They had been there only a few minutes, but to some it is a lifetime, and for others the end of their lifetime.

"It is a bloody chaos...(German) *machine gunners and snipers seem to be targeting officers...* (the officers removed) *badges of rank...The majority of the assault troops are leaderless, confused and terrified...Of the 272 engineers* (sent to Omaha to blow gaps in the beach obstacles) *111 were killed...within the first 30 minutes...One man explodes as the TNT he is carrying is hit by a bullet."* One soldier would later recall the chaos on Bloody Omaha as having inflicted, *a mass paralysis.*[150]

On Omaha Beach, the first wave lost enough men that the dead, dying and wounded were turning the ocean red from their blood. Some men were killed instantly, others dying on the landing crafts, others drowned, many were wounded and died with little or no medical attention, and others just seemed to disappear, vaporized as artillery bursts claimed men in violent heat filled explosions.

Years later, Major Stanley Bach, 1st Infantry Division, recalled: *"...heavy mortar and 88s* (German cannon) *fire on the beach, from east end to west end...at burst of shell, two Navy men went flying through the air...direct hit on LCM,* (Landing Craft Mechanized) *flames everywhere men burning alive..."*[151]

US Army Ranger Jack Burke added his experiences on Omaha Beach: *"...you begin to experience the worst day of your life...murderous machine guns...the 88s and 105s* (German artillery guns) *shelling the beach...I will never see anything like it again..."*[152]

Yet, with such horror unfolding all around them not all was lost. At the eastern end, some of the veteran of the Big Red One organized into small teams and began to do the job they were sent to do. They had to charge across the beach to find cover at the shingle, the narrow space at the bottom of the bluffs. Some incredibly managed to survive the tempest of German fire and found one another amongst the unparalleled carnage.

Lieutenant Huch made it to the shingle with a run and cover approach. He moved when he could, and hit the beach near the obstacles, and repeated that

---

[150] Mayo. D-Day: Minute by Minute. Pp. 148–191.

[151] Baloski, Joseph. Omaha Beach: D-Day, June 6, 1944. Mechanicsburg, PA: Stackpole, 2004. Page 308.

[152] Sterne, Gary. The Cover-Up at Omaha Beach New York: Skyhorse Publishing, 2013. P. 38.

until he reached the shingle. Looking back, he noticed: "*It was awful, people lying all over the place—the wounded unable to move and being drowned by the incoming tide.*"

That in itself must have been inconceivable just a few minutes earlier in the landing craft, but he continues: "*At least 80% of our weapons wouldn't work* (my own included) ..."[153] They had managed to survive and get to the shingle and the vast majority had no weapons other than their undaunted courage.

Captain Fred Hall realized that he and his men had landed off-course. When Hall hit the beach, it was chaos: "*It was everyman for himself crossing the open beach where we were under fire...And the noise...small arms, artillery, and mortar fire...the shouting and cries of the wounded.* Hall lost nearly half the men in his landing craft on the beach."[154]

Meanwhile, one platoon landed nearly intact and was making its way through the savage battle to the seawall. When the Germans realized the Americans were there, they opened up with their machine guns on the sheltering soldiers. The men discovered a path that led up the bluff, and Platoon leader Lt. John Spaulding and his men carefully advanced across a mine field into a German trench. Spaulding and his men located the machine gun firing on them and captured the gunner, he was not a German.

They next continued climbing up the bluff and once on top assaulted the German gun positions from behind. Spaulding and his men did the impossible. Yet, beneath them the battle for Omaha Beach was still raging at the shoreline for most of the American Army.

By 08:00 hours, an hour and half into the struggle the commander of the 16th Infantry Regiment, of the 1st Infantry division landed on the beach. The 16th was the regiment chosen to be the first attackers of Omaha Beach and they were the men in the first wave on the eastern end of the beaches.

Colonel George Taylor (1899–1969) arrived with the second wave of men from his regiment. Colonel Taylor was surprised at the chaos and destruction in men and equipment he found on the beach. His soldiers were leaderless, and desperately trying to stay alive under the unabated German fire.

Shocked by what he saw, he wasted no time organizing the soldiers frozen at the water's edge. Without regard to his safety, he went to the seawall and

---

[153] McManus. The Dead and Those About to Die. Pp. 84-85.
[154] Ambrose. D-Day June 6th... Page 349.

found more men desperately clinging to the perceived notion they could stay there.

Unabashed by the dangers that surrounded him, Taylor got his men moving, as he famously told them: *"There are two kinds of people who are staying on this beach: those who are dead and those who are going to die! Now, let's get the hell out of here."*[155]

Taylor was awarded the Distinguished Service Cross, for his inspirational actions on Omaha Beach. The citation reads in part,

"...for extraordinary heroism...Colonel Taylor landed during the most crucial and threatening period of the invasion operation. Thousands of men lay huddled on a narrow beachhead, their organizations and leaders cut down by the disastrous enemy fire. Without hesitation, unmindful of the sniper and machine gun fire which was sweeping the beach, Colonel Taylor began to reorganize the units. While continuously exposed to this murderous fire..."[156]

---

[155] Whitlock, Flint. The Fighting First: The Unknown Story of the Big Red One on D-Day. Westview Press: Cambridge, 2004 Print. Page 178. https://www.google.com/books/edition/The_Fighting_First/ Retrieved January 2021.
[156] Hall of Valor website. George A. Taylor, Distinguished Service Cross Citation, 1 July 1944. https://valor.militarytimes.com/hero/22725 Retrieved January 2021.

American Cemetery above Omaha Beach with rainbow

Part V: The Unimaginable Price

"Into the jaws of Death,
Into the mouth of hell."

Alfred, Lord Tennyson, Poet Laureate (1809–1892)

Meanwhile, at the western end of Omaha Beach, things were the same or maybe worse for the men of the 116th Infantry Regiment. They were part of the 29th Infantry Division which was landing at the *Charlie* and *Dog Green* sectors of Bloody Omaha Beach.

On D-Day, the 116th Infantry Regiment was older than the United States itself. It was formed in 1742 as a Virginia Militia unit and has remained in service ever since. The 116th fought in the American Revolution, and during our Civil War when they fought for the Confederacy, fighting at the Battle of

Gettysburg. They served again in World War I at Verdun and on D-Day they fought against Hitlers Nazis on Omaha Beach.[157]

The 116th had company when they landed on Omaha Beach. A group of US Army Rangers who should have gone to Pointe-du-Hoc, were sent to the western end of Omaha Beach. That put them close to Pointe-du-Hoc where Colonel James Rudder and his US Army Rangers landed on D-Day.

The struggle of the Rangers landing with the 116th Regiment has been immortalized in the motion picture, *Saving Private Ryan* which illustrates in breathtaking clarity the events of Omaha Beach at its west end on D-Day morning.

It was a perfect storm of failed US plans and determined German resistance, multiplied by the undamaged defensive structure. This maelstrom nearly overwhelmed the American soldiers who were sent to attack Hitler's vaunted Atlantic Wall.

Rommel knew Hitler's extolled Atlantic Wall would not stop the Allies. So, he was determined to add to it, and that meant covering the spaces the Atlantic Wall did not reach—the beaches. His goal was to slow and stop the invaders, and kill them at the water's edge. In France, Rommel was low on materials, equipment, supplies, and quality fighting troops. However, he was not low on ideas.

Like his legendary defense of El Alamein in North Africa, he used his skill and cunning against the incredible advantage the Allies had in men and material. The western end of Omaha Beach was built by Rommel's troops with one of his Normandy axioms in mind.

The war will be won or lost on the beaches. We'll have only one chance to stop the enemy and that's while he's in the water struggling to get ashore.[158]

The western end of Omaha Beach was in front of the town of Vierville-sur-Mer, and on D-Day it had a long flat section of beach filled with undisturbed obstacles, including some topped by mines and old artillery shells. Its beaches were flat, and extended to the sheer bluffs raising over one hundred feet high, the perfect place for Rommel's defenders.

There was a concrete gun emplacement that is still there, and it still has the 8.8 mm gun that tore apart the men, landing crafts, tanks, and ships landing on

---

[157] The 116th Infantry Regiment Foundation, Inc. 116th Infantry Home Page. https://116thfoundation.org/# Retrieved January 2021.

[158] Mayo. D-Day: Minute by Minute. Page 146

the beach. It was very heavily defended because it had a hard packed road leading up a hill, onto a main road leading into the Normandy countryside, perfect for the advance of armored units inland.

The western end, like the eastern end of Omaha Beach was defended by soldiers of a veteran German Division. They had been in Normandy for months but were further inland not close to the beaches. Then just days before the landings, parts of the German 352 Infantry Division moved up towards the coast. The D-Day planners did not know of this recent and important change, and not all the American field commanders were told of this change.

But one commander, and his closest staff members did know of this change—albeit just a few days before D-Day. General Bradley and his staff knew the veteran 352 ID had been moved to defend Omaha Beach. That was distressing news to the man planning on quickly conquering the French Coast.

Field Marshal Rommel was saddled with many *Static Divisions* in Normandy. That meant they had little or no way of moving. Often these Static Divisions used horses to move or deliver supplies. Yes, in Normandy, the German Army used many horses.

Remember the horse with the fat rider delivering food in the movie, *The Longest Day?* Remember the hose drawn wagons that are attacked by the soldiers in *Band of Brothers* in Episode 2, *Day of Days?* The Germans did not want them, the static troops, to move because many of these Static Divisions were not Germans at all.

Many of the soldiers in these divisions were from the countries Germany had invaded and occupied. They were from as near as Italy, and as far as Asia They were Russians, Ukrainians, and Georgians. They did not speak German and were not armed until the invasion began.

The Germans were desperate for manpower, so desperate they offered these foreigners either POW camps and being worked to death, or limited roles in the German army.

These were just desperate men who were trying to stay alive and defending the Fatherland was the last thing on their minds. Many of these men stayed and defended the Normandy coast, but once their German controllers were killed or fled, they quickly ran or surrendered.

If you have ever seen the movie *Saving Private Ryan*, after the Rangers, led by Captain John Miller (Tom Hanks) cross the beach and fight to reach the top of the bluffs they encounter two unarmed "Germans" trying to surrender.

The unarmed soldiers are pleading for their lives. The "Germans" are not speaking German.

The Americans do not care. They shoot their enemy, killing the two men. The two men trying to surrender are speaking Czechoslovakian, and Spielberg included that event so the audience might understand that many of the soldiers the American's faced on the D-Day beaches were not German at all. [159]

But the 352nd German Infantry Division was a group of battle-hardened German veterans mostly from the Eastern Front. They moved up to defend the beaches in direct support of the static troops already there. The 352nd was the difference between Bradley's envisioned easy beach landing, and the Hell he released his armies into.

"In the first few hours on OMAHA Beach, the OVERLORD operation faced its gravest crisis...instead of attacking...one regiment of an overextended static division as expected...troops hit on the front of...the 352, whose presence in the coastal zone had been missed by Allied Intelligence."

Gordon A Harrison wrote that in his influential, collective work, Cross-Channel Attack in 1951. He labeled the intelligence failure as *"...one of the more interesting failures of the war..."* It was more tragic than "interesting." Later in a footnote he acknowledges the grave fact: *"It should not be surprising if we discovered...* (that the) *352 had one up* (a regiment on the beach) *and two* (in reserve or already deployed to the beaches) *to play..."*[160]

It was reported in the days before the landings that the 352nd had moved up to Omaha Beach. The ULTRA decrypts that remained classified into the 1970s revealed: *"Thus the 352 Division, a field division of good quality which moved into the Côtentin* (Normandy area) *in March and right up to Omaha Beach a few days before the landings, received only a single mention before the fighting began..."*[161]

[159] Hooton, Christopher. The Saving Private Ryan detail you might have missed that makes the film even more brutal. https://www.independent.co.uk/arts-entertainment/films/news/saving-private-ryan-film-1998-steven-speilberg-german-soldiers-czech-translation-surrender-dialogue-a7582926.html 16 February 2017. Retrieved January 2021.

[160] Harrison. Cross-Channel Attack. Page 319. Includes footnote #75 on same page.

[161] Bennett, Ralph. ULTRA in the WEST: The Normandy Campaign of 1944-1945. New York: Charles Scribner's Sons. 1979. Print. Page 45.

The truth is that many years later what Harrison had labeled "*more interesting failures*" was a much greater failure then he realized.

Within the first few hours of the landings, it became obvious with deadly clarity something was wrong. What was wrong was another failure, but this was a different type of failure than the aerial and naval bombardments, this was a costly personal mistake.

Its genesis goes back to January 1944, in the planning stages of the invasion back in England. British Royal Engineer Captain Logan Scott-Bowden had personally inspected Omaha Beach. He had been sent to the Omaha region by secret mini-sub, and he swam ashore to inspect the quality of the compacted sands of Omaha Beach.

He found that the sands were perfect for landing wheeled and tracked vehicles. He also found a wide-open beach with no natural obstacles, no cover whatsoever for the invading troops. He was so apprehensive about the prospect of a disaster on Omaha Beach he told General Bradley: "*Sir, I hope you don't mind me saying it, but this beach is a very formidable proposition indeed and there are bound to be tremendous casualties.*" Bradley only offered a brief reply, "*I know my boy.*"[162]

In April and May of 1944, Bradley's direct superior General Montgomery was warned by his Chief of Intelligence, Brigadier General Edgar Williams: "*The chief gaps in our knowledge of the enemy in the* (Landing Beaches areas) *are the strength and location of the...352 Division.*"

By his own admission General Williams identified: "*The evidence about the 352 is...flimsy.* General Williams concluded: (the) *352* (could be) *a significant reinforcement of Omaha Beach.*"[163]

The simple truth written by historian Joseph Balkoski reads: "*Since the end of the Second World War, history has largely failed to record that late on June 4, the highest levels of Allied Intelligence had correctly deduced the enemy's 352 Division was positioned on the coast...and would surely*(be) *involved in the D-Day fighting...on Omaha...*"[164]

With the deployment of parts of the 352, the force defending Omaha Beach nearly doubled. But it was the quality and experience of the additional troops that was so disruptive. Instead of 600 poor caliber static non-German troops,

---

[162] Kershaw. Landing on the Edge of Eternity. Page 78

[163] Ibid. Page 70.

[164] Balkoski. Omaha Beach. Page 49.

Bradley's forces would face 1,100 troops including veteran killers from the Eastern Front.

What could General Bradley have done? Each time I walk the western end of Omaha Beach, that is the most haunting question I ask, and do not accept he was powerless on 6 June 1944. To the contrary, he was the man who could have, but didn't change a thing as he sent hundreds then thousands into a place he acknowledged later in his memoirs as, *"a nightmare."*

General Omar Bradley did not alter any plans for the assault. He had 30 hours, from June 4 to early 6 June to do something to answer for the changes that, he fully understood, awaited his troops on Omaha Beach. He did nothing and from 12 miles offshore safely aboard his command ship he watched as remarkable American soldiers' rode: *"Into the jaws of Death, into the mouth of hell."*

As the Americans rode towards the shoreline at Vierville-sur-Mer at Omaha's western end, it was stone cold quiet. Just like other parts of Omaha the German defenders had no ammunition to waste.

They waited in total silence as the first boats approached the shore; they waited and held their aim; they waited until the boats stopped; and they waited until the ramps splashed down exposing the men in the landing craft. It was 06:30 hours, when the first landing crafts arrived—they never had a chance. The first men ashore were the men of A Company, 116th Infantry Regiment, 29th Infantry Division, a group of men nearly completely wiped out.

At H-Hour, it was a disaster for the men of Company A. German defenders were in place, and ready as they exacted an unimaginable price upon the Americans.

"A stream of bullets coming from two angles (Remember that an MG 42 can shoot 20 bullets per second) *hits the first men on the ramps...it is a bloody chaos...men are diving into the sea; others scrambling over the sides of the landing craft...Some are drowning...Some are crawling onto the beach hiding behind Rommel's obstacles...*(others) *trying to dig holes in the sand...*(Some of the tanks) *that have made it to Omaha are preferring to stay half hidden in the surf...The majority of assault troops are leaderless, confused and terrified...Most landing craft have beached in the wrong place...The official*

regimental account will state, 'Company A ceased to be an assault company...'[165] Company A suffered over 90% casualties on the beach.

All along the western end of Omaha Beach the men landed right on time, but not on course. Many landed out of place, like the men at the eastern end of Omaha. They found a well-entrenched enemy determined to kill them at the water's edge. Bradley got a report stating: *"...the situation is chaotic...congestion on the beach from troops, jeeps, tanks, half-tracks, and wreckage's so bad...no more boats to land until it's cleared..."*[166]

It was up to those already there to get inland and off the murderous beaches. The men at the western end of Omaha Beach, with the exception of some US Army Rangers had never been in combat, this was their baptism. One Ranger said: *"We went onto the beach, and the Germans had us zeroed in."*[167]

It was no different for the other men landing on the shore. Men in Company G of the 116th, and the men in company F landed in front of the undamaged German defenders. They met the same fate as many Rangers and the men of Company A, 116th: "(they were) *cut down the moment the enemy opened fire.*"[168]

It was a perfect storm of bullets and shells, killing, wounding, maiming and paralyzing the soldiers stuck at the water's edge. All of that horror was accompanied by a cacophony of murderous sounds as men screamed, cried and begged for help, as bullets made a pinging sound from metal, and a thud from the ones that found the bodies of the dead and living.

Shells arriving from cannons and mortars barley whistling as they rapidly descended onto the beach, then exploding in a thunderous clap that traveled with a deafening blast wave that robbed many of their hearing and immersed them into an eerie disorienting world of silence in the middle of a wild battlefield.

One Combat Engineer Company *suffered 73% casualties* just landing. Another soldier, released far from shore, waded in deep water towards the beach. He noticed the German machine gun bullets hitting the water all around him. He recognized that the Germans were firing tracer bullets, which meant every fifth bullet was white hot and could be seen even in daylight.

---

[165] Mayo. D-Day: Minute by Minute. Page 148.

[166] Ibid. Page 203.

[167] Balkoski. Omaha Beach. Page 116.

[168] Ibid. Page 126.

The tracers assured all the gunners knew where their shots were landing, dramatically increasing the shots that maimed and killed.

"All of a sudden, all hell broke loose. Machine gun fire crisscrossed over my head...There is no way I can use words to explain all that was going on...I could see...men trying to come in and getting shot like fish in a barrel."[169]

The Army and Navy sent in demolition teams to land the full length of Omaha Beach. They were to blow open fifty-yard gaps in the beach obstacles, clearing paths so more and more ships could land. The Navy men were to work on anything they needed to blow up in the water or at its edge.

The Army demolition specialists were to advance and destroy obstacles more inland, creating paths to and opening the beach exits. They had some of the most dangerous work on all of D-Day.

The demolition men floated in with rubber rafts full of TNT and fuses. This is an accounting of the fate of some of the US Army demolition teams: *"Team 11—over 50% casualties...Team 13—Eight Navy got off the LCM with the loaded rubber boat. Artillery shell exploded* (hitting the rubber boat) *three dead...Team 15—Mortar scored a direct hit on rubber boat...three men killed and several wounded..."*[170]

These were teams of men, all were needed, and all the explosives were needed for the job to be done. Without these gaps in Rommel's belts of obstacles, the incoming landing crafts and ships were paralyzed out at sea, or worse yet, hit an obstacle and were stuck in place, making them easy targets.

In another account of another Naval Combat Demolition team *"...as we approached the beaches, we were subjected to heavy enemy gunfire of 88 mm, 75s,* (German cannons) *.50* (caliber) *machine gun and rifle fire...we suffered 41% casualties..."*[171]

The fate of the Demolition teams on Omaha Beach was summed up this way: *"The casualties among the demolition teams within the first thirty minutes...were so great that no historical account of their work can ever be completed...of the sixteen...breaches the mission called for...*(They) *probably finished six (37.5%) ...The cost in casualties* (for the failures to blow open

---

[169] Bowman. Bloody Beaches. Pp. 32-33.

[170] Balkoski. Omaha Beach. Page 149

[171] Bowman. Bloody Beaches. Page 42.

needed the gaps)...*was more than one-third of the 1,000 soldiers and sailors who landed among the first waves...*"[172]

The author claims hundreds of casualties on the beaches were the results of the lack of landing areas being opened for landing crafts, tanks and ships. On a day full of failures, this was another damming, deadly reaction that began with the faulty execution of the bombardments of Omaha Beach.

Like the eastern end, the western end of Omaha Beach had men who managed to escape the wrath of Rommel's defenders and breach the Atlantic Wall. US Army Rangers, men of the 29 Infantry Division and a fearless general led the way off the beach.

In the first wave at the western end, some of the men of the 116th Regiment, while under incessant machine gun, rifle, mortar and artillery shell fire finally fought, and crawled from obstacle to obstacle until after nearly an hour they made it to the shingle—sea wall. Most of their men were dead in the surf, or dying on the beach, but some managed to get off the beach and begin attacking the Germans.

US Army Rangers, Second Battalion, C Company, as portrayed in the movie, *Saving Private Ryan*, landed with the first group of 116th guys. They were all mixed together, and most needed leaders and functional weapons to replace what they had lost landing.

The Second Rangers that landed early suffered over 50% casualties just getting off the beach to the sea wall. Once at the wall, like the *Saving Private Ryan* Rangers, they did what they were trained to do, and slowly fought their way to the top of the bluffs and behind the Germans.

The second wave of 116th Regiment landing were also landing with Rangers, but these were 5th Ranger Battalion troops. They landed further east than the first wave did and met less resistance. Along with the mixed infantry and Rangers was the 29th Infantry Division deputy commander, Brigadier General Norman Cota (1893–1971). With less resistance, they headed straight for the sea wall.

With no regard for his personal safety, fifty-one-year-old General Cota, exposed himself to German gunfire and began to organize the men into attack groups. Once General Cota realized that he had Rangers in his groups he

---

[172] Balkoski, Omaha Beach. Pp. 151-152.

famously quipped, *Rangers! Lead The Way!*[173] That is still the motto of the US Army Rangers. The Rangers moved out and attacked up the bluffs.

For his actions on Omaha Beach, General Cota was awarded the US *Distinguished Service Cross* and *Silver Star*. He was also personally decorated by British General Montgomery with the *Distinguished Service Order*. The citation for his Distinguished Service Cross reads,

"General Cota landed on the beach shortly after the first assault wave of troops had landed. At this time the beach was under heavy enemy rifle, machine gun, mortar and artillery fire. Numerous casualties had been suffered…With complete disregard for his own safety, General Cota moved up and down the fire-swept beach reorganizing units and coordinating their action…"[174]

The bravery of few was not enough as the battle for Omaha Beach raged with most soldiers stuck at the shoreline. The western end of Omaha Beach, like the eastern end was protected by a series of well camouflaged, well dug-in, well-armed *Widerstandsnestern*, or resistance nests. At the western end, the Vierville exit was so important it was protected by two resistance nests, WN-71, and WN-72 flanking each side of the hard surface road that led inland.

Also, WN-70 was just a few hundred yards easterly, and WN-73 was a few hundred yards westerly so both those positions could influence any attempt at the Vierville beach exit.

In some places, the violence became very personal—medieval. Where the Americans had engaged the Germans there were no constraints, only violence that defined the horror of the first few hours on that beach. A German soldier noticed gun flashes around his position and realized the American were attacking his position from the sides and rear.

---

[173] Lt. Colonel (Ret) Bradbeer, Thomas. Major General Norman Cota and the Battle of Hürtgen Forest. Internet Achieve. https://web.archive.org/web/20101210191052/http://www.cgsc.edu/repository/dcl_M GCota.pdf Retrieved February 2021.

[174] Military Hall of Honor. MG Norman Daniel Cota, Sr. Distinguished Service Cross Citation   https://militaryhallofhonor.com/honoree-record.php?id=2378   Retrieved February 2021.

The Americans were as merciless as the Germans had been moments before. They were incensed, nearly out their minds remembering the deaths on the beach, just minutes before. A German soldier tried to make a break from his position: *"We could see smoke belching from some of our strongpoints, while others had fallen silent...Ammunition was desperately short...He looked...in disbelief* (he was) *standing amid...spent cartridges...some 15,000 rounds..."* The German ran out of his bunker and could not believe what he saw.

The 2nd Rangers, C Company was attacking his position: *"The ferocity of the fighting astonished me. Men were lunging at each other with fixed bayonets, and with their rifle stocks, and even entrenching tools or shovels. The Americans were charging upon the German gunners...men were in flames, and other men were shooting or stabbing them as they staggered on fire."*[175]

The struggles on the beaches had raged for just two and half hours. The sea was red with American blood, the shoreline a morass of immoveable men and machines. Gasoline from hit vehicles ignited and burned on the surface of the water creating an image comparable only to the fires of damnation in hell. Omaha Beach was a catastrophe of immeasurable consequences.

Bradley was confined to his command ship as he recognized he has lost control of the battle on the beaches. British General Montgomery informs Bradley that he can land forces at Gold Beach, it is open and available. As a matter of fact, at the very moment, men were being slaughtered on Omaha, *"the British were brewing tea on Sword Beach."*[176]

When word reaches Eisenhower, in England, of the crisis at the shoreline on Omaha Beach, he ordered the US Army Air Force to return to France and bomb Omaha Beach. Wisely, the US Army Air Force was unable to complete Ike's request to bomb a beach already covered with American soldiers—dead and alive.

For all their power, these powerful men were utterly powerless. They were useless. The task of liberating the liberators on Omaha Beach would have to fall to others.

Just before 09:00 hours at the height of the crisis on Omaha Beach, US Navy warships slowly moved towards the beach. The Navy observers had

---

[175] Kershaw. Landing on the Edge of Eternity. Pp. 290-291.
[176] Mayo. D-Day: Minute by Minute. Page 194.

watched the landings become a disaster and they had had enough. The Navy ships began to deliberately break their orders to hold their fire.

That order was issued at 06:30 hours as the diminutive 30 minutes allotted the Navy to bomb the beaches expired. Now, they moved in as time was only a consequence for the men trapped on Omaha Beach.

Could they hold on a little longer?

German gun still in bunker on Omaha Beach.

Part VI: The US Navy at Omaha Beach

"They that had fought so well
Came through the jaws of Death,
Back from the mouth of hell,
All that was left of them."

Alfred, Lord Tennyson, Poet Laureate (1809–1892)

Widerstandsnest 62, (Resistance Nest 62) or WN-62 was the largest German position defending Omaha Beach. Heinrich Severloh was one of only twenty-seven German soldiers from the 352 Infantry Division permanently assigned to WN-62. Heinrich, or Hein was a twenty-year-old machine gunner.

In his memoirs, he wrote a chapter called, *In the Hell of Omaha*, and he recalled years later what he experienced on D-Day morning: *"It was almost completely quiet…not a single shot being fired. We had strict orders to wait until the GI's were only 400 meters…"*

Earlier, he described the massive and unsuccessful aerial and naval bombardments. When the bombardments ended, his position was nearly unscathed, and he prepared for the arrival of the American soldiers.

"(before long) the Americans reached the shallow water…I moved the safety lock of my machine gun to the off position and began to fire…Soon the first corpses drifted about in the waves."

He then remembers he was oblivious to the other German guns firing including the falling artillery shells. He was solely focused on the Americans landing on the beach. Until he noticed a commotion on a ship larger than a landing craft.

Suddenly, his eyes were transfixed on a ship at the shoreline as an LCI (Landing Craft Infantry) a ship with 150 soldiers on board. The LCI had stairways leading from the deck to the water, landed.

The German saw what he thought was an odd occurrence: *"I noticed that tumultuous scenes were playing on the deck…It was clear the GI's who had seen what happened to their comrades were refusing to go down and jump into the blood-colored water.* But they had to go down—and I began to fire again…"*

Heinrich Severloh then saw more landing craft coming into his kill zone, the ramps went down, the soldiers tried to rush out, *"I began to fire again…"* He noticed the rising tide brought the American boats closer to his position, he watched them slow, stop and drop their ramps: *"Each time one (ramp) fell I began to fire."*

As time passed, he continued to shoot, kill, wound, and maim American soldiers.

"…it occurred to me…how many dead there were down there on the beach…there were hundreds and hundreds of lifeless bodies of American soldiers."[177]

---

[177] Severloh, Heinrich. WN62 A German Soldier's Memories of the Defense of Omaha Beach Normandy, June 6, 1944. Pp. 56-65.

The incident of the LCI landing on Omaha Beach at 06:30, in advance of the first wave has been questioned by some writers; it is not reported in the official U.S. accounts of D-Day, and there is speculation that such an incident may have occurred at a different time. WN62 A German soldiers Memories of the Defense of Omaha Beach. Front inside cover note: Robert R. Wolf.

Another of the German soldiers inside WN-62 was Private Franz Gockel. He was a young German machine gunner with the 352 Infantry Division, and he fired on the landing Americans at the eastern end of Omaha Beach. He watched men seek cover behind obstacles that only made them better targets as they stopped for the German gunners.

He watched men fight, crawl, and claw until they reached the sea wall believing they had found shelter. They had only found a dryer place to die. The Germans *"...had waited for this moment and began to lay deadly fire on preset coordinates along the sea wall."*

With young Americans being killed at the water's edge and at the seawall, Franz Gockel noticed something very unexpected, the landing craft headed to beaches turned away. *"Gockel and his comrades thought the Americans were beginning to withdraw."*[178]

The observation the German soldier made was partially correct. The small landing craft were ordered by General Bradley, and US Naval personnel on the beach not to land. There was no room for them to do anything other than join the dead and dying on eastern end of Omaha Beach.

The incoming tide was pushing the American's closer to the Germans. The tide at Omaha beach had been incoming since H-Hour. It was rising an inch every minute, every minute the blood red surface was pushing the soldiers closer to the Germans and closer to death.

The commander of the destroyer, USS Satterlee remembered: *"It was galling and depressing...to lie widely a few hundred yards off the beaches and watch our troops...being heavily shelled."*[179]

At 08:30 hours, the USS Carmick broke from the constraints imposed on the Navy at H-Hour. For two hours, her commander watched in horror as men,

---

[178] Shepard, Joshua. D-Day Landing At Omaha Beach. Warfare History Network. https://warfarehistorynetwork.com/2020/01/28/d-day-landing-at-omaha-beach/ Retrieved February 2021.

[179] Ambrose. D-Day June 6, 1944...Page 384.

tanks, LCVP (Landing Craft Vehicles Personnel), LCA (Landing Craft Assault), LCI (landing Craft Infantry), and LCT (Landing Craft Tank) were being shelled and fired upon by dug-in German defenders. The Carmick's skipper noticed that the Americans trapped on the beach were firing at one spot, so he decided to do the same.

He ordered his 5" guns to open fire. At 08:39 hours, the skipper of the USS McCook noticed that the troops at the western end of Omaha in front of the Vierville exit were stuck on the beach. He noticed men trapped at the base seawall and he too decided that it was time to fight back.

He ordered his 5" guns to open fire on the German positions that were desperately defending the beach exit.

"Commenced firing on pillbox which was delivering fire against beach. 08:58 Ceased firing on pillbox. Pillbox demolished."[180]

At 09:00 hours, the Captain of the US Navy destroyer USS Frankford, moved closer to the beach. What he observed as he closed in on the beach was shocking. He could see the casualties in the swells near the shore. He wasted no time and got on the radio and ordered: *"...all destroyers to close the beach as far as possible and support the assaulting troops"*[181]

Before long, the man in charge of the US Navy gunfire support on Omaha Beach went all-in to relieve the men still living in the blood red surf along Omaha Beach. Admiral C.F. Bryant, also broke radio silence as he ordered his ships, *"Get on them, men! Get on them! They are raising hell with the men on the beach, and we can't have any more of that! We must stop it!"*[182]

With that message the US Navy sent the cavalry to Omaha Beach as all warships in the group responded. It was the beginning of end of the crisis on Bradley's unconquered beach.

Without regard for their own well-being, the Navy's ships closed to the beaches, some just touching bottom as they moved into place closer and closer to open fire. Whether directed by signals from the remaining shore party fire

---

[180] Kirkland, William B. Jr. Destroyers at Normandy: Naval Gunfire at Omaha Beach. Washington, DC: Naval Historical Foundation. 1994. Digital version. https://www.history.navy.mil/research/library/online-reading-room/title-list-alphabetically/d/destroyers-at-normandy.html Retrieved February 2021. Page 33.

[181] Kirkland, William B. Jr. Destroyers at Normandy... Page 46

[182] Ambrose. D-day June 6, 1944... Page 386.

control officers, or following the gunfire of the American soldiers or just hitting targets of opportunity, the ships opened fire.

"Every possible mound or emplacement and everything that looked like a hole in the cliff was taken under fire..."

If it was a gun, any type of gun firing from the bluffs the US Navy opened fire, in one report they simply wrote, "(after firing) ...*gun was not seen any longer...*" They fired their 4" and 5" guns non-stop, raking the suspected bluffs as unmercifully as the Germans had fired on the beach invaders mere moment ago.

"Commenced firing on two guns that were set into the cliffs...one gun plunged from the cliff, other flew into the air."[183]

The destroyers kept moving and firing, until they were less than 1,000 yards from shore. They were within machine gun, mortar, artillery and rifle range of the Germans who could not believe what they were witnessing. Ships steaming towards shore like tanks, but with 4" and 5" deadly powerful and accurate cannons.

The Germans fired back with their own artillery because the destroyers were well within range. The sailors could hear the German guns shots pinging off the ships, and see and feel the explosions all around them. Aboard the USS Shubrick seaman Edward Duffy thought he was in a: *"Dodge city shootout...*(He) *smoked two packs of cigarettes...*(drank) *a dozen cups of coffee...in three hours...We could hear the* (German) *projectiles exploding in the water around us."*

It was a nerve-racking place to be, and the US Navy ships stayed at the water's edge, unyielding, defying the deadly German fire. Duffy said: *"I was scared. I expected at any moment to hear a shell come crashing through the bulkhead."* Then, seaman Duffy saw something he had never seen before. One of the Shubrick's gun spotters saw a lone German officer on the bluffs.

The gun-spotter believed that the officer was a forward observer directing German artillery onto the beach. In a remarkable display of naval gunfire, he directed Shubrick's four 5" guns towards the German on the bluff. The 5" navy guns were sixteen feet long, fired fifty-five-pound shells at 2,600 feet per second.

---

[183] Kirkland, William B. Jr. Destroyers at Normandy... Page 47.

Fire! the order was given, and the guns fired at the cliffs at nearly point-blank range. The German officer and that part of the cliffs overlooking Omaha Beach disappeared forever. [184]

James Knight was a US Army Demolition Engineer, who was trapped at the water's edge for almost two hours on D-Day. He was slowly being pushed ashore by the relentless rising tide, being driven ever closer to his German enemies. Knight saw a destroyer heading for shore.

He thought it was another loss on a day of losses, the hopeless Knight was sure the ship was headed to the shore to beach itself, just another Omaha Beach casualty. He was wrong.

The USS Frankford was not damaged, but it was headed directly towards Omaha Beach when it suddenly turned. USS Frankford turned hard to the west and lined up parallel to the shoreline, so close to land she should have scraped bottom. Just as she finished her turn all four of her 5" guns, and 40 mm guns opened up simultaneously.

The Frankford steamed down the beach guns blazing. Then, rather than turn out to sea, she stopped, reversed her engines and fearlessly steamed backwards while continuing to fire again, and again, and again. Not satisfied, the skipper repeated his actions.

He stopped, moved the ship forward with all guns firing on the beach. *"Fired at a pillbox target destroyed...firing on* (gun) *battery...direct hit...Commenced firing* (at two machine gun nests) *stopped all machine gun fire..."*[185]

It was not just the Navy's destroyers that attacked the beaches. Remarkably, the battleships USS Texas and USS Arkansas added their massive guns to the naval chorus of deadly accurate fire. From less than four thousand yards, the Texas fired at point blank range at the Germans near the Vierville exit.

Her massive 14" guns were lying horizontal and just above the ship's decks as they fired round after massive round, just over the heads of the Americans on the beach. The concussions from the shells impacting the bluffs were felt by the men on the Beach. Whatever they hit was blown into the air in a million pieces. Those watching from the beaches or on the other ships just watched in amazement at something they had never seen.

---

[184] Ambrose. D-Day June 6, 1944... Pp. 386-387.

[185] Kirkland, William B. Jr. Destroyers at Normandy... Page 50.

One Navy LCI (Landing Craft Infantry) was told do not land on beach. The skipper waited offshore and watched as the Germans were firing everything they had: *"Enemy fire on the beaches was terrific. 105 mm, 88 mm, 40 mm, mortars, machine guns…everything."* Into that maelstrom of German artillery fire, rushed the USS McCook. The USS McCook sailed straight into the western end of Omaha Beach, headed for the heavy action at the Vierville exit.

McCook's guns opened up *"…hitting gun positions, pillboxes, buildings, and dug-in cliff positions."* McCook fired at anything that moved near the beach exit, and on the bluffs. At one point, she fired into a German gun position and caused the men manning the gun to display a white flag to the ship.

When the McCook stopped firing, the Germans filed down the bluffs and surrendered. Before she stopped firing the McCook fired 975 shells, USS Shubrick fired 440 shells, USS Satterlee fired 638, and USS Carmick fired 1,127 shells at Omaha Beach on D-Day. [186]

The Destroyers fired until the men were able to get off the beach. They fired all day and into the evening as they were called upon to help the men of the 1st and 29th Infantry Divisions who were slowly moving inland.

When it was over, Colonel S.B. Mason, Chief of Staff of the 1st Infantry Division wrote a letter to Admiral John Hall, the veteran US Navy warrior who had tried to warn the planners of their planned errors at Omaha Beach. Mason wrote, *"I am now firmly convinced that our supporting naval gunfire got us in; that without that gunfire, we positively could not have crossed those beaches."*

When word reached Field Marshal Rommel as to how his beach was breached, he had to report to his superiors: *"Our operations in Normandy are tremendously hampered…by…the…superiority of the enemy air force…*(and) *the effect of heavy naval guns."*[187]

The victory at Omaha Beach belonged to the US Navy, and the dog-faced infantry soldiers, who despite all the failures beyond their control would not, could not give up to the Germans on Bloody Omaha Beach.

[186] Ambrose. D-Day June 6, 1944… Pp. 385-388
[187] Kirkland, William B. Jr. Destroyers at Normandy… Page 76.

I Quietly said to her as we
walked amongst the acres of
dead Americans,
*"They were ALL
a Mother's son."*
Author

Part VII: Conclusion

"When can their glory fade?

O the wild charge they made!
All the world wondered.
Honor the charge they made."

Alfred, Lord Tennyson, Poet Laureate (1809–1892)

On D-Day, freedom and tyranny were separated by the width of a beach in
a foreign country, being violently occupied by a foreign power, which was
defeated by an invading foreign army sent to destroy the occupiers and liberate

269

the foreign country. Never before or since has the world seen such a sacrifice of one country on the shores of another. Remarkable.

On D-Day, an American literary giant was just offshore watching the disaster unfolding on Omaha Beach. He was a legend in his own lifetime and could hardly believe what he saw from a Navy supply ship just a few thousand yards removed from the violence on Omaha Beach.

He talked his way off the ship, and onto a landing craft and a ride into Omaha Beach. He promised he would stay on the landing craft, and he did. He didn't have to go to the beach, his writers' eyes saw enough even from a few hundred yards offshore.

Ernest Hemingway observed, "...*the first, second, third, fourth and fifth waves lay where they had fallen, looking like so many heavily burdened bundles on the flat pebbly stretch between the sea and the first cover.*"[188]

On D-Day, Hemingway was not the only journalist not allowed on Omaha Beach. America's favorite war correspondent, Ernie Pyle walked Omaha Beach the day after the battle. His remarks were published in the United States about a week or so after D-Day.

His words, like Hemingway's words were the first to bring home the horror that was Omaha Beach, "*It was a lovely day for strolling along the seashore. Men were sleeping on the sand, some of them sleeping forever. Men were floating in the water, but they didn't know they were in the water, for they were dead...The wreckage was vast and startling. The awful waste and destruction of war...On the beach lay, expended, sufficient men and mechanism for a small war. They were gone forever now...*"[189]

On D-Day, and the immediate days afterward there were men who searched for the Omaha Beach story in all its appalling truthfulness. One such was historian was one of the US Army's own historians, Lt. Colonel S.L.A. Marshall. He was in Normandy and conducted hundreds of interviews and drew many conclusions.

---

[188] Reynolds, Michael. Hemingway the Final Years. New York: W.W. Norton. 1999. Print. Pp. 97-98

[189] Gelarden, Joe. D-Day plus 75 years - Ramblings from an old scribbler. Boothbay Harbor, ME: Boothbay Register. June 5, 2019.
https://www.boothbayregister.com/article/d-day-plus-75-years/119113   Retrieved February 2021.

This conclusion he did not publish until after his Army career ended in retirement in 1960. Interestingly, 1960 was the last year of the administration of President Dwight D. Eisenhower. In 1944, General Eisenhower was the Supreme Allied Commander on D-Day. The fame and notoriety of being the overall commander on D-Day catapulted General Eisenhower into becoming the 34th President of the United States.

From D-Day to the oval office was just a short eight-year victory lap for the Supreme Allied Commander. Retired General and historian S.L.A. Marshall wrote of Omaha Beach in November of 1960: *"There is for the Normandy landing as a whole no accurate figure for the first hour or first day. The circumstances precluded it...the passing of the years and the retelling of the story have softened the horror of Omaha Beach on D Day...their ordeal has gone unmarked...in a situation which was largely characterized by tragic failure."*[190]

On D-Day, according to the Department of Defense web site, you will find the following accounting of the dead, on Utah Beach.

"...only 197 were killed or wounded." Read on and you will see that the Department of Defense claims that on Omaha Beach, *"The Americans suffered 2,400 casualties."*[191] If you visit the website for the National D-Day Memorial they claim, *"success came at the cost of about 3,000 casualties...that landed on Omaha the first day."*[192]

On D-Day, according to respected author and historian, Joseph Balkoski who writing in Appendix I on page 350 in his excellent 2004 book, *Omaha Beach: D-Day, June 1944*, claims: *Grand Total* (casualties) *"4,720,"* That is a casualty rate 25% higher than Pearl Harbor on 7 December 1941, and it makes D-Day on Omaha Beach, the deadliest day and place for American fighting men in the entire Second World War.

---

[190] Marshal, S.L.A. General US Army. First wave at Omaha Beach. The Atlantic. November 1960.

[191] U.S. Department of Defense. D-Day the Beaches. Headquarters United States European Command.
https://dod.defense.gov/Portals/1/features/2016/0516_dday/docs/d-day-fact-sheet-the-beaches.pdf retrieved February 2021.

[192] National D-Day Memorial. June 6, 1944. https://www.dday.org/june-6-1944/ Retrieved January 2021.

Time has a way of sealing off parts of a story we find troublesome. Yet, in a rich irony, time's uncomfortable constants themselves are only diminished with the passing of time, leaving some to accept the *proposed* narrative, while others question what seems hardly authentic.

We will never know the exact number of men who died on that beach on D-Day. But we can never forget those men who were sent to that beach in hopes of liberating an enslaved continent. Soldiers sent in our names.

Walk Omaha Beach, you will never forget it. Go when the tide is low, walk out to the water's edge and remember them, those that were killed, and those that survived—they were all broken on Omaha Beach. The long dark shadows of those remarkably bloody hours, haunts our individual and collective consciences.

Stand on Omaha Beach with the wind and sand blowing on you, stand there until you feel the truth. And then, travel to the American Cemetery above Omaha Beach, walk amongst the thousands of American soldiers and when you are ready—stand there until you see the truth of Bloody Omaha Beach.

Bibliography

Ambrose, Stephen E. *D-Day 6 June 1944: The Climatic Battle of World War II*. Simon and Schuster: New York. Print 1994.

Astor, Gerald. *June 6, 1944: The Voices of D-Day*. Random House: New York. Digital Version

Balkoski, Joseph. *Omaha Beach: D-Day June 6, 1944*. Stackpole Books: Mechanicsburg, PA. 2004. Print

Bennett, Ralph. *ULTRA in the WEST: The Normandy Campaign of 1944–1945*. New York: Charles Scribner's Sons. 1979. Print.

Bowman Martin W. *Air War D-Day: Volume 4 Bloody Beaches*. Pen & Sword Books: South Yorkshire, England Print. 2013

Bradbeer, Thomas Lt. Colonel (Ret). *Major General Norman Cota and the Battle of Hürtgen Forest*. Internet Achieve. https://web.archive.org/web/20101210191052/http://www.cgsc.edu/repository/dcl_MGCota.pdf

Butler, Daniel Allen. *Field Marshal: The Life and Death of Erwin Rommel*. Casemeate: Havertown, PA Print 2015.

Evans, Mark L. *Arkansas III (Battleship No. 33)1912–1946*. Naval History and Heritage Command. June 2020

Gelarden, Joe. D-Day plus 75 years—Ramblings from an old scribbler. Boothbay Harbor, ME: Boothbay Register. June 5, 2019. https://www.boothbayregister.com/article/d-day-plus-75-years/119113

Harrison, A. Gordon. *Cross Channel Attack.* The Center of Military History, United States Army: Washington, D.C. 1951. Print.

Hewitt, Henry Admiral. *The Memoirs of Admiral H. Kent Hewitt.* Edited by Evelyn M. Cherpak. Naval War College Press: Newport, Rhode Island. 2004.

Kershaw, Robert. *Landing on the Edge of Eternity: Twenty-Four Hours at Omaha Beach.* Pegasus Books: New York. 2018. Print.

Lewis, Adrian R. *Omaha Beach: A Flawed Victory.* University of North Carolina Press: Chapel Hill, NC. 2001. Print.

Mayo, Jonathan. *D-Day: Minute by Minute* Marble arch Press: New York. 2014. Print.

McManus, John C. *The Dead And Those About to Die: D-Day: The Big Red One at Omaha Beach.* New York: NAL Caliber. 2014. Print.

Raaen. John C, JR. *Intact: First Hand Account of the D-Day Invasion from a 5th Rangers Company Commander.* St. Louis: Reedy Press. 2012. Print.

Reynolds, Michael. *Hemingway the Final Years.* New York: W.W. Norton. 1999. Print.

Ryan, Cornelius. *The Longest Day: June 6, 1944.* Simon & Schuster: New York. 1959. Print.

Shepard, Joshua. *D-Day Landing at Omaha Beach.* Warfare History Network. https://warfarehistorynetwork.com/2020/01/28/d-day-landing-at-omaha-beach/

Severloh, Heinrich. WN62 A German Soldier's Memories of the Defense of Omaha Beach Normandy, June 6, 1944.

Stern, Gary. *The Cover-up at Omaha Beach*. New York: Skyhorse Publishing. 2014. Print.

Tillman, Barrett. *Brassey's D-Day encyclopedia: the Normandy invasion A-Z.* Internet Archive.

Whitlock, Flint. *The Fighting First: The Unknown Story of the Big Red One on D-Day.* Westview Press: Cambridge, 2004 Print. *https://www.google.com/books/edition/The_Fighting_First/*

Hall of Valor website. *George A. Taylor, Distinguished Service Cross Citation*, 1 July 1944. https://valor.militarytimes.com/hero/22725

The 116th Infantry Regiment Foundation, Inc. Home Page. https://116thfoundation.org/# Retrieved January 2021.

Collections, Small Arms, Light Machine Guns *MG 42*
Light Machine Guns *MG 42* https://norfolktankmuseum.co.uk/mg-42/

Military Hall of Honor. *MG Norman Daniel Cota, Sr. Distinguished Service Cross Citation* https://militaryhallofhonor.com/honoree-record.php?id=2378 Retrieved February 2021.

The Battleship Texas BB35 *Invasion of Normandy, France 16 April to 18 June 1944. History.*
https://web.archive.org/web/20060923092736/http://users3.ev1.net/~cfmoore/history/1944normandy.html

U.S. Department of Defense. *D-Day the Beaches*. Headquarters United States European Command.
https://dod.defense.gov/Portals/1/features/2016/_0516_dday/docs/d-day-fact-sheet-the-beaches.pdf
National D-Day Memorial. June 6, 1944. https://www.dday.org/june-6-1944/

Afterword: Still, She Stood

The ride away from Oradour-sur-Glane was sullen, my heart filled with despair like the feeling we get when a loved one dies unexpectedly. I was torn between driving and grieving, listening to a GPS tell where to go, and being unable to shake where I had been.

My ride was to be pleasant enough as the sun still shined brightly on an early French evening in the country-side. My destination was a beautiful old bed and breakfast less than an hour from Oradour-sur-Glane. The road was easy to drive and reminded me of scenes from a French grand prix.

The journey was winding and provided glances along the picturesque Vienne River a tributary river to the more famous Loire River. Slowly my presence was returned to the present, as I distanced myself from the horror of Oradour-sur-Glane. Before long, the cool breeze through the open window, and the knowledge I was nearly at my destination was welcomed as I was hungry and tired.

He met us at the door and was a perfect French gentleman. He welcomed us in and was pleased to have guests late in the holiday season. His English was very good, and his warm smile and French accent completed a flawless introduction. We were his only guests this day, and he showed us to our room, up the old highly decorated stairway.

The art, and portraits felt as old as the *manoir* itself. As we walked, our host pointed out his French descendants, making note of their place in the local history. It was a history I knew nothing of, but his explanations delivered with a sense of pride, wrapped in his charming accent was very entertaining. I hoped our walk together would last longer than it did.

We found our room and he left us to relax. When we asked about a good French meal, he directed us to some local restaurants ensuring the cuisine would be quite pleasing. He gave us the key to the front door, explaining he sometimes falls asleep.

"Let yourselves in, but please lock the door behind you," he requested. He finished by adding: *"Perhaps, my son will be home when you return. If so, he will let you in and lock up."*

We went into town, sipped our wine and were determined to have a slow reflective dinner. We were surrounded by locals speaking French, laughing, eating, and drinking. They were the remedy I needed to shake way the ghosts of Oradour. I was pleased and reflection turned to recognition that these wonderful French people made me feel a thousand miles, and over half a century away from Oradour-sur-Glane.

Waking up the next morning, we met the Madame of the manoir, and she was every bit as charming her husband. She had prepared a breakfast feast, full of county-side goodies including fresh coffee, eggs, fruit, bread, homemade jams, jellies, and pastries that covered her beautiful linen table cloth.

She explained our culinary options in English delivered with a French accent that seemed right out of central casting. She left us to our sumptuous feast.

The Madame returned to check on our progress, and we were just sitting there drinking coffee. She asked us where we were from, we said Boston, and she offered that had never visited Boston, or for that matter she had never been to the United States. She asked about our travels in her beloved France.

I told her I was thinking of writing a book on the Americans in Normandy in 1944. Eventually, she inquired what had brought us so far from Normandy. She asked: *"You are hundreds of kilometers from Normandy. What has brought you here near the Vienne River?"*

I told her, "Yes, we *are hundreds of kilometers from Sainte-Mere-Eglise, and it was a tragic story that had drawn me here. I am here for the story of the village of Oradour-sur-Glane. The Germans who destroyed the village were on their way to Normandy to fight against the Americans who had landed on D-Day."*

She acknowledged what I said, and a silence fell between us. She looked at me over the table still covered in her decorations and the abundance of food. *"I know the story,"* she said and continued, *"We all know that story."*

She breathed a sigh and told me one woman had escaped the burning church. *"I met her many years ago. She was my mother's age."* She said she had also met the young boy who escaped, and that as he grew, he would speak to the children in all the villages near Oradour. *"He told us of that terrible day,"* she said with her words trailing as she finished.

Looking at her, I wondered if she would have been alive on that 10 June 1944, *"Do you remember that day? I asked quietly."*

She answered: *"I was very young and have little memories of the day. I was with my mother and grandmother. My mother knew something was wrong."*

She was still standing but her eyes were fixed away from mine, she was looking down. *"Were you here at this house in June of 1944?"* I inquired. I knew we were currently about 20 kilometers from Oradour and was curious how the adults knew something was wrong.

Looking at her looking down, I wondered if I should let our conversation end. She was almost transfixed, and she seemed to be breathing slowly. But the door was opened and I needed to know more of the story of Oradour-sur-Glane..

I felt it essential that I hear her story. I had walked amongst the silent wreckage of Oradour, its existence taxed my emotions and offended my senses. The sights at Oradour were like a silent horror movie.

Now, perhaps her words would be my soundtrack and complete the chaos and carnage from over three quarters of a century past. I had not heard a voice beyond those in my head. I had to hear a French voice, and this was probably my only chance.

"I was here at this house; it was my mother's house." I quickly injected, *"We are nearly 20 kilometers form Oradour."* She stood beside her table in her beautiful French dining room.

Still, she stood, motionless and silent as if suddenly inhabited by something otherworldly.

I asked with the reverence she and the residents of Oradour had earned. My words were delivered softly: *"How did your mother and grandmother know something was wrong?"* She did not look up at me, but looked up at the wall across from her, *"The Smoke,"* she said. That answered the question, they burned down the entire town. It was my turn to look down and let the stillness between us grow.

Unexpectedly she spoke: *"The smoke...it carried...a terrible smell."* She continued, *"I asked my mother what that smell was."* It would take her years to explain her answer, *"burning bodies,"* she said.

It was a reminder that not only had the murderous monsters killed everyone, but they burned everybody in the town they burnt to the ground. My eyes teared up, her pain was as real as the bread and fruit on the table. I was without words and looking at her I thought she was without words as *still, she stood.*

After my visit to Oradour-sur-Glane, and the charming bed and breakfast I still have fond memories of, I began to understand that I wanted to write a book. The unshakeable sadness that Oradour still carries, the pain such a place still harbors after nearly three quarters of a century is tough to shake.

After Oradour, I returned to Normandy, and walking in the footsteps of my American heroes, I was washed with pride that my country, the United States of America, had helped rid the world of Hitler and his Nazi monsters. Writing this book and other books about America's finest—her soldiers, has been a very profound honor.

Recommended Reading

I recommend these excellent books:

Adams, Perter Caddick. *Monty and Rommel Parallel Lives*. Overlook Press: New York. 2012. Print.

Ambrose, Stephen E. *D-Day June 6, 1944: The Climatic Battle of World War II*. Simon and Schuster: New York. Print 1994.

Balkoski, Joseph. *Omaha Beach: D-Day June 6, 1944*. Stackpole Books: Mechanicsburg, PA. 2004. Print

Balkoski, Joseph. *Utah Beach*. Mechanicsburg, PA: Stackpole Books. 2005. Print.

Beck, Phillip. *Oradour: The Massacre and Aftermath*. Print. Pen & Sword: South Yorkshire, UK. 2011. Print.

Brinkley, Douglas. *The Boys of Pointe du Hoc*. HarperCollins: New York. 2005. Print.

D'Este, Carlo. *Decision in Normandy*. E. P. Dutton: New York. 1983. Print

Dinardo, R.L., *Mechanized Juggernaut or Military Anachronism?: Horses and the German Army in World War II*. Stackpole Books: Mechanicsville, PA. Print. 2008.

Hargreaves, Richard. *The Germans in Normandy: Death Reaped a Terrible Harvest*. Pen & Sword Military: South Yorkshire, UK. 2009 Print.

Lewis, Adrian R. *Omaha Beach: A Flawed Victory.* University of North Carolina Press: Chapel Hill, NC. 2001.

Lord, Walter. *The Miracle at Dunkirk.* The Viking Press; New York. 1983.

Luck, Hans von. *Panzer Commander.* Memoirs of a Panzer Commander. Praeger: New York. 1989.

Marshall, Charles. *Discovering The Rommel Murder: The Life and Death of the Desert Fox.* Mechanicsburg, PA: *Stackpole Books, 2002*

Mayo, Jonathan. *D-Day: Minute by Minute* Marble arch Press: New York. Print. 2014.

McManus, John C. *The Dead and Those About to Die: D-Day: The Big Red One at Omaha Beach.* New York: NAL Caliber. 2014. Print.

Mitcham, Samuel W. Jr. *Rommel's Desert War: The Life and Death of the Afrika Korps.* Mechanicsburg, PA: Stackpole Books, 2007. Print

O'Donnell, Patrick K. *Dog Company:* The Boys of Pointe-du-Hoc. De Capo: Boston. 2012. Print.

Ryan, Cornelius. *The Longest Day: June 6, 1944.* Simon & Schuster: New York. 1959. Print.

Stern, Gary. *The Cover-up at Omaha Beach.* New York: Skyhorse Publishing. 2014. Print

Walker, Robert W. *The Namesake: Biography of Theodore Roosevelt Jr.* New York: Brick Tower Press. 2008. Print.

CPSIA information can be obtained
at www.ICGtesting.com
Printed in the USA
LVHW011927260723
753100LV00002B/148